THE
HEROIC
ENTERPRISE

BUSINESS AND THE COMMON GOOD

JOHN M. HOOD

THE FREE PRESS

NEW YORK   LONDON   TORONTO   SYDNEY   SINGAPORE

THE FREE PRESS
A Division of Simon & Schuster Inc.
1230 Avenue of the Americas
New York, NY 10020

THE FREE PRESS and colophon are trademarks
of Simon & Schuster Inc.

Designed by Carla Bolte

Manufactured in the United States of America

10   9   8   7   6   5   4   3   2   1

Library of Congress Cataloging-in-Publication Data

Hood, John, 1966–
The heroic enterprise: business and the common good/John Hood.
p.   cm.
Includes bibliographical references and index.
ISBN 0–684–82762–X
1. Social responsibility of business. 2. Common good.   I. Title.
HD60.H66   1996
658.4'08—dc20

                                                   95–26703
                                                   CIP

ISBN 0–684–82762–X

To my wife, Lisa,

Love of my life,

With whom all things are possible,

And without whom they would never be attempted

CONTENTS

ACKNOWLEDGMENTS

Without the aid of family, friends, and colleagues, I would never have been able to attempt a project of this magnitude. The following is by no means an exhaustive list of those who deserve my heartfelt thanks.

The Heritage Foundation in Washington, D.C., and the Lynde and Harry Bradley Foundation in Milwaukee, Wisconsin, provided me with a visiting fellowship and the support necessary to research and write the book. I am especially indebted to Heritage Vice President Adam Meyerson, who conceived the idea for *The Heroic Enterprise* and, as director of the Bradley Fellow program, shepherded me through the dangerous topography of first-time authorship. Joe Loconte, David Miller, Kathy Moffett, Stephen Glass, Jennifer Soininen, and Brendan O'Scannlain of the *Policy Review* staff gave me invaluable aid and advice during my year in their office, and numerous Heritage executives and researchers— among them Tom Atwood, Herb Berkowitz, Margaret Bonilla, Marshall Breger, Stuart Butler, Tucker Carlson, David Mason, Kristie Reed, Terri Ruddy, John Shanahan, Adam Thierer, Allyson Tucker, Bridgett Wagner, and Mark Wilson—gave generously of their time and ideas.

Researchers and writers at other publications and institutions also gave me important information, insights, and comments. They include Stephen Moore of the Cato Institute, Stuart Nolan of the Capital Research Center, John Miller of the Center for Equal Opportunity, Virginia Postrel and Rick Henderson of *Reason* magazine, Karl Zinsmeister of *The American Enterprise,* Mark Cunningham and Chris Warden of *Investors' Business Daily,* Fred Smith and Jonathan Adler of the Competitive Enterprise Institute, and Laura Litvan of *Nation's Business.*

This book would also have not been possible without the aid, advice, and forbearance of the John Locke Foundation family in North Carolina, including Marc Rotterman, Don Carrington, Andrew Cline, Marilyn Avila, and Joey Stansbury. Special thanks to the Locke Foundation's board of directors and chairman, Art Pope, who provided me with both leave time and ideas.

Thanks to Bob Wallace and the rest of the folks at The Free Press for helping to guide my work in progress and for transforming the result into something readable and comprehensible.

Those who read my manuscript in its early stages deserve both gratitude and apologies. They include Michael Lowrey, Jeff Taylor, David Hood, Hal Hood, my parents, Harold and June Hood, and my wife, Lisa—whose contribution to *The Heroic Enterprise* surpasses all others, in that she allowed me to spend a sizable part of our first year of marriage writing a book in another state. Her patience and love, and the assistance of my family and friends, make me feel fortunate and deeply grateful.

INTRODUCTION

In 1947, a slim volume written by a relatively obscure General Motors corporate executive was issued by a small publishing house under the title *The Mainspring of Human Progress*. The book began with an intriguing chapter entitled "Puzzling Questions of Vital Concern to 2,155,000,000 Individuals," led off with this curious paragraph:

> For 60 known centuries, this planet that we call Earth has been inhabited by human beings not much different from ourselves. Their desire to live has been just as strong as ours. They have had at least as much physical strength as the average person of today, and among them have been men and women of great intelligence. But down through the ages, most human beings have gone hungry, and many have always starved.[1]

The author, Henry Grady Weaver, served as director of customer research for GM. Blind in one eye, he nevertheless spent much of his life peering over data. He was a number-cruncher, not a philosopher or polemicist; his writing experience had consisted mainly of penning articles on psychological research. But *The Mainspring of Human Progress,* an amateur's paean to freedom and individual ingenuity, remains one of the finest discussions of the impact of business on society that has ever been written.

Weaver was writing to an American public that had just endured almost two decades of desperate economic hardship, social upheaval, and war. There was a sense of euphoria after the surrender of Germany and Japan in 1945, a commonly held belief that the United States had managed to extricate itself from turmoil and disaster to achieve unparalleled strength and influence around the world. At the same time, however, doubts were beginning to surface about some of America's traditional institutions and principles. The apparent vitality of the Soviet Union, which had itself fought back from the brink of destruction to a glorious victory, was unsettling. The lingering economic controversies from the New Deal—about the role of the federal government in society, and the ability of capitalism to provide jobs and opportunities for the common man—had been left unresolved during a half decade of world war. Indeed, the growth of the federal government during World War II and the unprecedented role it assumed of directing and managing the wartime economy was just being recognized and debated.

Weaver was a practical man as well as a vigorous defender of American business. He understood that in order to persuade his readers that the free enterprise system was worth preserving, he would have to eschew elaborate theory and focus instead on historic fact and common sense. So he began his book with a discussion of the state shared by most human beings throughout most of human history: hunger. The ancient civilizations extolled by historians and philosophers, Weaver pointed out, consistently failed to keep their people fed. Egyptians and Greeks sometimes killed their babies because they couldn't feed them. The Roman Empire collapsed in famine. French peasants were dying of hunger when Thomas Jefferson bought Louisiana from Napoleon Bonaparte. As late as 1846, the Irish were starving to death from a potato famine. In Weaver's day, famines continued to plague significant portions of Asia and Africa, but in the United States there were only periodic, geographically limited episodes of hunger.[2] And after Weaver's time (he died in 1949), the "green revolution" of unparalleled agricultural productivity in the 1960s essentially eradicated hunger as a serious problem not only in the United States but throughout much of the developed and developing world (except in those regions where war or politics disrupts agriculture and commerce).[3]

Weaver was fascinated with the sudden, amazing productivity of agriculture, as well as with other pleasant surprises of modern life. "Why did men, women, and children eke out their meager existence for 6,000 years [of recorded history], toiling desperately from dawn to dark—barefoot, half-naked, unwashed, unshaved, uncombed, with lousy hair, mangy skins, and rotting teeth—then suddenly, in one place on Earth there is an abundance of such things as rayon underwear, nylon hose, shower baths, safety razors, ice cream sodas, lipsticks, and permanent waves?" he asked.[4] Imagine what Weaver might think of American society today, where a family of modest means might have access to a cornucopia of foods and treats, dozens of television channels, thousands of movies, inexpensive clothes and cosmetics, a luxurious (by the standards of 1947) home with air conditioning, microwave ovens, digital stereo, a medicine chest full of lifesaving or pain-alleviating drugs, several reliable automobiles, and a magical desktop machine capable of balancing a checkbook, drawing a picture, publishing a newspaper, playing a game, and sending a letter instantaneously to another city or even another country. Indeed, the average American now consumes about twice as many goods and services as families did in Weaver's day—and he thought his contemporaries enjoyed an extremely high and unprecedented standard of living! (We might well say the same today: Studies of household consumption show that *poor* families today live very much like middle-income families did in the 1950s in terms of housing and amenities.[5])

A devout Southern Baptist, husband, and father of two, Weaver was no materialist. He would not (nor should anyone) interpret the mere possession of conveniences and luxuries as proof of social well-being. At the same time, however, Weaver lacked the elitist's disdain for the importance of material comfort. He carefully studied human nature—specifically, consumer preferences—and understood the revolutionary impact of economic progress on the lives of the middle class and poor. Nor did Weaver have much patience for those who tried to interpret American progress in ethnic or racial terms. "That sounds fine in after-dinner oratory and goes over big at election time," he wrote perceptively, "but the argument is difficult to support. Our own ancestors, including the Anglo-Saxons, have starved right along with everyone else."[6] Instead, Weaver argued, the mainspring of human progress was freedom itself. The United States, by allowing the most individual freedom to produce goods and services and sell them to consumers for profit, had unleashed the greatest degree of invention and ingenuity, resulting in social benefits for all.

In Weaver's time, this simple statement of the virtues of a capitalist economy, while increasingly rare in the ivory towers of American academia, was hardly incongruent with public sentiment. During the 1940s and 1950s most Americans held business as an institution in high esteem (as

well as, it should be noted, such other institutions as government, organized religion, and the press). The media, too, often viewed business and
corporate leaders with at least equanimity, if not actual approval. Media
analysts Robert Lichter, Linda Lichter, and Stanley Rothman point out
that many television and motion-picture plots of the 1950s featured businessmen in positive, sometimes heroic roles. Wise, honest, and trustwor-
thy fathers Jim Anderson of "Father Knows Best" and Ward Cleaver of
"Leave It To Beaver" were an insurance salesman and an accountant,
respectively. Nick Charles, "The Thin Man," was a publisher. Herbert
Philbrick, the hero of the popular 1950s TV adventure series "I Led
Three Lives," was a pipe-smoking advertising executive, a Communist
Party worker, and an FBI counterspy. Bruce Wayne (also known as Batman) was a wealthy industrialist. Even into the 1960s, television series
continued to portray those in business as "good guys." Westerns were a
surprising source of positive images about business; Ben Cartwright of
"Bonanza," after all, ran a sprawling ranching and mining empire on the
family's thousand-acre Ponderosa estate.[7]

In most cases, however, while these business characters were portrayed positively, they were rarely portrayed in the actual practice of
doing business. The Beaver spent little time at his father's accounting
firm. Bruce Wayne even donned a mask and fought crime at night so as to
distinguish Batman from the CEO of Wayne Enterprises. There were
some notable exceptions. The hit 1954 film *Sabrina*—in which brothers
played by Humphrey Bogart and William Holden vied for the affections
of Audrey Hepburn—has several memorable scenes with both major and
minor characters bouncing up and down on a new plastic, to be manufactured out of sugar cane and sold by Bogart's and Holden's family firm.
Holden, a hedonist with little interest in business, asks his workaholic
brother why he was spending so much time dabbling with plastic rather
than having fun. "What will that prove?" he demands, pointing to the
strip of plastic. Bogart replies as follows:

Prove? Nothing much. A new product has been found, something of use to
the world. So a new industry moves into an underdeveloped area. . . . People
who never saw a dime before suddenly have a dollar, and barefoot kids wear
shoes and have their teeth fixed and their faces washed. What's wrong with
the kind of an urge that gives people hospitals, libraries, baseball diamonds,
and movies on a Saturday night?[8]

Needless to say, if Weaver had lived long enough to see *Sabrina,* he would have rooted for Bogart's crusty but insightful businessman over Holden's irresponsible playboy. Nor would he have been alone: Movie audiences were *supposed* to root for Bogart, who gets the girl in the end (while Holden learns responsibility and prepares to shoulder his weight in the family business).

THE BACKLASH AGAINST BUSINESS

But even in the comparatively conservative 1950s, there was a significant undercurrent of skepticism and revisionist thinking about the role of business in society. These ideas flowed through universities, then bubbled up through the legal system in a series of court decisions that redefined the purpose and responsibilities of the American corporation. Social movements, responding to problems such as racial injustice and environmental degradation, began to view business as a corrupt, amoral institution in which a few greedy individuals profited at the expense of the broader community. By the 1960s and 1970s, the undercurrent of revisionism about business became a raging river of criticism, protests, and hostility.

The mass media both reflected and influenced these public perceptions. Investigative journalism became an heroic, even romantic, calling, with the name of the game being to catch greedy corporations in the act of polluting the water, selling shoddy and overpriced products, exploiting workers and families, and sacrificing the public's health, safety, and welfare to make a quick buck. On television and in the movies, business executives increasingly became the villains, to be challenged by heroic lawyers, policemen, reporters, and activists. In a study of the hundred highest-grossing films (selected from *Variety* listings), researchers found that nearly nine out of ten business characters were portrayed positively before 1965, but two out of three were portrayed negatively thereafter. After 1975, the proportion of negative business characters rose to three out of four.[9] Such films as *The China Syndrome, Norma Rae, Silkwood,* and *Wall Street* are examples of this trend, in which antisocial or even criminal corporate behavior could be challenged only by the heroic actions of crusading lawyers and journalists or brave whistle-blowers. Lichter, Lichter, and Rothman found the same pattern for television characters. While small-business owners were treated about the same over the decades, the percentage of big-business characters portrayed as villains rose from 31 percent before 1965 to 58 percent afterward. The authors compared, for example, the positive portrayals of the Cartwright family in "Bonanza" to the largely corrupt and immoral Ewing family of "Dallas."[10]

Public sentiment toward business, influenced by social activism and media images, also began to change. In 1965 almost 60 percent of Americans believed that businesses made a "reasonable profit," whereas 24 percent thought businesses made too much. By 1975 the trend lines had reversed, with more Americans calling profits excessive rather than reasonable.[11] Even in 1939, as the economic stagnation of the Great Depression lingered, 56 percent of Americans said that the interests of employers and employees were "basically the same," while only 25 percent said they were opposed. But by 1994, more Americans thought the interests of the two groups clashed than thought they coincided.[12] Much of the change has occurred in public perception of big business; in one 1992 poll, 64 percent of Americans rated the moral and ethical standards of small-business owners as excellent or good, while only 31 percent said the same about "business executives."[13]

It was during this same period of social upheaval and changing media images about business that a movement began among business scholars, journalists, issue-oriented activist groups, and some corporate executives to shift the goals and principles of American business away from profits and return to shareholders and toward the interests of a broader constituency of so-called stakeholders—workers, customers, neighbors, and society at large.[14] Variously called "corporate social responsibility" or "socially responsible business," the modern movement is dated by many of its adherents to 1953, with the publication of *Social Responsibilities of the Businessman* by Howard Bowen. In 1963 came *Business and Society,* a textbook for colleges and universities by business professor Joseph McGuire, and by the 1970s the field was a full-fledged academic discipline that could boast programs in major business schools and dozens of important books.[15] Today corporate social responsibility is not only an academic field of inquiry and a guiding philosophy for many social activists but a major issue among corporate managers whose deep concerns about corporate image, public relations, environmental liability, lawsuits, relations with governments, and worker morale—and, it should be said, about the many lingering problems in American society often spotlighted by business critics—have melded into a search for a coherent set of ethical and managerial principles to guide economic enterprises in the 1990s and beyond.

Of course, corporate social responsibility as a late twentieth-century American movement is only a modern manifestation of an ancient debate among philosophers and theologians in many lands and cultures about the morality of commerce itself. Is economic competition the enemy of compassion and community? Is commercial activity a necessary evil or a desirable good? To whom do traders and merchants owe their loyalty? Do capitalists exploit their workers and the poor? Is it moral to sell basic human necessities at a profit? The greatest thinkers of human history have wrestled with these questions. Aristotle wrote about trading and business profits in his *Nicomachean Ethics* and *Politics*. Major portions of Old Testament books such as Deuteronomy contain rules for ethical business practice. Adam Smith's *The Wealth of Nations* is usually thought of as a treatise on economics, but it also discusses in depth the social context and impact of commercial activity. Smith was, after all, a theologian and ethicist, not a businessman or economist. Karl Marx was no economist either, and had never set foot in a factory, but his critical analysis of business behavior changed the course of history.

In the United States of the late nineteenth century, the issue sharpened as defenders and critics of the "robber barons" clashed over the role of profit, exploitation, and immoral business practices in the development of the West, the growth of industry, and the accumulation of vast fortunes. Over the next century, the debate about such controversial businessmen as Cornelius Vanderbilt, Leland Stanford, Jay Gould, J. J. Hill, J. P. Morgan, and John D. Rockefeller raged on. Were these men exemplars of the evils of unfettered, greedy capitalism, or were they instead great innovators whose impact on society justified their wealth? (In actuality, the story of the "robber baron" period is more complicated than either of these propositions would allow, as described in such works as *Entrepreneurs vs. the State* by Burton W. Folsom, Jr.[16])

In the modern corporate social responsibility movement, the key issues of contention include the following:

- The supposedly declining prospects of American workers (in terms of wages, job satisfaction, and leisure time)
- Worker access to health insurance and other benefits
- Health and safety issues for both workers and consumers

- Corporate discrimination against minorities, women, the disabled, and other aggrieved groups
- The impact of business on families and children
- The relationship between business and other social institutions such as schools and charities
- Environmental degradation

An example of how activists of the 1990s critique corporate behavior can be found in *Absence of the Sacred,* written by former advertising executive and business analyst Jerry Mander and published by Sierra Club Books in 1991. Corporations, Mander argued, are essentially amoral institutions who sacrifice the common good in pursuit of mindless profits. While this occurs across a range of corporate actions, the most serious problem is ecological. In modern industrial production, he said, "metals from the ground are converted into cars. Trees are converted into boards and then into houses, furniture, and paper products. Oil is converted into energy. In all such activity, a piece of nature is taken from where it belongs and processed into a new form." Mander even resurrected the old "labor theory of value" to indict the concept of corporate profit itself:

> All corporate profit is obtained by a simple formula: Profit equals the difference between the amount paid to an employee and the economic value of the employee's output, and/or the difference between the amount paid for raw materials used in product (including costs of processing) and the ultimate sales price of the processed raw materials. Karl Marx was right: A worker is not compensated for the full value of his or her labor, [and] neither is the raw material supplier. The owners of capital skim off part of the value as profit. Profit is based on underpayment. . . . this is called exploitation.[17]

One might view Mander's attack on corporate behavior in America as extreme and atypical of business critics. But allegations of corporate misbehavior, irresponsibility, exploitation, and greed are commonplace in the mainstream media of the 1990s: in morning newspapers, in evening TV newsmagazines, in movies and popular music, and even in children's cartoon programs like "Captain Planet and the Planeteers." Just to take one example, during early 1995 there were a spate of stories on TV newscasts and in major newspapers and magazines about the "overworked American." The cover story for the March 6 *Newsweek,* entitled "Breaking Point," chronicled the supposed inability of American workers to keep up with the demands of their downsizing, profit-chasing employers while also trying to rear families and enjoy leisure time. "We are fast becoming the nation of the quick, or the dead-tired," the magazine proclaimed.[18] Yet in actuality the average workweek of Americans has been *falling* for decades; leisure time, as well as participation in a wide variety of leisure and recreational activities, has been increasing.[19] In opinion polls, most Americans express satisfaction with both their jobs and their family lives, and few say they would be willing to work fewer hours if it would mean less income.[20]

In a cover story in the April 1992 issue of *Inc.* magazine, a popular publication among entrepreneurs and business owners, Paul Hawken—the founder of Smith & Hawken, a garden catalog company, and a prominent activist and hero in the corporate social responsibility movement—called for a new "Ecology of Commerce." He wrote matter-of-factly that "we can say in no uncertain terms that business is destroying the world." This catastrophe could be averted, Hawken continued, if business would work to reduce consumption, raise wages, and reduce its impact on the world environment. "Either we see business as a restorative undertaking, or we, as businesspeople, will march the entire race to the undertaker."[21] What was amazing about Hawken's polemic was not its ideology but the fact that the editors of a business magazine apparently thought his views to be both serious and of interest to a business audience. After all, *Inc.* presumably is no less concerned than its competitors about maintaining and expanding its readership (those greedy profiteers!). Are America's entrepreneurs likely to agree, "in no uncertain terms," that business is destroying the world?

The situation is hardly bleak. The corporate social responsibility movement has its critics and combatants, both within business and without. Corporate public relations, a massive industry in its own right, has made social responsibility a major theme in advertising, promotions, article placements, and events. In economics, free-market thinkers from Smith to Milton Friedman have argued that the pursuit of profit by economic enterprises generates tremendous social benefits. And in politics, impassioned arguments against heavy regulation and in favor of business freedom and competitiveness seem to have found an audience among many policymakers and voters, who still view business with greater respect than other institutions such as government or the press.

But this public respect for business is abstract in nature; it doesn't extend to all of the complaints of the social responsibility movement. A Roper Organization poll in 1991 asked respondents to rank the responsibilities of business. At the top of the list were both tasks Americans believed corporations were doing well (such as producing good-quality products and services, and protecting the health and safety of workers) and tasks Americans believed corporations were doing poorly (such as cleaning up pollution). Lower on the list of perceived business responsibilities were "developing new products and services" and "keeping profits at reasonable levels." Neither omission is surprising. The innovation and invention inherent in business, and so crucial to social progress, rarely gets much press or public attention. And on the latter point, Americans have for many years exaggerated the size of corporate profits, telling pollsters that they believe the average profit of U.S. firms is 34 percent when in reality it is only about 4 percent.[22]

A DIFFERENT APPROACH

I approach the issues surrounding business behavior and the common good in a very different way than have most analysts of corporate social responsibility. First and foremost, I spend very little time on theoretical discussion; I merely summarize the major viewpoints and disagreements in the corporate social responsibility debate. Nor is this book primarily an analysis of the history of business, since such analyses can already be found in numerous works of scholarship and journalism. Instead, this book describes the conduct and social effects of business in America today. It examines many areas of greater concern to scholars, business executives, and the general public, but it does so through the lens of actual experience. Interviews with business executives and case studies of how businesses address and solve problems help to define the issue of corporate social responsibility more sharply, leading to several clear (and to some, no doubt, surprising) conclusions about the moral and ethical aspects of commerce and the key tenets of the corporate social responsibility movement.

One of the fundamental distinctions in philosophy and ethics is the "is–ought" dichotomy. To describe what *is* does not necessarily describe what *ought* to be; however, sometimes a descriptive discussion can lead to normative conclusions. Most philosophers and ethicists give at least some attention to tradition—to the bundle of beliefs and behaviors that evolve in a particular society or institution over time, as human beings struggle to understand and cope with the problems they face in their everyday lives. I contend in this book that corporate social responsibility can be judged by examining in detail how actual companies, in their day-to-day operations, confer broad and measurable benefits to the society in which they operate. In this approach, I borrow from the technique of Weaver and of Adam Smith, who introduced his subject in *The Wealth of Nations* in descriptive terms and discussed at length the actual operation of capital markets and foreign trade in eighteenth-century Europe. His views about what we would today call corporate social responsibility are expressed as the lesson not of ethical reasoning but of his own experience: "I have never known much good done by those who affected to trade for the public good."[23]

My purpose is simply to update and revise this discussion in the context of late twentieth-century American commerce, providing students of corporate social responsibility—in the academy, in the boardroom, in the newsroom, or in the legislative chamber—with specific examples of how businesses can and do serve society through the pursuit of excellence, worker performance, competitiveness, innovation, and profit.[24] Whether business, due to its demonstrable contributions to the common good, can and will be viewed as "heroic" as are other professions or callings is a matter of great importance if free enterprise is to survive and thrive. Henry Grady Weaver, in the heady and unsettling days after World War II, understood this well. Writing about great American entrepreneurs such as Eli Whitney (the father of not only the cotton gin but much of mass production itself), John Deere, Thomas Edison, and Henry Ford, Weaver argued that their contributions to American society were greater, in his judgment, than those of many political or military leaders who were better known to the public. Indeed, even such early American political heroes as Benjamin Franklin, Thomas Jefferson, and Thomas Paine were important inventors and entrepreneurs in their own right.[25]

Americans were and are an inventive people, Weaver wrote, because of the very system of free economic competition based on profit and reward. "No matter how much money John Deere may have made," he observed, "it would be insignificant in comparison with the tremendous overall benefits shared by millions of people" from his innovative steel plow that made prairie agriculture, and thus westward expansion, viable.

"It's just possible that good old John Deere wouldn't have bothered his head about the plowing problem if he hadn't been living in a free country, where an ambitious blacksmith had a chance to become a prosperous manufacturer."[26]

In reality, the business world is populated more by heroes like John Deere than by the villains who make the morning newspapers, are vilified on the evening newsmagazines, or appear in Hollywood's unrealistic and silly fantasies about American society. Few tasks are more important than exploring this world and trying to explain how it actually works.

CHAPTER 1

RESPONSIBLE TO WHOM?

In June 1992 a new business organization was created in Washington, D.C. It joined long-established groups in the nation's capital such as the U.S. Chamber of Commerce, the National Association of Manufacturers, and the National Federation of Independent Business. But the agenda of this new group, called Businesses for Social Responsibility, was very different from that of the traditional business lobby. Its founding members—including Aveda Corporation, Ben & Jerry's Homemade Inc., The Body Shop, Calvert Group Ltd., Esprit de Corp, Hasbro, Lotus Development, Philadelphia Coca-Cola Bottling Co., Reebok, Rhino Records, Stride Rite Corporation, and Working Assets—were well-known as advocates of political causes such as environmentalism, equal rights, nonviolence, and economic equity. The organization's stated goal, to be accomplished through lobbying and public relations efforts, was "integrating" into corporate decision-making such concerns as "social equity and environmental responsibility" and "developing a sustainable economy." Despite its location in the seat of federal government power, Businesses for Social Responsibility did not target government officials as its main audience. "A lot of what we're talking about is dealing with other companies, not public policy," said the organization's executive director, Michael Levett.[1]

Businesses are used to hearing criticism from those in government, the media, academia, or the nonprofit sector. Complaints that American com-

1

panies sacrifice the common good in their pursuit of profit—by laying off workers and paying remaining workers poorly, abandoning inner cities, polluting the environment, endangering consumers, and perpetuating social inequality—have long been reliable applause lines and attention-getters in the speeches of politicians, the editorials of major newspapers, the books of self-styled consumer and environmental activists, and the briefs of crusading public-interest attorneys. But with the development of the modern social responsibility movement and the creation of Businesses for Social Responsibility, executives of some well-known and successful companies have joined the chorus of corporate critics. This has had the result of making a defense of traditional views of corporate responsibility more difficult; as one corporate manager remarked, when a corporate executive attacks the profit motive and the record of business in promoting social progress, the event takes on a "Nixon goes to China" dimension that is irresistible to the media.[2] With the creation of the new organization, corporate social responsibility—long the doctrine of researchers and activists, and increasingly part of the curriculum in America's schools of business and management—had established itself as a political and social force to be reckoned with. "Social awareness is the lifestyle fashion" for the 1990s, said Esprit de Corp founder Susie Tompkins.[3]

The gist of the corporate social responsibility thesis is that firms should have responsibilities beyond those of economic self-interest. Instead of having a goal of maximizing return to owners or shareholders, corporate social responsibility advocates say, responsible and ethical companies must balance profit-seeking and other social goals. Richard Evans, external affairs director of British corporation Traidcraft Plc, stated that "ethics, with its concern for the common good of all people and its attempt at a coherent analysis of how this can be achieved, cannot allow business to define itself in purely economic terms and to ignore the ethical implications of its involvement in the lives of individuals and society as a whole in many other areas."[4]

Furthermore, "socially responsible" businesses often assert that it is sometimes their duty to sacrifice profit for the sake of either the environment or society at large. Yvon Chouinard, president of the outdoor-wear company Patagonia, announced in a 1992 catalog that "everything we make pollutes." Polyester clothing comes from petroleum, a nonrenewable resource. Cotton is sprayed with pesticides to combat the boll weevil and frequently treated with formaldehyde, a human carcinogen. Wool relies on large flocks of sheep that denude fragile, arid areas of the earth. Chouinard promised that Patagonia would reduce its product offerings, thus reducing its need for raw materials, with the ultimate goal of halting the firm's growth altogether.[5] Most business executives who embrace social responsibility aren't willing to take their ecological or other concerns as far as Chouinard has, but nevertheless they believe that profit maximization is a poor guide for evaluating the ethical and social dimensions of business decisions.

The corporate social responsibility movement in the United States today has its roots in legal and academic debates of decades past. Before addressing the specific charges lodged against American business, a brief history of these debates is in order.

DEFINING THE CORPORATION

Corporate social responsibility, despite its title, does not necessarily refer only to the behavior of corporations. Many of the arguments advanced against the actions of huge, multinational corporations such as Exxon apply equally well to small businesses such as family-owned service stations. Both supposedly contribute to the destruction of the world environment by dispensing petroleum, which must be drilled, transported, refined, and sold—at each step potentially harming the environment. If commercial activities are perceived to be unethical or destructive, it doesn't matter what type of business enterprise engages in them; they are still irresponsible. So when they indict the ethics of American business, social responsibility advocates are really discussing not only the corporate businesses that account for 60 percent of U.S. gross national product but also the noncorporate businesses that generate 25 percent (governments, nonprofits, and households account for the remainder).[6]

But corporations—and in particular the publicly traded corporations that represent only a small fraction of U.S. corporations but generate most corporate income—are the subject of most social responsibility discussions because of how they are created and managed. Corporate social responsibility scholars note that since corporations are "fictitious persons," created by law and sustained by grants of limited liability for individual shareholders, they have obligations to society that surpass those of sole proprietorships or partnerships. One such scholar, business professor Thomas M. Jones, explained that "the corporation which acts in a responsible manner may simply be paying society back for the social costs of doing business, costs for which the firms rarely receive an invoice."[7]

This view is hardly new. In fact, it was accepted doctrine in the United States and other Western societies until the nineteenth century that the right to conduct business in corporate form was a matter of royal or state prerogative, not of private economic interest. Monarchs issued charters to public-stock corporations that promised public benefits, such as exploration and colonization of the New World. Individuals could own shares of the corporation and sell them (with some limitations), but the purpose of the corporation was not merely to serve the interests of stockholders. In America, the earliest business corporations established during the 1700s were founded to perform such services as building transportation infrastructure, supplying water, fighting fires, and providing insurance. These early corporations were rare and closely regulated in size, scope, and property holdings.[8]

After the break from England, however, American states began to pass charters that allowed self-incorporation rather than incorporation by special legislative act. At first these corporations could be created only for religious, charitable, or municipal functions. The first private incorporation statute, passed by the North Carolina state legislature in 1795, applied only to canal builders, and the canals had to revert to state ownership. Later, however, states broadened the scope of self-incorporation to the point where corporations began to arise throughout the economy for the clear purpose of conducting private business. One reason for this liberalization of corporate codes was competition among states for the revenues from incorporation fees. By encouraging enterprises to incorporate in their state, legislatures could obtain higher tax returns. Eventually, minimum capital requirements and "public purpose" rules were dropped to maximize corporate formation. By the late 1800s the corporation as an independent, private business enterprise run for the benefit of its shareholders had established itself as a mainstream form of economic organization in America.[9]

During the late 1800s and early 1990s, the implicit assumption underlying the economy as well as state corporate law was that the purpose of a corporation was to make money for shareholders. This consensus was rarely challenged. The first important legal test of the responsibilities of corporate directors came in the influential 1919 case of *Dodge v. Ford*. Despite its name, the case had nothing to do with competition between automakers; instead it had to do with the intended largess of Henry Ford, president and controlling shareholder of the Ford Motor Company. In August 1916 Ford owned 58 percent of company stock, and the Dodge brothers owned 10 percent. Rather than pay out both regular dividends and special dividends, as the company had done in previous years, Ford announced that only regular dividends would be paid. The remaining profits would be used to expand production capacity, increase worker wages, and offset expected losses from a reduced sales price for Ford's popular cars. Many analysts have interpreted Henry Ford's decision to increase investment, raise wages, and reduce prices as an astute business decision calculated to increase the profits of the company in the longer run—but that was not his stated purpose. Ford proclaimed broader social goals, stating that "my intention is to employ still more men; to spread the benefits of this industrial system to the greatest possible number, to help them build up their lives and their homes." The Dodge brothers sued, claiming that Ford was using shareholder equity to pursue his own personal philanthropic goals. The Michigan supreme court, while professing to respect Ford's business judgment, agreed with the Dodges:

> There should be no confusion . . . of the duties which Mr. Ford conceives that he and the stockholders owe to the general public and the duties which in law he and his co-directors owe to a protesting minority of stockholders. A business corporation is organized and carried on primarily for the profit of shareholders. The powers of directors are to be employed for that end. The discretion of the directors is to be exercised in the *choice of the means to attain that end*, and does not extend to a *change in the end itself*, and to the reduction of profits or the non-distribution of profits among shareholders in order to devote them to other purposes.[10] [emphasis added]

The court went on to say that corporate behavior such as charitable giving could pass legal scrutiny as long as it had a legitimate relationship to corporate profits. There was a decided difference, the court continued, between "an incidental humanitarian expenditure of corporate funds for the benefit of the employees, like the building of a hospital for their use and the employment of agencies for the betterment of their condition, and a general purpose and plan to benefit mankind at the expense of others." Other state courts codified this standard by upholding corporate expenditures such as gifts to local training schools, community chests, recreational facilities, hospitals, and even churches. Expenditures designed to attract customers and advance corporate interests by obtaining "goodwill and prestige" also passed muster.[11] As a practical matter, then, *Dodge v. Ford* and similar cases throughout the early twentieth century gave corporate managers a lot of discretion about how to go about serving corporate interests.

Nevertheless, *Dodge v. Ford* did serve to establish in the minds of corporate managers and others the notion of private corporations having *direct* responsibilities only to their shareholders. After the Great Depression and throughout the 1940s, this notion came under fire from several fronts. First, a number of scholars and observers of business came to advance the proposition that corporations, far from being owned and thus controlled by their shareholders, were really accountable to no one but their managers. Adolf Berle and Gardiner Means, in their influential 1932 book *The Modern Corporation and Private Property*, argued that shareholders were passive owners at best, effectively exercising only the power to sell their shares if they were dissatisfied with corporate policies or performance. (Like-minded analysts have added that the growth of institutional ownership of corporations—in which mutual funds or pension plans buy shares on behalf of individuals—has made this point even more relevant today. Just from 1950 to 1994, the percentage of total corporate equity owned by institutions rose from 6.1 percent to 46.6 percent.[12] Social responsibility scholars say this means there is even less effective control exercised over today's corporations by shareholders who may not even realize what stocks they own or, in the case of pensions and insurance, upon which stocks their financial futures depend.[13]) "By surrendering control and responsibility," Berle and Means wrote, shareholders had "surrendered the right that the corporation should be operated in their sole interest." Their book was published in November 1932, the same month of Franklin Roosevelt's election, and helped justify the economic regulations imposed in the early New Deal period.[14]

Another argument was that corporations, during the decades since the *Dodge v. Ford* decision, had grown so large and amassed such power over the economy and society that previous formulations of their social responsibilities had simply become outdated.[15] This was the view stated by the New Jersey supreme court in *A.P. Smith Manufacturing Co. v. Barlow*, the 1953 case that helped redefine the purpose of corporations in the minds of many executives, judges, and scholars. In 1951 the board of directors of A.P. Smith, a manufacturer of valves and fire hydrants, adopted a resolution to contribute $1,500 to Princeton University. Corporate shareholders challenged the donation as being outside the proper scope of corporate expenditure. The court disagreed and upheld the contribution. Part of the decision argued that the donation to Princeton could be justified as in the interest of the firm, because the "survival of the corporation in a free enterprise system" depended "in no insignificant part upon free and vigorous nongovernment institutions of learning." But as one commentator has observed, this defense of the relationship between the act and its goal (a $1,500 gift to Princeton and the survival of free enterprise) "while perhaps perceptible, is still remote, almost fanciful."[16] Practically speaking, this explanation of vague and indirect benefit could be applied to virtually any corporate expenditure, thus eliminating judicial oversight over corporate philanthropy and other forms of "socially responsible" activity altogether.

But the court went even further. Referring back to the original royal corporate charters, the court stated as follows:

> Just as the conditions prevailing when corporations were originally created required that they serve public as well as private interests, modern conditions require the corporations acknowledge and discharge social as well as private responsibilities as members of the communities within which they operate. . . . Clearly, then, the [shareholders,] whose private interests rest entirely upon the well-being of the corporation, ought not to be permitted to close their eyes to present-day realities and thwart the long-visioned corporate action in recognizing and voluntarily discharging its high obligations as a constituent of our modern social structure.[17]

Around the same time, other court decisions and new state corporate statutes recognized the power of corporations to make donations to the public welfare or for charitable, scientific, or educational purposes. Corporate social responsibility advocates began to argue that if philanthropic giving was a legitimate corporate activity fulfilling the social responsibilities of corporations, then perhaps other activities that place social goals over shareholder return were also legitimate, such as abandoning profitable but (in their view) socially or environmentally destructive product lines. One can argue that the actual legal status of corporate social responsibility did not change a great deal between *Dodge v. Ford* and *Smith v. Barlow*, since corporate managers had always enjoyed a substantial amount of discretion as to how to serve the economic interest of corporations. But the court in *Smith v. Barlow*—as well as other legal and academic commentators—suggested that the corporate interest *itself* had changed. Because they controlled institutions of economic power and social influence, the argument went, responsible corporate managers should consider a host of goals other than profit maximization. There was no longer a legal need, at least, to relate a proposed corporate action to the goal of increasing shareholder value. And if there were such a need, the discretion allowed corporate managers was so broad that any asserted relationship, no matter how tenuous, would suffice.

REACTION AND COUNTERACTION

There were many business leaders, scholars, and thinkers who viewed the corporate social responsibility movement with alarm. The most famous critic is probably Milton Friedman, scholar at Stanford University's Hoover Institution, Nobel Prize–winning economist, and author of *Capitalism and Freedom*, columns for *Newsweek*, and perhaps the most widely cited (and criticized) essay on corporate social responsibility since the mid-1960s.

"The Social Responsibility of Business Is to Increase Its Profits" was a modest, five-page article in the September 13, 1970, issue of the *New York Times Magazine*. In it, Friedman stated matter-of-factly that "only people have responsibilities"; businesses have no responsibilities as such. So to state that a corporation has a responsibility to pursue a social good is really to state that persons affiliated with the corporation, be they managers or workers or shareholders, bear that responsibility. Clarifying this point, Friedman said, helped to expose the legal and ethical issues involved. If a corporation makes a donation to charity, for example, it is really corporate managers who are making donations of assets that ultimately belong to corporate shareholders. Unless those shareholders express their desire to make such a donation, the manager's decision to support the donation is a case of one person "spending someone else's money." Far better would be a decision to return the money to shareholders as dividends (or capital gains, realized if and when they sell their stock) and let them decide which charities to support. Similarly, if corporate social responsibilities are to be fulfilled with money that would otherwise go to employees in the form of wages, or that is collected by raising prices for consumers, then the corporate manager is spending their money without consent as well.[18]

In Friedman's view, the purpose of the corporation was clear. "There is one and only one social responsibility of business—to use its resources and engage in activities designed to increase its profits," he stated, "so long as it stays within the rules of the game, which is to say, engages in open and free competition without deception or fraud."[19] This last proviso is extremely important in the philosophy of Friedman and other market-oriented thinkers. Profit is the purpose of the corporation, but it cannot justify individual acts of violence or fraud. These acts violate the basic laws of a free society, as well as make truly free exchange in the marketplace impossible. So, in reality, the proper function of the corporation is to pursue *justly obtained* profits.

For Friedman, the most destructive element of the corporate social responsibility movement was its impact on business executives themselves. Calling the pronouncements of some "socially responsible" businesses "pure and unadulterated socialism," Friedman wrote that "businessmen who talk [about social responsibilities] are unwitting puppets of the intellectual forces that have been undermining the basis of a free society these past decades."[20] Friedman added, however, that in one sense he could understand why even reasonable business executives might make public comments about social responsibility. If enough people in society began to view corporations as having social responsibilities other than those involving profit, then corporate managers, as a function of their responsibility to the survival and profitability of the business, might be justified in embracing and advertising social goals. "If our institutions, and the attitudes of the public, make it in their self-interest to cloak their actions in this way, I cannot summon much indignation to denounce them," Friedman stated. "At the same time, I can express admiration for those individual proprietors or owners of closely held corporations or stockholders of more broadly held corporations who disdain such tactics as approaching fraud."[21]

This is an interesting passage, fraught with implications that Friedman's critics have seized upon, but it is hardly the only controversial issue to arise out of this article. It is no exaggeration to say that, with very few exceptions, every major article on or analysis of corporate social responsibility since the publication of the *New York Times Magazine* piece has cited it, mentioned it, or challenged it. Some critics maintain that Friedman's understanding of corporate ownership is badly dated;

since shareholders are passive or even unknowing investors in particular companies, they don't exercise the type of control that real owners of property do. "With the dissolution of ownership in the traditional sense," wrote one legal scholar, "the dichotomy between shareholder and societal member must be reconsidered." In essence, since stockholders increasingly invest in diversified mutual funds or pension plans, their conscious interest is more in the health of business and society as a whole rather than in the health of particular firms. Thus, the argument continues, a firm will actually fulfill the true desires of shareholders by making investments in institutions that make the economy or society better off generally, even if the firm sacrifices its own profits to do so.[22]

Another argument lodged against Friedman's view is that he oversimplifies the nature of business activity. One prominent religious scholar wrote that dividing profit-seeking business activity from the larger world of political, legal, and social decision-making is impossible. "In order to find [Friedman] credible at all, we must overlook the massive involvement of business in the realm of law," the professor wrote. "Far from specializing in pure economic activity, with law being left to the separate socio-political domain, business is heavily involved in the realm of law in both its legislative and judicial dimensions."[23] Similarly, without good schools, infrastructure, peaceful and safe communities, solid families, and a prosperous public with money to spend, business cannot thrive—so its economic responsibilities are so intertwined with social responsibilities (to fund social, economic, or educational programs and press for political change) that the two cannot be distinguished. Once again, Friedman is said to be living in the past or in the world of abstract theory rather than reality. "Role specialization, while perhaps desirable, does not and cannot exist in our modern industrial economy," Thomas Jones stated. "Corporations play a political role; governments play an economic role. Profit alone no longer implies preferred behavior. . . . Corporations are social institutions and as such must live up to society's standards; society has changed the standards for corporations, as it has every right to do."[24] Still another argument is that corporate shareholders often are merely bystanders and should not expect to benefit from the success of a company as much as groups with more direct influence on company performance, such as workers. "Being basically capitalists and not genuine entrepreneurs, stockholders therefore do not deserve the profits their investments generate," wrote one British scholar.[25]

Political or economic liberals have not been Friedman's only critics. Conservatives, too, have questioned the notion that a corporation's only social responsibility is to increase profits. Some prominent conservative politicians and intellectuals, for example, have criticized media companies for producing music, television programs, motion pictures, and other forms of entertainment containing antisocial content (for example, pornography or violence). These conservatives use terms such as "corporate citizenship" to express their views about business responsibilities to society, terms that anthropomorphize corporations and blur the distinction between *persons* and, in contrast, the *institutions* created by persons to achieve certain ends.

Friedman has answered these kinds of criticisms in the years since his famous article. Changes in the economy and society have not invalidated the distinction between corporations and other institutions, Friedman argues, nor is the relationship between shareholder and corporate manager anything but an owner–employee or principal–agent relationship. To suggest otherwise is merely to substitute one's judgment for the judgment of shareholders, who, after all, voluntarily decide whether to invest their funds. They (or their agents among money managers) will sell stock of companies from which they no longer expect competitive returns.[26] Indeed, the proliferation of stock ownership through institutional investors has merely reinforced the responsibility of corporate managers to focus like a laser beam on profit as an objective. Corporate social responsibility scholars may not like the implications of this trend, but that does not justify their attempts to second-guess the desires of shareholders for economic return. A defender of Friedman's position once pointed out that the Bible provides an example of how passive ownership is, nevertheless, clearly ownership:

Consider the Parable of the Talents. A master entrusted assets to three servants. He then left the country. By doing so, the master created both legal and physical separation of ownership and control. Two of the servants invested the assets in productive uses, doubling their value, and were rewarded when the master returned. The third, however, simply returned the master's assets without even having earned interest on them and was punished. . . . The parable was effective because its hearers understood that the departed master retained his ownership rights even though the stewards had been entrusted with control over the property. Those of us who find the parable effective today do so because we see a separation of ownership and control in a host of secular settings and because we still understand that separating control from ownership does not divest the owner of his rights.[27]

About objections that a single-minded pursuit of profit would allow corporations to make and sell all sorts of socially destructive things, Friedman points out that individual employees, consumers, and shareholders have the right—indeed, the responsibility—to refuse to participate in economic activities whose social effects they fear or that violate their personal ethical or religious beliefs. "If a chemist feels it is immoral to make napalm," Friedman said in an interview, "he can solve his problem by getting a job where he doesn't have to."[28] One might add other examples: a religious person need not work for the *Humanist*; an orthodox Jew need not work for Oscar Mayer; and those who believe that violent and pornographic entertainment are causing significant social harm need not work for, buy from, or own stock in companies that produce it. In each case, if enough people make their views clear through personal action, corporations who seek economic return will have to rethink their activities. This reliance on such issues as labor availability, cost, and consumer demand—rather than the whims and personal opinions of corporate managers—is helpful because it allows corporate decisions about social or moral issues to be based on real information about the society in which they operate. "This is another way in which the free market does provide a much more sensitive and subtle voting mechanism than does the political system," Friedman concluded.[29]

SHIFTING THE FOCUS OF DEBATE

Most proponents and opponents of corporate social responsibility have spent a great deal of time debating such issues as the true nature of corporate ownership in America today and the legal or fiduciary responsibilities of corporate managers in business transactions such as takeovers and mergers. But for the purposes of this book, there remain a couple of points from Friedman's discussion of corporate social responsibility that stand out as crucial, though unappreciated, issues for corporate managers and other interested persons to think about.

One is the important notion that corporations do not exist in physical reality. This has implications beyond Friedman's contention that corporations, as artificial persons, cannot really have social responsibilities. Consider that corporations consist of more than simply the land, plants, machinery, inventory, and products owned by the corporation. The value of a corporation—at least in the minds of those who buy, hold, or sell its stock—is based on both tangible and intangible assets. A company with few assets today but a great idea for a new product may dominate the marketplace tomorrow, while a company with millions of dollars in assets and a large market share in a soon-to-be obsolete industry may be destined for failure. Hard-to-quantify characteristics such as worker morale, management style, systems for promoting internal innovation, and an ability to foresee future trends determine the expected value of corporate stock.

Can individual shareholders of a corporation really be viewed as "owners" of such corporate assets as the brainpower and work ethic of employees, or the goodwill and confidence of consumers? Perhaps, but a more meaningful way to think about corporations may be that they are bundles of ever-changing and variably valuable private agreements between individual persons. Coca-Cola, for example, might be reasonably thought of as a set of bilateral and multilateral agreements between such groups as corn growers, factory workers, plastic designers, bauxite miners, graphic artists, bank lenders, bond buyers, managers, retailers, soda drinkers, and celebrity endorsers. All these individuals (and many others) enter into contracts with "Coca-Cola" in which they agree to provide something of value in exchange for something else of value.

Stockholders are no different; they agree to risk their wealth as equity owners of the corporation in exchange for the promise of a profitable return on their investment. There is nothing greedy or socially undesirable about this emphasis on profit. While some stockholders might fit the stereotype of the wealthy, East Coast capitalist seeking to add to his million-dollar fortune, most do not. Many American families rely on investments in stocks or mutual funds to pay the down payment on their first home, to send their kids to college, or to live decently in retirement. The median household income of a corporate shareholder was $43,800 in 1990, and the median age was forty-three. Fully one out of every four adult Americans owns corporate stock, either directly or through a stock mutual fund. Millions more own stock less directly by being vested in employer pension plans, which collectively own about a quarter of all corporate equity. Still others benefit from stock profitability as customers of insurance companies. Geographically, corporate stockholders are dispersed throughout the United States; only 5 percent live in New York City.[30] Shareholders of U.S. corporations seek profit in the same way that other sizable groups of Americans seek higher wages as workers, higher interest rates as lenders, lower interest rates as borrowers, and lower prices as consumers. Corporations serve as the venue where these sometimes-compatible, sometimes-conflicting interests are accommodated in ever-changing, but always mutually satisfactory, ways.

Stephen Bainbridge, a professor at the University of Illinois College of Law, has suggested that this "nexus of contracts" view of corporations, arising among economists and legal scholars mostly after Friedman's 1970 essay, establishes a firmer defense of profit as the goal of corporations than the traditional understanding of shareholder "ownership" Friedman employs. After all, shareholders of publicly traded companies, at least, do differ from owners of other property in some easily recognizable ways. Someone who buys a few shares in Coca-Cola and is subsequently caught breaking into a bottling plant cannot defend himself by proclaiming that since he is an "owner" of Coca-Cola, he has a perfect right to enter the premises of a company plant without permission. Thinking of the responsibility of corporate managers to corporate stockholders as stemming from a contract with a specified goal—the maximization of profitable return on investment—might be more helpful than thinking about property ownership per se. Embracing the contractual definition of a corporation, Bainbridge is able to argue that state laws allowing incorporation are not special public favors to corporate shareholders, justifying special public expectations of social obligation from those shareholders. Instead, they are merely "default rules"—rules for establishing contracts between buyers and sellers of equity that would come about in the marketplace anyway, but at a high transaction cost. Rather than having every corporation and potential shareholder negotiate and sign contracts, the law recognizes a baseline corporate contract that everyone is presumed to agree to unless otherwise specified. "Refusing to hold shareholders personally liable for firm debts thus is the precise equivalent of enforcing a standard form sales contract, nothing more and nothing less," Bainbridge contends.[31]

Another of Friedman's points that deserves greater attention is his suggestion that "the people who preach the doctrine of social responsibility are concealing something: the great virtue of the private enterprise system is precisely that by maximizing corporate profits, corporate executives contribute far more to the social welfare than they do by spending stockholders' money on what they as individuals regard as worthwhile activity."[32] Here we are at the crux of the matter. The assumption that profit is inconsistent with the common good of the society is predicated on a tension between making money and serving one's fellow man. But if the pursuit of profit really does, as Adam Smith said centuries go, act as "an invisible hand" guiding human action toward socially beneficial endeavors, then surely to abandon that pursuit is to lose social benefits that would otherwise exist.

In other words, perhaps commercial activity—as distinguished from such other forms of behavior as personal philanthropy or government action—confers unique benefits on society. Realistically, all sorts of problems in society can be viewed as within the purview of corporate activity. But in Friedman's view, the response of corporations to these problems will and must be different because of the nature of profit-seeking business: "The crucial question for a corporation is not whether some action is in the interest of the corporation, but whether it is enough in its interest to justify the money spent."[33] Companies, then, bring a search for efficiency and economy to the task of solving problems. This search represents a fundamentally different way of addressing social problems than the means employed by governments, charities, churches, or families. Therefore, Friedman concluded, social responsibility means something very different to businesses than it does to other social institutions. In the next chapter I will clarify this distinction further, in the specific case of charitable giving.

CHAPTER 2

A SOCIAL INVESTMENT
BALANCE SHEET

B y anyone's definition, Jerome Lemelson would be called a great philanthropist. Born in 1923, Lemelson has donated tens of millions of dollars over the years to organizations ranging from the Massachusetts Institute of Technology to local charities across the country. A great deal of his philanthropy has been devoted to extolling the virtues of invention and innovation in America. He has given millions of dollars to universities and the Smithsonian Institution in Washington to create programs to teach and promote invention. In 1995 the first annual Lemelson-MIT Prize—a $500,000 award for oustanding American inventors—was awarded at the Smithsonian.[1] At his death, the Lemelson Foundation is expected to be worth at least $300 million.[2]

By endowing university chairs in innovation and funding inventor awards, Lemelson's philanthropy merely reflects his life's work. Jerome Lemelson holds more patents than any living human being. Since 1949, when he began tinkering with inventions as a New York University student (inventing the typewriter eraser as a class project), Lemelson has patented some five hundred inventions, ranging from video telephones, audiocassette players, and videocassette records to spark plugs, syringes, ice skates, and Silly Putty. Only Thomas Edison, Elihu Thomson, and Edwin Land (who invented the Polaroid camera) have more patents. By licensing and marketing his many valuable inventions, Lemelson, now a resident of Incline Village, Nevada, has become a millionaire many times over.[3]

We associate inventors with gadgets and gee-whiz discoveries to such an extent that we often forget how important their innovations are to the everyday economy. Lemelson, for example, invented the flexible manu-facturing system, now the standard in manufacturing enterprises the world over. Before this innovation, assembly lines were fixed and unchangeable; now, when a manufacturer wants to change the design of a product, it need not install a whole new assembly line. The efficiency gains from this development would be difficult to overestimate. No matter how hard Lemelson tries, there is no possible way that he can give enough money away to make his charitable contribution to American society approach the value of his contributions as an innovator and entrepreneur.

Take just one of his inventions, an automated system for reading bar-code labels. Without this modest-sounding technology, which Lemelson helped to pioneer, a large segment of modern industry simply would not exist.[4] Manufacturers such as automakers and computer companies rely on bar codes to track the flow of parts in factories and the movement of finished goods into the distribution chain. When most Americans encounter bar codes every day at checkout lines in grocery stores and retail establishments, cashiers merely swipe the bar code past a reader to record a product's price in the cash register; they do not see how this information then travels to central processing units in store offices, ware-houses, and corporate headquarters, allowing companies to adjust pro-duction and distribution to changing desires of consumers. This seemingly simple and commonplace technology allowed new retailers with daily information about consumer demand as well as their own inventories to cut prices, increase product offerings, and, generally speaking, serve customers better beyond merely speeding up lines and reducing checkout-line errors. Wal-Mart, Toys 'R' Us, Blockbuster, and Home Depot all owe a large portion of their growth and success to the revolutionary impact of bar-code readers.[5] Measuring the impact of this in value added to the economy would be virtually impossible, but you would clearly be talking about many billions of dollars, at least. Lemel-son's philanthropic activities, while praiseworthy, pale by comparison.

Lemelson understands the social value of entrepreneurship. "Innova-tion and invention have helped build the greatest industrial economy the world has ever known," he said, "but inventors have always been left on their own. My goal is to make Americans more conscious of innovation."[6] Until he and others succeed at this important task, however, the debate about the responsibility of business to society will continue to be focused to a strange and even absurd extent on noncommercial activities that are deemed socially beneficial, rather than on what firms actually make and sell. So Vermont-based Ben & Jerry's is thought of by many to be almost the prototype of a socially responsible corporation because it gives away 7.5 percent of its corporate profits as philanthropy (the average for U.S. corporations is a little over 1 percent), limits the salaries of top executives, and identifies its marketing and public statements with social causes from homelessness to saving the world's rainforests.[7] Yet it actually spends most of its time making and selling ice cream, which is purely a luxury good (unlike, say, rice or shoes or electric power) and which, it might be argued, contributes to the poor health of many Americans by filling their bellies with fat and sugar.

Is Ben & Jerry's, by virtue of its philanthropy and social activism, really more socially responsible than, say, a manufacturer of plastic 55-gallon drums, with a tiny corporate giving program and no political causes to champion? The company's drums might safely and cheaply store yarns for transport from one floor of a factory to another floor, or from textile mills to apparel manufacturers, reducing the retail price of clothing and thus making a family's scarce dollars stretch a little further. But according to the standards that many social responsibility analysts employ, such a company would hardly merit a mention—or perhaps even a negative one, since it uses "non-renewable resources" such as plastic to make its products.

PHILANTHROPY AND RESPONSIBILITY

Of all the issues related to corporate social responsibility, perhaps the most straightforward is philanthropy. Most advocates of social responsibility point to philanthropic activities as typifying their vision of corporate citizenship. Moreover, as discussed in the previous chapter, the legal history of corporate social responsibility is closely intertwined with changes in corporate giving. The major rulings of the 1950s that delinked corporate decision-making from traditional standards of corporate responsibility, at least in the minds of many executives and analysts, also effectively protected all but the most egregious cases of corporate malfeasance from judicial review. Managers were empowered to use their own discretion to serve not only the interests of shareholders but also those of society as a whole.

It is important to realize, though, that corporate philanthropy has been standard business practice throughout American history. During the nineteenth century and the first half of the twentieth century, American businesses practiced various forms of corporate giving. Firms not only built and funded hospitals and schools, they essentially created such national nonprofit organizations as the YMCA. But these activities, conducted under the legal standard later codified in the 1919 *Dodge v. Ford* case, were intended to serve the *direct* business interests of the firms. Companies created hospitals in areas where their employees lived so that their future workforces would be healthy. They funded community chests devoted to social, educational, and recreational amenities for employees and even gave money to employees' churches so their spiritual needs would be met. Railroad companies built a system of local YMCAs to give itinerant employees a place to stay the night and get a hot meal.[8] These expenditures were relatively easy to defend to directors and shareholders, because the connection between them and the profits of the business were clear. At the same time, the amount of money donated to charity by corporations remained modest.

The nature of corporate giving changed during the 1950s and 1960s. Perceiving less of a responsibility to serve shareholders exclusively, corporate managers expanded the scope of giving programs to faraway universities, orchestras, food banks, and other charities previously funded exclusively by individuals and estates. Major corporations created their own in-house foundations, which built up large endowments. The Exxon Education Foundation, for example, funded programs for decades that bore no relation to Exxon's main line of business. The outside directors of the foundation were not necessarily company employees or family members, and they made decisions on the basis of social and humanitarian goals, not corporate goals.[9]

The *magnitude* of corporate philanthropy, however, has not changed dramatically since World War II. Corporate giving as a share of total philanthropy in the United States was small before the 1950s and has remained so. It has fluctuated over the years, but it seems to have tracked economic growth more than social or legal trends. In the thirty years (from

1963 to 1993) examined by *Giving USA 1994*, a publication of the American Association of Fund Raising Councils, corporate giving as a share of total giving stayed in the middle single digits, falling below 4 percent during the economic turmoil from 1970 to 1976 and rising above 6 percent during the economic boom of the mid-1980s. In 1993 corporate philanthropy (including corporation-funded foundations) totaled $5.9 billion, or a modest 4.7 percent of all giving. By comparison, individuals accounted for the lion's share (81 percent) of American philanthropy, with both grant-making foundations and bequests playing a larger role in philanthropy than corporations.[10]

In the previous chapter I dealt largely with the theory of corporate social responsibility. In the case of philanthropy, at least, reality intrudes. As (1) the world economy has become increasingly competitive, (2) the role of savvy institutional investors acting on behalf of yield-seeking individuals has expanded, and (3) corporations have reviewed their decades of experience with post–*Smith v. Barlow* giving programs, an interesting reversal has taken place. Even as managers have retained their broad discretion over the use of corporate funds, corporate philanthropy has been gradually and steadily returning to the old "business interest" model that predates the modern corporate social responsibility movement. At most American companies today, philanthropy is no longer considered a sacrosanct element of a "social contract" in which corporations have a duty to serve "stakeholders" through giving and other activities. Instead, corporations view philanthropy as an integral part of their operations, in some cases even moving giving programs into their marketing or advertising divisions. Philanthropy is undertaken now largely because of direct, tangible benefits a firm and its shareholders can expect to receive. Today, as Amoco Foundation executive director Patricia Wright put it, "anyone involved in the corporate world knows that it is necessary to have a strong strategic link between charitable giving and the corporation's bottom line."[11] The Amoco Foundation had traditionally given money to a host of causes, from the arts to medical research. In 1992, Amoco decided to focus philanthropy in just two areas: education and inner cities. Wright explained that the need for well-trained workers had inspired the choice of education, while Amoco had a large market share in inner-city markets.[12]

Menlo Smith, chairman of the Sunmark Capital Corporation in St. Louis and founder of the Sunmark Foundation, has long practiced this form of corporate philanthropy. "Because our shareholders will always have different charitable interests, we concluded long ago that any giving done by Sunmark should have a very direct business purpose, and that if it does not, the giving should then be done individually by the shareholders, and not the corporation," he said.[13] This concept, often called *strategic philanthropy*, is increasingly being embraced by American business executives. It represents the triumph of market pressures and common sense over judicial speculation and academic theory. Milton Friedman and similar critics may have lost the legal or academic battle over the propriety of corporate philanthropy (given the statements of some judges and scholars on the subject), but their views are being vindicated by actual corporate behavior.

PHILANTHROPY AND THE PROFIT IMPERATIVE

Strategic philanthropy is implemented differently by different firms. For some corporations, it involves the introduction of formal cost-benefit analyses, which set performance goals for social or charitable activities and carefully track progress toward those goals. General Electric, for example, hired the Rand Corporation to track student performance at urban high schools receiving $20 million in funds from the company foundation.[14] For other corporations, strategic philanthropy simply involves ongoing consideration of how philanthropy ties into the firm's need to attract good employees, enthusiastic investors, and loyal customers. No longer are a company's business goals and philanthropy goals formulated separately by different groups of decision-makers. As Curtis G. Weeden, vice president for corporate contributions at Johnson & Johnson, explains: "It is essential that corporate giving is linked to business goals. An effective philanthropy program should be clearly connected to the high-priority concerns of the company."[15]

Critics view with trepidation the return of "business interest" as a guiding force in corporate philanthropy, but if their concern is with actually making social progress—rather than maximizing the flow of corporate funds into charities—then strategic philanthropy fits the bill nicely. The reason is that when businesses have a legitimate role to play in addressing a social problem, they tend to deploy all of their resources in the effort. "For the first time," says corporate giving analyst Craig Smith, "businesses are backing philanthropic initiatives with real corporate muscle."[16] So in addition to giving away cash, corporations are giving non-

profit organizations managerial advice, technological and communication support, and teams of employee volunteers. Moving beyond traditional practices of pitching corporate funds toward the favorite causes of
individual managers or board members, corporations are actually trying
to solve problems—a more limited slate of problems, granted, but that is
how it should be.[17]

So what legitimate business interests can be served through corporate
philanthropy? Below I discuss four major objectives of corporate giving
programs, and how companies try to reach them.

Attracting Loyal Customers

Perhaps the most straightforward use of corporate philanthropy is to market a firm's goods and services to customers whose charitable impulses
or social values inform their buying decisions. Two large U.S. firms that
pioneered this approach are American Express and AT & T. American
Express developed its "cause-related marketing" strategy during the early
1980s separately from its more traditional philanthropic foundation. The
ideas was to link card usage to corporate giving: whenever a consumer
used the American Express card to make a purchase, the company would
make a contribution to a charity valued by the consumer. "By giving people a local cause to rally around," said Jerry Welsh, the company executive who engineered the program, "we hoped to spark cardholders into
using their cards for local purchases."[18]

American Express tried the approach first in the California market in
the spring of 1981. California was and remains one the most competitive
credit card markets in the country (indeed, the first widely distributed
multiple-use credit card in the country was the BankAmericard—later to
become Visa—issued by San Francisco–based Bank of America). In an
effort to increase American Express Card usage in the Bay Area, the
company pledged during a three-month period to donate two cents to the
San Francisco Arts Festival every time local customers used their credit
cards. After the company exceeded its marketing goals (and the arts festival received $100,000 in contributions), American Express replicated the
strategy in local markets across the country, linking card usage to support
for ballets, symphonies, opera companies, and other community arts
organizations. A 1983 national campaign linked to company support for
the Statue of Liberty restoration project pledged a penny for every use of

the card and a dollar each time a new customer applied for a card. Card usage increased 20 percent during the quarter of the promotional campaign over the same period the previous year, the number of new cardholders rose more than 45 percent, and the campaign generated $1.7 million for the statue's restoration. "We're giving away money, but we're doing it in a way that builds business," Welsh said.[19] Interestingly, American Express wasn't the first company to tie promotions to the Statue of Liberty. Joseph Pulitzer helped fund the construction of the statue's pedestal more than a century ago by offering to print the name of each contributor in his New York newspaper, a tactic that not only raised plenty of money but also increased circulation.[20]

At AT & T, corporate funding for the arts and cultural institutions represents a targeted effort to compete with other long-distance telephone companies for the business of upscale customers. By changing AT & T's long-established image as an old, stodgy company, executives sought to attract the young, upwardly mobile professionals who were heavy users of long distance. In the mid-1980s AT & T marketing and foundation executives began to meet with artists to discuss common interests, and by 1989 the company had developed the "AT & T: OnStage" program. Production costs and operating support for nonprofit drama, music, and dance productions come from the corporate foundation, while the marketing division helps advertise productions. The company has enjoyed success by picking productions likely to win critical acclaim and the interest of potential customers. As its expenditures on the program have risen, AT & T has been able to rely less on traditional advertising.[21] "There is a higher percentage of the types of people we want to reach in the arts," said AT & T vice president Edward Block. "You think in terms of what it costs you to reach whatever kind of person you're trying to reach, and clearly our support of orchestras is a very attractive business proposition."[22]

Many other American companies, large and small, use sponsorships and product tie-ins to make their philanthropy serve their interests as well as those of beneficiaries. When Barnett Banks opened a new branch outside of Jacksonville, Florida, it advertised a program to donate $1 to a local preservation society for every $100 received in deposits during the first week of operations. The branch received $1 million in deposits, making it the bank's fastest-growing office.[23] McDonald's Corporation has found that its Ronald McDonald Houses, created in the mid-1970s for sick children and families, have yielded tremendous social and financial benefits. The company provides seed money for each Ronald McDonald House; local franchisees serve on house boards and collect most of the funding for the program from restaurant customers. McDonald's suppliers, such as Coca-Cola, also provide contributions. Franchisers have found that after they run a Ronald McDonald House promotion in their restaurants, sales in that community increase significantly.[24] "We can become more competitive not only with our product but also through the work we do in the community," said Ken Barun, president and CEO of Ronald McDonald Children's Charities. "People may decide to eat at McDonald's—versus one of our competitors—because of their emotional responses to our charitable activities."[25]

Rockport was a relatively small shoe manufacturer in Marlborough, Massachusetts, before it discovered the power of cause-related marketing. In 1982, the company began an intensive program to promote the health benefits of walking, distributing more than 2 million brochures and founding the Rockport Walking Institute. The company's efforts helped the fitness-walking craze of the 1980s gain momentum, and Rockport saw its own sales of walking shoes increase twentyfold.[26] The process of finding a link between product and cause can yield some interesting results. Ralston Purina Company, for example, funds a campaign to help senior citizens adopt pets.[27]

Some corporate giving has become so intermingled with advertising campaigns that it has become almost impossible to distinguish the two. Sponsoring sports events, for example, can mean spending a few hundred dollars to buy uniforms for a Little League team (with the sponsor's name on the back, of course) to spending millions of dollars on major attractions. In recent years, college football bowl games have become the equivalent of huge billboards advertising corporate sponsors, yielding such names as the USF & G Sugar Bowl, the Federal Express Orange Bowl, the Outback Steakhouse Gator Bowl, the XIBM OS/2 Fiesta Bowl, and the John Hancock Bowl (which abandoned its non-corporate name altogether).[28] Slightly less famous endeavors along the same lines include the Ken-L Ration Kids' Dog Show, USTA–Michelob Light League Tennis, and the Pepsi-Cola Hot Shot Basketball Program.[29]

Of course, cause-related marketing only works when a company can offer a good or service that is competitive in quality and price. "The research that says people will pay more for socially responsible goods simply isn't true," said Jeffrey Hollender, chief executive officer of Seventh Generation Inc. Hollender found, for example, that the only way to make his "environmentally friendly" dishwashing detergent competitive in the market was to use a petroleum-based cleaning agent. Reformulating the product, which had previously contained no petrochemicals, reduced its price dramatically, leading to a 20 percent increase in sales.[30]

Studies show that *on the margin*—that is, once consumers are choosing among products similar in price and quality—images and feelings about companies can play a role in the final decision. One Roper Organization poll found that when choosing between products of equal price and quality, 78 percent of respondents said they would buy the one made by a company that contributes to medical research, education, and the like. Two-thirds said they would switch brands to a manufacturer that began to support a cause they deemed worthy. Nevertheless, most respondents said that advertising had more of an influence on them than corporate social activism.[31] In other words, it is not enough for companies to spend shareholder funds to support charitable activities; for the best results, these activities must be related in some direct and memorable way to the company's products. Also, in corporate giving it is extremely important that the public know about the company's good works. Without such knowledge, the business interest is not served.

Until relatively recently, corporate managers thought that this strategy was too obviously self-serving and might actually turn off current or potential customers.[32] "It took business a while to reconcile the fact the society understood strategic, targeted giving," said Archie Carroll, a management professor and public relations analyst at the University of Georgia. "In fact, corporate understanding lagged public sophistication in this regard." Customers do not mind the corporate interest, Carroll adds.[33] Contrast the extensive but unpublicized philanthropy by the late Robert Woodruff, founding chairman of Coca-Cola whose nickname among Georgia charity circles was "Mr. Anonymous," with the company's giving program today. As the Conference Board's magazine noted, "It now attempts to run a high-profile program, based on clearly defined guidelines that are intended to enhance overall corporate goals—that is, sell more Coca-Cola."[34] This need for publicity underscores the qualitative difference between corporate philanthropy (when properly used, a narrow but useful function) and individual philanthropy, where we satisfy the vast majority of our charitable or altruistic yearnings, and where modesty typically is valued over self-promotion.

Attracting and Building a Productive Workforce

In the competitive world economy, the search for productivity represents the key activity of successful companies. This quest for the holy grail of more and better output at lower cost is prosecuted on numerous fronts, but one common approach, particularly when trying to attract skilled workers to an existing facility, is to make donations to organizations or causes that improve the amenities of the community surrounding the facility. Just as the railroad companies of the nineteenth century funded YMCAs and schools for their employees, so today many companies give funds to local chapters of the Boy Scouts, to schools and universities, and to local human services agencies. Many of these activities are discussed in subsequent chapters.

One proven strategy for improving employee performance at the workplace is to build a sense of teamwork and corporate mission through volunteer activities. Traditionally, team sports have been used for this purpose, but firms have learned that other programs might accomplish similar goals and allow more employees—including those not so athletically inclined—to participate. Connecticut-based GE Plastics has used several community-service projects in which volunteer teams have helped renovate a homeless shelter, a boys' club, and a YMCA. The idea was to take "the tremendous energy and creativity of four hundred people and do something to help other people," said Joel Hutt, marketing communication manager for the company; the goal "was to get to know each other by sharing a hard day's work for a good cause." Similarly, Questar Corporation, a natural gas company in Salt Lake City, researches and publishes a list of local volunteer opportunities for employees. "Our morale is higher and our employees are more productive because they are involved with the community," said community affairs director Jan Bates.[35]

Union Planters National Bank in Memphis, Tennessee, runs a volunteer program called IMPACT (Individuals Making Progress And Changing Tomorrow). The bank informs employees about local opportunities where they can donate funds or time to worthwhile causes such as literacy training, building low-income housing, and sponsoring local schools. Union Planters recognizes its employee volunteers with IMPACT license plates, T-shirts, and special prizes for its most devoted workers. In 1992, more than half of the bank's employees participated in the program, donating forty thousand volunteer hours to more than two hundred agencies throughout Tennessee. "I look at the IMPACT program as a benefit," said one employee participant. "It gives Union Planters one more notch on its belt to show why it's a great organization to be affiliated with."[36] Merchants National Bank in Montgomery, West Virginia, found that the process of getting employees together from all its divisions to plan and carry out community projects was useful. "One of the benefits of our meetings is getting to know employees from other branches and departments," said one Merchants employee; another said that "working together creates a bond between the employees that otherwise might not exist."[37]

These sorts of benefits from volunteer programs are quantifiable. A study conducted by IBM and the Graduate School of Business at Columbia University found a positive correlation between employee involvement in the community and such measures as return on assets, return on investment, and employee productivity. A 1993 report by the Conference Board made a similar point: that volunteer programs give companies a tool to attract and retain good employees, helping them develop valuable characteristics such as creativity, trust, teamwork, and persistence.[38]

Similarly, the small number of formal academic studies on corporate philanthropy in general have found that American companies seem to view the two profit-seeking behaviors described above—attracting customers and building a strong, productive workforce—as the primary motivations for giving. In particular, a study done by researchers from Texas A & M University and Emory University found that corporate expenditures on advertising and on charitable contributions are closely related. The study also found that companies such as retailers with a great deal of public contact tend to give more money to nonprofits (and, of course, spend more money on advertising) than do firms such as first-stage manufacturers with little public contact. These findings "refute the social responsibility rationale for corporate philanthropy," they wrote, and suggest that it is in the main a "profit-motivated expense" rather than a measure of "altruistic responses of corporations."[39]

Promoting the General Economic Interest of Firms

A great deal of corporate giving, especially the large amount of it directed toward institutions of higher learning, involves research or educational programs with an obvious connection to a donor firm's economic interest. The Ameritech Foundation, for instance, gave Ohio State

University $1 million in 1993 "to support research in how telecommunications can be used to improve education, health care, and international trade." That same year, IBM gave Purdue University $2.25 million to research "innovative uses of computing and engineering applications." Kimberly-Clark Corporation, a Dallas-based manufacturer of consumer and health care products, gave $1 million to the University of Texas for rehabilitation research aimed at "understanding disabilities and developing methods to help disabled people live productively." Johnson & Johnson spends a half-million dollars each year to send hospital executives and chief nurses to a grueling, three-week mini-MBA course at the University of Pennsylvania's Wharton School of Business. Besides learning valuable management skills, the participating hospital staffers—who are responsible for most buying decisions at their institutions—are also exposed to the company's brand name and products.[40] And Monsanto Agricultural Company gave $2 million to the American Red Cross for flood-relief activities in the Midwest, a region of the country with obvious importance to the firm.[41] Subsequent chapters in this book on education and health care explore this connection more fully.

Promoting Pro-Business Public Policy

Another legitimate "business interest" that corporate philanthropy can address is the firm's interest in public or political disputes. Obviously, American corporations, large and small, operate within a political environment. Decisions by local, state, and federal government have a significant direct or indirect impact on companies by reducing their profits, increasing their costs, curtailing their markets, and limiting their freedom. In a variety of ways, corporate managers use strategic philanthropy to advance the legitimate interests of their firms in this context. So, for example, many companies fund programs to teach students about free enterprise and the American economic system. Corporate-funded chairs in business, economics, entrepreneurship, sociology, and law often have the stated purpose of promoting market values and concepts. Furthermore, many corporations fund think tanks, associations, and other organizations in the public policy arena that research and promote capitalistic values and market-oriented public policies. Of course, some corporations also use donations to advance interests that clash with Friedman's proviso that force or fraud not be used to increase profits. Some firms seek government protection from competitors, while others seek government subsidies and special tax breaks. This important distinction is discussed in a later chapter.

Strategic philanthropy has not yet spread across the entire population of corporate givers, nor do all managers agree on how to carry it out. In fact, many companies operating in the public policy arena actually donate more money to organizations that work *against* corporate interests than those working to defend free enterprise. The Capital Research Center, a Washington-based research group, has for years documented this strange practice in a publication called *Patterns of Corporate Philanthropy*. Only a handful of large U.S. corporations give more money to market-oriented groups than they do to organizations hostile to economic freedom. And of the thirty-six nonprofit advocacy groups that received more than $250,000 in corporate contributions, twenty-seven had mostly anti-business agendas.[42] There are many reasons for this strange phenomenon, the most charitable (but hardly persuasive) being that corporate managers believe they are serving the interests of their shareholders by using generous donations to try to co-opt groups likely to oppose corporate interests. There is little evidence, however, that this strategy has succeeded. A more plausible explanation is that corporate philanthropy officers are not themselves enthusiastic advocates of free enterprise—and too many CEOs let such officers make giving decisions.

Even in less controversial ways, some American corporations continue to practice philanthropy the old-fashioned way, giving undifferentiated grants to local United Way chapters, giving to pet organizations or causes of executives, and making no attempt to connect philanthropy with the actual commercial activity of the firm. In an era of intense global competition for consumers and capital, these practices will likely be punished in the marketplace. "Far too many companies still have little to no strategy, and their donations efforts are akin to trying to spread a pound of butter from here to San Francisco," said a New York–based vice president for Hill & Knowlton. "Their giving is so scattered and unfocused that it is virtually invisible."[43] When telecommunications company US West decided to recast its giving program in 1988, it narrowed its focus and started thinking strategically. "Spreading money around like the good fairy didn't seem like a wise use," said Jane J. Prancan, executive director of the company foundation. The trend in corporate giving is definitely in that direction. A 1992 study of the hundred largest corporate donation programs by a Virginia philanthropy consultant found that more than half had developed strategic plans for giving, with thirty-eight implementing them only since 1990. As the process continues, companies that do not rethink their philanthropic practices will find themselves disadvantaged. "If we're perceived as people who just give away shareholders' money, we're not going to last very long," said Arco Foundation president Eugene R. Wilson.[44]

SOCIALLY RESPONSIBLE INVESTMENT

Strategic corporate philanthropy is sometimes referred to as *socially responsible investment* in the sense that companies, rather than simply giving away money, are making a conscious investment in a worthwhile social cause from which they expect to receive a return in the future. But there is a different meaning of the term that merits discussion here. It involves a conscious effort on the part of investors to buy and keep shares only of companies that meet certain tests of social responsibility, such as the refusal to produce or use products perceived to be environmentally destructive; a stated commitment to abortion rights, gay rights, or social justice; or the prevalence of philanthropy, affirmative action, day care subsidies, and health insurance for workers.[45]

Since the 1970s an increasing number of brokerages and mutual fund families have been offering funds with "social screens" that are supposed to exclude companies that pollute, oppress minorities and the poor, and do business with the Pentagon or unsavory foreign governments. Two of the oldest of these funds are the Pax World Fund (created by Pax World Management Corporation in 1971) and the Dreyfus Third Century fund (created by the Dreyfus Corporation in 1972). Calvert Asset Management Company operates a number of newer socially responsible funds, as do Parnassus Investments, Accrued Equities Inc., and Progressive Asset Management.[46] A parallel movement has been to pressure institutional investors such as pension funds and insurance companies to make socially responsible investments in such projects as low-income housing, small business development, and environmental waste management.[47]

There is, of course, nothing in a free society that precludes shareholders of companies from buying and holding their shares for whatever reason they choose. Similarly, if one wants to buy insurance or pension coverage from a company that practices "socially responsible investing," one certainly can. The problem for advocates of these investments, however, is the traditional—and really not debatable—presumption that unless an alternative is explicitly stated, the goal of shareholders, insurance subscribers, and pension recipients is financial. A worker who chooses an employer with a pension plan is most likely seeking to guarantee a stable source of postretirement income. A family that invests savings in a mutual fund is most likely trying to build a nest egg for retirement or children's college education. Neither the worker nor the family is likely to consider social or ideological agendas, even if they enthusiastically subscribe to them, to be as important as these objectives.[48] But proponents of socially responsible investing argue that these presumptions aren't true, or at least that there is no tension between the goal of profit maximization and the goal of advancing social or ideological causes. Peter Camejo, president of Progressive Asset Management, asserts that "the prevailing wisdom—[that you] sacrifice profits for principles—is wrong, dead wrong" when it comes to such investments.[49] Jerome S. Dodson, president of the Parnassus Fund, agreed that fund managers who screen investments on social criteria other than strict rate of return are not at a disadvantage.[50]

Fortunately, there is a test of which proposition is true: the market for investment. Almost without exception, "socially responsible" funds lag far behind the rest of the market in real returns to shareholders. Dreyfus Third Century, for example, is one of the largest of these funds, with $351 million in assets in 1995. As of that year, its annualized rate of return over the past five years was only 8.91 percent, compared with 12.1 percent for the average growth fund and 12.6 percent for the Standard & Poor's 500 Stock Index. Similarly, Pax World has posted a long-term return far below the market average. Of the socially responsible funds I was able to identify, only the Parnassus Fund has been a consistently high performer. More generally, most studies of social responsibility in business have found no correlation between the views and policies endorsed by the corporate social responsibility movement on the one hand and corporate profitability or stock performance on the other.[51] The underwhelming performance of "socially responsible" investing is hardly surprising. Social screening reduces the number of firms from which fund managers can choose, thus reducing the chances that they will pick a breakthrough company to propel the fund's yield to and above the market average. At the same time, the screening process itself can be costly.

Management fees, at least for the smaller funds in the socially responsible stable, are relatively high, further reducing the real rate of return.

These funds also can claim only a tiny percentage of total investment. In corporate equities, for example, the eight major socially responsible stock funds, as identified by *Business and Society Review*, could claim only $1.9 billion in total assets in 1995, less than three-hundredths of 1 percent of equity investment in the U.S. and about two-tenths of 1 percent of mutual fund equity holdings.[52] Socially responsible bond and money market funds also attract only a barely noticeable trickle of money. In other words, few investors seem interested in these socially screened investments, reinforcing the notion that for most shareholders, return is a much more important objective than fulfilling some ideological litmus test.

Whatever else may be true about these socially responsible investing firms and the criteria they use to evaluate companies, the facts seem to show that individuals who entrust their money to such firms are often sacrificing return on investment for some other social objective. That is, of course, their prerogative. In a sense, their investments are a form of philanthropy—they are supporting (as shareholders or lenders) companies that share their social or political concerns, by suffering an opportunity cost of lost potential returns. This is little different from simply giving cash to the same causes endorsed by the corporations in a "socially responsible" investor's portfolio.

CONCLUSION

One observation that can be made from the lackluster performance of socially responsible investments is that perhaps their managers are using a poor definition of social responsibility. Similarly, when critics say that corporations spend too little of their funds on philanthropy, they may be defining responsibility in a manner that does not really fit the institution they are studying.[53]

Individuals who give of their time and money to advance worthwhile causes are exhibiting some of the most noble and uplifting of human characteristics. Whether motivated by deep religious conviction or a secular sense of social justice and equality, these individuals are making and acting on value judgments about how they wish to spend their private lives. Corporations operate under a different set of conditions. Corporations are not human beings; they are bundles of contracts that human beings construct to perform certain tasks. Private, profit-seeking corporations that produce goods and services for sale exist to deliver some kind of tangible benefit to their shareholders (usually income, but possibly others such as a sense of achievement, personal glory, or the satisfaction of personal values). In a free economy where capital and investment flow without significant impediment, individuals are free to buy or sell shares of corporations according to how these corporations are meeting their personal goals at the time. As discussed in Chapter 1, American corporations are increasingly owned by passive investors who have entrusted the decision to buy, hold, or sell to agents (such as pension fund administrators and mutual fund managers) acting on their behalf. The vast majority of these agents have as their explicit charge the goal of maximizing economic returns on the investments entrusted to them.

To suggest, as many advocates of corporate social responsibility models do, that company executives should give a higher percentage of company revenues to charity—or that institutional investors should favor social goals over profit in managing their clients' assets—is to suggest that shareholders are unable or unwilling to make decisions for themselves. This, however, is not the case. In a competitive market, corporate managers or institutional investors who put other goals above profits are likely to see capital flow out of the "socially responsible" corporations and into alternative investments with a higher rate of return. Thus, as we have seen, the type and extent of corporate philanthropy have changed as the international market has grown more competitive. Company managers are finding that they cannot ignore the interests of company owners—be they a single person or hundreds of thousands of shareholders—when deciding how and where company funds will be spent. And two decades of attempts by "progressive" money managers to put other social interests above those of economic performance have resulted in mediocre returns and little interest on the part of most investors, who presumably prefer to make and act on their own value judgments about social causes with the proceeds of their profitably invested money.

There is, of course, a more direct and significant relationship between corporations and philanthropy than is rarely discussed by social responsibility proponents. When businesses are more profitable, individuals—be they owners, stockholders, executives, workers, and even consumers (if the profits stem from selling better products at lower prices)—can accumulate more wealth, with which they can make charitable donations or endow private foundations. This commonsense observation is often forgotten, even by those executives who run America's largest philanthropic foundations. As the Capital Research Center has often pointed out, such donors as the Ford Foundation, the Rockefeller Foundation, and the MacArthur Foundation fund projects and organizations that would have elicited strong objections from their capitalistic founders.[54] Richard B. McKenzie, a professor in the Graduate School of Management at the University of California, Irvine, wrote in a monograph for the Philanthropy Roundtable that "philanthropy is crucially dependent, both in theory and in fact, upon a well-oiled, efficiently operating market system."[55] Without such a system, less wealth will be generated for philanthropy. At the same time, without an efficient market system, there are likely to be more social problems (stemming from poverty and technological backwardness) on which philanthropists must spend their time and money.

Does the relatively small role of corporate philanthropy and so-called socially responsible investing in American society suggest that corporate responsibility is impossible or nonexistent? Does the search for profit preclude companies from making a positive impact on society? Certainly not. The debate about corporate social responsibility is one of *definition*. The extent of corporate philanthropy is simply not a useful or even reasonable measure of corporate responsibility. Indeed, regardless of its intentions or motivations, corporate philanthropy has been and probably will always be a small part of what corporations do and an even smaller part of the total amount of money given to charitable or social causes. To discover a more useful definition of corporate social responsibility, we must examine other aspects of the relationship between American companies and workers, consumers, investors, and society at large—distinguishing the many sweeping claims of corporate social responsibility analysts from the actual experience of American business.

CHAPTER 3

EMPLOYMENT, LAYOFFS, AND SOCIAL RESPONSIBILITY

Corporate social irresponsibility has often been exemplified by the image of a recently laid-off worker who, despite years or decades of devotion to an employer, is left with nothing more than a skimpy severance check, a company sweatshirt, and an uncertain or even undesirable future. A worker, for example, like Allen Stenhouse.

Stenhouse worked his way through night school at Georgia State University and put in twenty-four years in the insurance business, finally landing a $50,000-a-year job as business manager of a major insurance company's health care department and a $280,000 condo in West Hartford, Connecticut. But two days before Christmas in 1988, Stenhouse, then forty-eight, was laid off along witth two thousand other company employees. Unable to find similar work after months of searching, Stenhouse took a minimum-wage job stocking shelves at a discount store. He lost $13,000 of savings in a failed attempt to start a financial consulting business. His fourteen-year marriage collapsed. His condo was foreclosed on and auctioned off, and he owed the IRS some $22,000. By 1992 Stenhouse was living on Social Security disability payments in a cheap apartment and visiting a psychiatrist. "I have lost the fight to stay ahead in today's economy," he declared. "You can only be rejected so many times; then you start questioning your own self-worth."[1]

Surely, many analysts would say, any business that would pull the rug out from under such a loyal employee just to shave a few points off its operating costs cannot be considered socially responsible. Indeed, if Stenhouse—abandoned, dispossessed, despondent, unable to find solid employment and economic opportunity—were typical of American workers today, then there might be serious grounds for reconsidering not only the responsibility of particular firms to society but whether our economic system works at all. For every Allen Stenhouse, however, there is at least one Debora Kane. Kane was also earning $50,000 in 1988, as a computer systems analyst for Goldman Sachs in New York, when she got a layoff notice. She and her husband had just bought a new house and were new parents of a daughter, Susannah. Kane also tried to find work similar to what she had been doing for Goldman Sachs, to no avail. So, like Stenhouse, she decided to try her hand at self-employment. Unlike Stenhouse's, her bet panned out.

First Kane worked freelance and part-time for some small firms specializing in computer training programs for corporations. Then, emulating these firms' approaches, she opened her own training firm, PC Basics, in July 1989. Targeting her services toward institutions such as hospitals, small businesses, and nonprofit organizations that were underserved by other computer training firms, Kane found her previous employment experience and careful business planning paid off. By 1993 she was earning about the same salary she had once made at Goldman Sachs—only she also had the benefits and satisfaction of working for herself rather than someone else. She did have a concern, though: "Having more business than I can handle alone is becoming a problem."[2] Undoubtedly that is a problem Stenhouse would have loved to experience.

So which anecdote best reflects the reality of the American workforce during the last few years of downsizing and layoffs? One school of thought, embraced by many longtime denizens of the corporate social responsibility movement, is that layoffs have decimated the industrial workforce, leaving employees with little hope of job security or improving economic prospects while weakening the social compact between businesses and average citizens.

But another school of thought suggests that American companies, reacting to increased international competition with a relentless search for efficiency and quality, have found ways to produce more goods and services at lower cost—thus freeing up money for investment in new enterprises and for consumption of new goods and services. Social responsibility, in the minds of this school's adherents, represents a commitment not to waste the resources of the society at large in unprofitable plants or lines of business. Using new technology, management strategies, or other innovations to produce more with less, companies directly boost the fortunes of their owners or shareholders and indirectly enhance the fortunes of consumers paying lower prices for better-quality goods and services. This money does not just disappear; it makes itself visible as new investment and higher consumer demand, both of which actually create jobs. So to denigrate corporate restructuring and downsizing is to question the means by which businesses advance the broader public good. "In our zeal to afford protection for those immediately affected by a corporate change," wrote three Arizona State University researchers, "we may ultimately harm a broader base of individuals both immediately and over the long term."[3]

Testing which of these two schools of thought is right means examining long-term trends in worker compensation and employment, as well as the performance of companies implementing downsizing—or, more accurately, "rightsizing"—strategies to minimize costs and maximize profits. It also means describing the reality of workforce reduction in most American businesses, particularly how firms treat dislocated workers and what happens to them in the broader job market.

COMPANY PERFORMANCE

In October of 1993, Robert Reich—the former Harvard lecturer and author on business trends tapped by President Bill Clinton as U.S. Secretary of Labor—came to New York to speak to a gathering of the Council of Institutional Investors, which includes the nation's biggest pension fund investors. Reich's concern (not surprisingly, given his title) was jobs. Echoing the criticisms of many politicians and analysts during the 1980s and 1990s, the secretary told the investors that American business had gone overboard in its quest for lower labor costs and greater efficiency. By laying off workers, he argued, firms lose experienced personnel and run the risk of losing their competitive edge and ability to react to changing economic conditions. "I am questioning whether we have gone too far in corporate downsizing," he said at the meeting. "Cutting payrolls may not be the most effective way of improving corporate performance. There are a lot of nonfinancial criteria that don't show up on a balance sheet and are hard to get your hands on."[4]

About nonfinancial criteria predicting corporate success, Reich was hardly telling the pension fund investors something they did not already know. Financial analysts look at a host of factors (ranging from leadership and worker morale to public image and regulatory climate) when attempting to forecast what sort of return a company will provide its stockholders in the long run. Reich, whose comments and writings on corporate social responsibility extend back to the early 1980s, was advancing a more controversial point: that, on balance, the layoffs and workforce changes in American business over the past decade or so had harmed not only workers but the very companies implementing the policies.

Reich's observation is difficult to square with the relevant facts. Done correctly—that is, with an eye toward maintaining the morale of retained employees and boosting their productivity—layoffs seem to generate solid benefits for many firms. Consider the example of Arvin Industries, an automotive-parts manufacturer based in Columbus, Indiana. From 1990 to 1993 Arvin reduced its workforce by 10 percent (representing some 16,000 positions) as it restructured its production process and attempted to weather the storm of a general downturn in the auto industry. But in 1993, with the industry cycling back into a growth phase, Arvin saw its orders for shock absorbers and MacPherson struts jump and its profits forecast to grow by 20 percent a year through 1995. As the trend lines point upward, the company still plans to seek out savings in labor costs. "To remain globally competitive, we must continue to streamline operations and keep a tight rein on labor costs," said Arvin human resources director Ray Mack.[5] After assuming the helm in 1988 at Portec Inc., an Illinois-based builder of railroad and construction gear, Michael T. Yonker found the company had $34 million in losses on sales of $108 million, with $36 million in bank debt. By 1992 Yonker had reduced Portec's workforce by 31 percent and cut other costs. The firm had lower sales that year ($68 million), but it made a $5.5 million profit.[6] At Unisys Corporation, the Pennsylvania-based computer maker, the workforce shrank by 47 percent over five years, to 47,000 workers in 1994. During the same period, its operating profits rose 41 percent and revenue per employee grew 39 percent. "In this industry, we will have to continue to restructure every day," said vice president for investor relations John McHale.[7]

Firms that use rightsizing effectively not only improve productivity and profitability but also boost their attractiveness to investors. Connecticut-based chemical manufacturer Union Carbide began a restructuring effort in 1990 after years of lagging behind its competitors. The company sought to eliminate some $400 million a year from its costs and generate returns throughout the business cycle. By 1993 the company had reduced employment by 22 percent and decided to raise its cost-reduction target to $575 million by 1995. Investors responded enthusiastically to Union Carbide's cost savings, with the company's stock price almost doubling in 1992— making it the fastest-growing Dow Jones Industrial stock that year.[8]

Other companies have seen their stock prices rise after rightsizing efforts, confounding the conventional wisdom that layoffs must always signify trouble ahead. During 1993, for example, corporations such as IBM, Boeing, United Technologies, and Procter & Gamble all saw their stocks rise significantly faster than the Standard & Poor's 500 Index after making layoff announcements during the year totaling more than 100,000 jobs.[9] Part of the reason these stock prices have risen is that many companies announcing major restructuring plans choose to immediately write off expenses such as severance, relocation expenses for retained employees, and training programs for new or reassigned ones, even though the costs may extend into following years. Investors see these companies as starting with a "clean slate" by increasing efficiency and taking losses that would otherwise be a drag on earnings in the future.[10]

Research on the impact of layoff announcements themselves (separate from the long-term impact of rightsizing on production and sales) shows that the market's reaction depends on the reason for the layoff. One study divided layoff announcements from 1979 to 1987 into two groups: those caused by immediate financial distress, and those caused by strategic restructuring or consolidation. Announcements of financial-distress layoffs were on average preceded by several weeks of stock prices declining relative to their predicted trend, followed by a leveling off of the price by the fifth day after the announcement. Layoffs due to strategic reasons, though, were preceded and followed by *higher-than-predicted* prices. Layoffs, in other words, rarely appear out of the blue. Market observers have some idea of what's going on, and layoffs serve as a confirmation of trends already observed. For the average firm using rightsizing as a means of strategic restructuring or consolidation, investors seem to view the decision positively.[11]

When the American Management Association surveyed human resource managers at more than seven hundred major U.S. companies in 1994, it found that reducing the workforce was increasingly likely to be an attempt to reposition the company rather than simply a response to economic recession. The percentage of respondents citing "business downturn" as the reason for layoffs was about double that citing "improving staff utilization" in the recession year 1991, but the two percentages had come close to parity by 1994. Overall the survey found that businesses trimming their payrolls at least twice between 1989 and 1994 were the most likely firms in the survey to report higher profits (58 percent) and greater worker productivity (44 percent).[12]

These years of restructuring, reorganization, and rightsizing—painful as they might have been for some individuals—left the American business sector not hollowed out and reeling, but competitive and surging. Because firms rightsized and upgraded their technology, wrote Beth Belton in a late-1994 *USA Today* report on economic growth, "brisk demand for goods and services is being met by lean companies whose production costs are as low as any in the leading industrialized nations."[13] And there are many companies who, having undergone significant layoffs and restructuring pain in the late 1980s or early 1990s, eventually began to hire lots of new workers. Compaq Computer of Houston, Texas, was losing sales and profits in 1991 when its board brought on an aggressive new CEO, Eckhard Pfeiffer. Over the next three years the company cut prices an average of 30 percent annually and laid off 20 percent of its 11,250 employees. By 1994 sales had tripled, profits had increased even more rapidly, and Compaq's workforce stood at more than 14,000.[14]

WORKERS AND RIGHTSIZING

But even if companies and their owners or investors are benefiting from rightsizing, the question still remains: Are workers better off or worse off? The popular mythology is that prior to the early 1970s, most Americans were employed in stable jobs with constantly rising salaries and hopeful prospects about the future. Families could afford to plan for the future, buy homes, save for their children's educations, and move up the economic ladder. In the mid-1990s, however, the argument is that with the pressures of international competition, technological change, and demands by shareholders for immediate high yields on their investments, companies are cutting costs by cutting labor, regardless of the damage their actions cause among workers (whose incomes slide and opportunities vanish). "Over the past 20 years, economic anxiety has spread in ever-widening circles," wrote Ronald Brownstein in a particularly hyperbolic *Los Angeles Times Magazine* piece.[15] Despite similar pronouncements from many politicians and journalists, there is little evidence that the earnings and prospects of the American worker have declined in recent years, nor it is clear that Americans are much more worried today about their prospects than they used to be. Observers have been misled by flawed statistics and poll numbers that, on the surface, seem to show a decline. When you look carefully at the economic pessimists' case, though, it falls apart.

One often-overlooked issue is the extent of employee benefits. In most cases, critics cite statistics such as average weekly wages, as President Clinton did in his first State of the Union address, to advance the proposition that "for 20 years the wages of working people have been stagnant or declining." This statement might have been accurate if weekly wages were the only way that workers were compensated for their labor. But nonwage benefits such as health insurance, life insurance, government-mandated social insurance programs, pensions, stock ownership plans, paid vacations, and family assistance are also compensation, and these have been playing an increasingly important role in virtually every American company's payroll.

The U.S. Chamber of Commerce in Washington, D.C., annually surveys businesses across the country to find out what sort of benefits are provided to employees. Its latest *Employee Benefits* report found that on average, nonwage benefits paid to employees were valued at 39 percent of cash wages paid in 1992. So an average worker in an average firm with a nominal salary of $25,000 that year actually received $34,750 in total compensation. This percentage has changed significantly over the past four decades. In 1955 benefits made up only 17 percent of wages, and this figure grew to 22 percent in 1965, 30 percent in 1975, and 36 percent in 1986.[16] Overall, according to the U.S. Bureau of Labor Statistics, average hourly inflation-adjusted compensation, including wages and benefits, has risen in each decade since the 1950s and even edged up 3.5 percent from 1990 to 1993, when recession and layoffs were supposedly destroying the livelihood of average workers.[17]

There is another problem, however, with the wage numbers. The inflation adjustment used to show real wage decline is widely known to be wrong. For years, economists have recognized that the Consumer Price Index, the standard measurement of inflation, has been overstating the real rate of inflation by at least a full percentage point per year.[18] One reason is that federal statisticians could not keep up with the buying habits of consumers and product innovations by producers. Products such as calculators, computers, and CD players were not included in the CPI basket of commodities until years after they hit the market, so the price index did not accurately reflect the early drops in price typical of technology-based goods. Also, rises in consumer prices often reflect rises in quality rather than just inflation. The price of an automobile tire, for example, rose from $13 in the mid-1930s to about $70 in nearly 1994, reflecting a rise in the "tire price index" of about 1.5 percent a year. But today's steel-belted radials last more than ten times longer than tires from the 1930s; based on cost per thousand miles driven, tires actually sell for less today than they did during the Great Depression.[19] Yet another problem with the CPI was corrected after 1983, but many analysts continue to use the older, misleading numbers to exaggerate the inflation rates of the 1970s. The problem was that before 1983, the sales value of homes was included in the CPI. Since only a small percentage of families buys a home each year, though, most economists agreed that "rental value" rather than sales prices should be used.

Overall, studies of both wages and family incomes that make the requisite adjustments in inflation rates show an upward trajectory, with few dips, between 1970 and the mid-1990s.[20] And contrary to conventional wisdom, during the Reagan economic expansion of the 1980s, the poorest 20 percent of families actually saw their incomes rise faster than did the richest 20 percent of families.[21] Studies of household net worth, which arguably are more useful than looking at income flows by themselves, also show gains across the economic spectrum, particularly when the value of pensions and other retirement assets are included.[22]

Furthermore, even accurate comparisons of wages and compensation do not necessarily describe how workers view their changing situations. Becoming self-employed, for example, can sometimes entail at least a temporary loss of income—but at the same time reduce the cost of commuting, day care, buying work clothes, and eating out. Changing jobs or professions can also reduce stress, improve the work environment, and present workers with stimulating new challenges. A 1991 study of Vermont salaried workers laid off by General Electric found that 38 percent had become self-employed. Most were earning less than before and had fewer benefits, but an amazing 90 percent said their "current job was better than their GE job" and hoped to remain in it.[23]

Meanwhile, although corporate downsizing has led to a great deal of hand-wringing about the end of job security in the American economy, there is surprisingly little evidence that today's workers actually are less likely to stay in their jobs over time than were previous generations of workers. In fact, a study by the Wyatt Company, a large benefits consulting firm, shows that contrary to popular belief, the typical worker in America today has been at the same job longer than someone of comparable age twenty or thirty years ago. This trend has been particularly pronounced among women in the workforce.[24] And although workers could be forgiven for thinking, based on the popular images promulgated by politicians and the media, that their jobs are next on the chopping block for avaricious, irresponsible corporate downsizers, a majority of workers in a 1994 poll still said they felt like they had job security.[25]

When asked about their financial prospects, American workers today will usually say they would like to earn more money, but they also (accurately) view their economic prospects as good and admit that they are better off financially than their parents were at their age.[26] The Consumer Sentiment Index compiled by the University of Michigan Survey Research Center shows that in *every single year* since the early 1950s, more than 60 percent of Americans said they were better off financially than they were the previous year. Indeed, except for two brief periods— the Watergate and oil-shocks era of 1973–74 and the recession years of 1979–82—more than 70 percent of all Americans have said they were better off each year.[27] In a 1994 survey, 65 percent of American workers said they were satisfied with their current jobs, while just 10 percent said they were dissatisfied.[28] The image we often see or hear about of an anxiety-stricken, embittered, deeply pessimistic workforce with little hope for advancement is more a fantasy of political commentators and professional pessimists (both conservative and liberal) than it is the reality in America.

This is true even for those workers who have been directly affected by corporate downsizing. One Bureau of Labor Statistics study found that of 3.4 million workers laid off and then reemployed during the 1990–91 recession, about a third were reemployed at lower salaries or in part-time positions as of January 1992. (Many of these workers have no doubt seen compensation increases since then.) Meanwhile, 37 percent actually gained in salary from reemployment, with 18 percent seeing pay increases of at least one-fifth.[29] This snapshot, taken just after the end of the recession and thus understating income gains, shows how distorted the standard portrayal of corporate downsizing has been. Obviously a sizable percentage of workers experienced at least short-term losses from corporate restructuring, but an even larger number saw short-term gains.[30]

Finally, some critics have argued that layoffs have only increased the amount of time that retained employees must work in order to produce the same amount of goods or services. *Time* magazine presented this view of corporate downsizing in an October 24, 1994, cover story. "I'm doing the work of three people," one worker for New York's NYNEX telephone company told *Time*. Because the workforce in his division has been reduced from twenty-seven to twenty people, the worker complained that "all I have time for is a shower, dinner, and a little sleep. Then it's time to turn around and do it all over again."[31] But is this typical of American workplaces today? Hardly. In fact, the average workweek and workday fell steadily from 1950 to 1990, while average vacation and holiday time almost doubled. Annual hours worked per employee went from 1,903 in 1950 to 1,836 in 1960, 1,743 in 1973, and 1,562 in 1990. Just in the two decades since 1970, when corporations were supposedly imposing greater and greater burdens on their workers, work hours for the average American employee declined by 9.3 percent, the equivalent of twenty-three extra days a year in family or leisure time.[32]

LAYOFFS: BEYOND THE FIRST ACT

Bad news is usually good news, or so the old saying goes. Layoffs by a large business (for example, a member of the Fortune 500) attract front-page news coverage, as do similar restructuring efforts at smaller firms that may nevertheless dominate employment in a particular community. The focus of coverage is usually the human dimension—how many people are losing their jobs, how do they feel about it, and so forth. But rarely do media outlets follow these stories more than a few days. Nor do they tend to report hires as prominently as fires, particularly because new or growing enterprises often escape notice until they are huge. "Ever see any references to Wal-Mart hiring anyone?" commented Marvin Kosters, an economist at the American Enterprise Institute in Washington. "I never heard of Microsoft ever hiring a worker, but they must have." In fact, Wal-Mart grew from 1,500 employees in 1971 to 400,000 in 1993, while Microsoft went from 2 to 18,000.[33]

Readers and viewers get no context within which to evaluate the layoff announcements. They are not told what happens to the laid-off workers, except in general terms about employees having to take sizable pay cuts or remaining unemployed for long periods of time. So given that average compensation is not dropping off and employment rates remain high, what is really happening to all those laid-off workers? A few examples of where they end up are explained below.

Other Businesses

At the same time that larger firms have been rightsizing and reorganizing, small- to medium-sized companies have been hiring at a furious pace. Of the 4.6 million net new jobs created from 1989 to 1993, only 300,000 were created by the Forbes 500.[34] From 1980 to 1994, the share of the workforce employed by the Fortune 500 companies fell to 10.9 percent from more than 20 percent.[35] It is true that most of the employment growth (70 percent or so in 1993) has occurred in the service sector,[36] but that hardly means that the bulk of new jobs created are low-skill, low-wage positions. The service sector includes insurance, finance, health care, and social services—some of the fastest-growing and highest-paying industries in the country. The stereotype, in other words, of a long-time factory worker losing his job and ending up flipping hamburgers in a "McJob" is not typical of what is going on in the labor market.

Just from 1988 to 1993, which includes a recession, the service-sector category of jobs with the largest net increase in jobs was managerial/professional, with 2.9 million new positions created. These jobs paid more than twice the median weekly wage of the sales or service categories.[37] Other studies show that job growth in both services and manufacturing followed similar patterns during the 1980s. Obviously there are millions of Americans who are unprepared to fill these high-wage jobs—as evidenced by the high demand in many communities for skilled construction laborers, engineers, information workers, physical therapists, and other positions—but that is mostly a public policy failing (in education and social programs) rather than one of corporate decision-making.

The exodus from big business to smaller organizations extends to the very top of the pay scale. George Conrades spent three decades at IBM, starting as a systems engineer in 1961 and ending up as manager of the computer company's U.S. operations, with $26 billion in revenues and one hundred thousand employees. In 1992, though, corporate restructuring cost Conrades his job. Rather than accepting offers at other large computer firms, he decided to take the job of CEO at Bolt Beranek & Newman, a contract research firm based in Cambridge, Massachusetts. BBN scientists had been instrumental in the development of electronic mail and the Internet, but the company needed help translating its innovations into commercial business. Conrades welcomed the challenge. "I'd already seen the big company movie and I know a lot about it," he said. "But it's as if you've already read *War and Peace,* then some rainy day comes and you reach for *War and Peace* again. I'd much rather read something new."[38]

For lower-level workers, a common post-layoff destination has been the so-called contingent workforce. This includes both part-time work in traditional manufacturing and service businesses as well as consulting and work for temporary-help agencies. The latter has been portrayed in the most ominous light, but temp agencies offer people steady, varied work, the prospect of making contacts with potential employers, and—in an increasing number of cases—full benefits such as health insurance, life insurance, paid vacations, and training programs. While big national firms such as Manpower Inc. and Kelly are well-known, most temporary employment is with medium-sized or small firms with a local or regional focus. Tampa-based Action Staffing, for example, contracted out some 11,200 workers to six hundred different companies in thirty-five states in 1992. Home Corporation of Montgomery, Alabama—an owner and manager of upscale apartment complexes in ten states—hired Action workers to staff all its complexes, with positions ranging from minimum-wage groundskeepers to $32,000-a-year resident managers. Action employees receive fully employer-paid health care and disability insurance, plus a 401(k) retirement plan.[39]

The "contingent workforce" is a popular target for Reich, labor union leaders, and corporate responsibility mavens. In 1994, for example, the *Dallas Morning News* wept that "thousands of unemployed workers, particularly those just out of college, have been forced to accept part-time jobs with no health insurance, no sick days, and declining opportunities for upward mobility."[40] *Time* magazine breathlessly proclaimed that the "disposable work force is the most important trend in business today, and it is fundamentally changing the relationship between Americans and their jobs."[41] But the fact is that critics often misinterpret the composition of the workforce and ignore its positive elements. First of all, there is no evidence that more workers are "contingent" today than before; indeed, there were slightly more in 1983 than in 1993.[42] Of the 35 million Americans identified by the Labor Department in 1994 as part of the "contingent workforce," about 11 million were really self-employed in jobs ranging from doctors to gardeners. (More about them later.) Another 6.4 million worked for contractors or temp agencies, many working forty hours a week or more, learning useful skills, and finding permanent jobs with the companies for whom they temped (38 percent of Manpower's temps, for example, were offered permanent positions in 1993). The remaining 22 million were part-time workers, but three-quarters of those workers were part-timers by choice because they were rearing children, going to school, or pursuing other interests. The number of people working part-time *involuntarily* actually peaked in the early 1980s.[43]

Are these part-timers being exploited by firms unwilling to make permanent hires? That may happen sometimes, but according to a study by Marvin Kosters and Deidre McCullough of the American Enterprise Institute, the part-time character of jobs does not make a critical difference in wages paid per hour worked.[44] Part-timers do tend to receive fewer non-wage benefits from their employers than their full-time coworkers do, but that doesn't necessarily mean they go without health insurance or retirement plans. Many part-time workers live in households where another wage-earner—be it a spouse, parent, or other family member—works full-time and receives family benefits. In fact, a 1992 study by the Employee Benefit Research Institute found that only 14.5 percent of voluntary part-timers (who make up the vast majority of those working part-time) lacked health insurance, compared to 16 percent of full-time workers.[45]

The myth of the "contingent workforce," like much of the discussion of employers' social responsibility, is largely a political rather than an economic construct. "To portray these . . . workers as a phenomenon that is either new, sinister, or fast-growing poses quite a challenge," wrote Ida L. Walters in a revealing *Reason* magazine piece. "'Temporary' has to be made synonymous with 'contingent,' and the workers profiled have to be cast as 'living on the edge,' which means ignoring the tens of millions of 'contingents' who are planted securely on economic terra firma. Otherwise, the story falls apart."[46]

Start-Ups

Many displaced workers—ranging from top corporate managers to mid-level managers to production or administrative personnel—reenter the workforce as owners of their own small businesses. This trend intensified during the late 1970s and throughout the 1980s. Prior to 1975, the rate of new business incorporations tended to track the overall growth rate of the economy. But since then, the incorporation rate has exploded. In 1991, a recession year, more than 630,000 new companies incorporated—double the number of new firms in 1975.[47] Harvey Kinzelberg, chairman and founder of the Entrepreneurial Institute of America in Deerfield, Illinois, remarked that "from our experience in talking to people, we're noting a substantial number—perhaps 10 to 15 percent of outplaced individuals— who either are totally frustrated with corporate America or have decided that they no longer want to trust their fate to the corporate world. These people are at the point in their careers where they want to take the risk for control of their own lives, and they seem to want to choose an entrepreneurial future."[48]

The growth of the American franchise sector, including restaurants, copy shops, and similar service firms, reflects part of this phenomenon. The International Franchising Association estimates that 30 percent to 50 percent of new franchise applicants are people who have lost their jobs due to corporate restructuring efforts. Louis Minella was a store planner for Sears, Roebuck & Company when restructuring in 1993 led him to take early retirement at age fifty-three and open a Mail Boxes Etc. franchise in Thornwood, New York, a year later. The store offers mailbox rental, faxing, copying, and other services to customers needing a kind of "branch office." Minella's reasons for starting his own business were as much personal as anything else: "I just said, 'Oh gee, with the few years I have left I'd like to do something that I could be the boss of, and in charge of, and hopefully make it so I can come and go as I please.' . . .After 31 years in the corporate world, it was time to do something different."[49]

Laid-off workers who become entrepreneurs have opened every sort of business imaginable. Frequently, work experience gained at the very company from which they have been laid off has been critical to their self-employment success. After being laid off from the Burlington Northern Railroad, geologist Thomas Ballard of Northglenn, Colorado, started his own limited partnership to acquire properties and lease them to large mining companies. Lila Hexner left her job as a manager at Northern Energy Corporation in Cambridge, Massachusetts, when the company's business outlook turned sour. Assembling a database of experts in many fields, she formed The Consulting Exchange to broker their services to corporations.[50] Bernard Kear and Larry McCandlish were fired from Exxon's research and development division in 1987 as the company refocused its research activities. But Kear, a specialist in nanostructure technology (breaking down materials), simply applied his expertise to developing new ways to improve cutting tools and drilling equipment at Nanodyne Inc., the firm he created with McCandlish in 1990.[51] Mary Anne Jackson lost her job as director of business-and-operations planning for the Swift/Eckrich division of Beatrice Foods in a 1986 leveraged buyout. She used her organizational expertise to start My Own Meals, which produces children's meals and other food products. Jackson says that getting fired gave her the push she needed to take a risk. "Starting your own business is like getting married," she said. "You never know when you're ready. And you never think you're quite ready."[52]

Not all start-up businesses will succeed as well as these have, of course. But that is no reason to think that entrepreneurship by laid-off workers will not result in significant success, income gains, and job creation. In fact, the riskiness of small business has consistently been exaggerated. A 1995 study of 800,000 small businesses by Dun & Bradstreet found that 70 percent survived at least eight years—and most of those that ceased operations did so voluntarily, due to retirement or better economic opportunities elsewhere. "The chances of starting a business and failing are much, much lower than people believe," commented William Dennis, a senior research fellow at the National Federation of Independent Business.[53]

Home Work

Many workers leave their jobs with valuable skills, contacts, and experience. By becoming self-employed consultants and contractors, they can use these strengths to earn a good living while enjoying the benefits of working for themselves from their homes. It is impossible to understand the new American economy without recognizing that we are currently in a self-employment boom centered in work-from-home businesses. Studies by Link Resources, a New York market research firm, show that during the economic slowdown and recession years of 1989–91 home-based self-employment grew by an average of 12.7 percent per year.[54] From an estimate of 6 million home offices in 1980, the ranks of the home-based self-employed grew to 32 million in 1993—representing more people than live in either California or Canada. Not all of these self-employed individuals are full-timers; some hold other jobs outside the home. Nevertheless, write Paul and Sarah Edwards of Working From Home Forum, "By the end of the '90s, perhaps as many as one of every two workers will be engaged in a full-time or part-time home-based business or doing salaried work at home during normal working hours." Already, one out of every three new businesses today is started at home.[55]

Some newly self-employed consultants and contractors are rehired by the very firms that originally laid them off. Vita Gray had served as vice president of professional services for St. Joseph's Hospital and Medical Center in Phoenix, overseeing five hundred employees in ten departments and labs. Then she found out she was being laid off. Gray continued to work diligently during the last six months of her regular employment; the day after she left the hospital's payroll, she was back with a one-year contract to help coordinate a $100 million renovation and construction project. A University of Michigan study found that Gray's case wasn't unique: of two hundred companies undergoing layoffs, 35 percent called former workers back temporarily or on a contract basis.[56] Indeed, the entire magnitude of corporate downsizing has been consistently exaggerated in that press coverage focuses on the number of workers no longer employed by a firm but fails to track how the services once provided by in-house departments are now provided by outside contractors, often staffed by the very people who used to work inside.

Other home-based entrepreneurs use their skills and experience to attract clients from across the country. Henry Davis of Natick, Massachusetts, actually began his career in the computer industry as an independent contractor, designing software part-time while attending Furman University and the New Mexico Institute of Mining and Technology. Then he went into the semiconductor business, working for several firms, large and small, before being laid off for the last time from a management position at a small computer company. "I asked myself why I should beat my brains out making money for someone else," Davis said, "when I could beat half my brains out and make money for myself, plus have more time with my family." He founded a strategic marketing and consulting firm for high-tech clients out of his home; he now has two independent contractors working with him (both laid off from computer firms themselves), contracts across the country, and earnings that are five times what he was making before. In his experience, Davis said, "most people are accepting that it's okay to be self-employed," and potential customers don't care whether he works from home or has a plush office space thirty or forty-five minutes away. Davis, though, does care: "I'm working about the same number of hours I did before, but the time is distributed differently." He does not have to commute, can spend more time with his family, and can take a vacation whenever he wishes to.[57]

Bill Spees of South Bend, Indiana, joined four colleagues to found Legendary Systems Inc., a successful engineering consulting firm. "We started this business after we were forced into early retirement by the recent economic unpleasantness," he said. Working from their homes, Spees (a licensed professional engineer) and his partners travel only to consult on-site with clients.[58] Landscape architect C. Thomas Fitzwilliam lost his job when the Arlington, Texas, landscaping company he worked for followed the Texas economy into the tank. He now operates Fitzwilliam Landscaping and Irrigation from his Arlington home.[59]

Early Retirement

Lastly, a significant number of workers who have lost their jobs in recent years have found that the benefits of retiring early far outweigh those of rejoining the workforce. Given the generous severance and pension benefits available from many firms, these retirees are enjoying a comfortable standard of living and lots of time to spend with their families, to further their education, and to pursue hobbies or recreation. Patrick Volpe, for example, is fifty-one and an early retiree from the General Motors plant in Linden, New Jersey. He started as a messenger in 1961 and handled company cars before he retired. Selling his New Jersey home for $233,000 (he bought it in 1965 for $32,000) and grossing $3,000 a month from GM pensions and investments, he and his family moved to a four-bedroom house in Hernando, Florida. Volpe lives a life of leisure, if not opulence. "I'm never going to be rich; I might as well be happy," he says.[60]

Volpe is not alone. The number of Americans retired from work rose from 13.3 million in 1970 to 25.3 million in 1990, an increase not accounted for simply by the aging of the population. One reason why some laid-off workers—particularly those in their fifties and early sixties—can afford to retire is that, like Volpe, they have accumulated significant wealth through appreciating home prices and investments. Median household net worth adjusted for inflation has doubled just since 1970.[61] At the same time, more employees today are eligible for pension benefits, including partial payments for early retirement, than ever before.[62]

LAYOFFS AND RESPONSIBLE FIRMS

Even if corporate layoffs and rightsizing programs are not irresponsible per se, as is often alleged, it may still be possible to criticize the way in which many firms conduct their restructuring efforts. The typical case is of a worker who has been let go suddenly, without warning, and without good explanation from a job he or she has held for years. During his fifteen years in the semiconductor business, Henry Davis was on the giving as well as the receiving end of layoffs, and he remarked that too many firms he was familiar with had held "pink slip Fridays" in which employees were told not to report for work the following Monday. "Instead of being open with people, these [corporations] wouldn't tell their employees whose jobs were in danger and why," he said.[63] That is the kind of corporate decision that many people have in mind when they call layoffs socially irresponsible.

But is this sudden-death approach to layoffs the norm in the American workplace today? No. Most company executives realize that it is in the interest of the firm as well as the displaced worker to make sure that worker has adequate time, help, and resources to become reemployed or self-sufficient. This is why companies usually offer some form of severance or outplacement benefits to laid-off workers. A 1990 survey of corporate severance policies by Right Associates, a Philadelphia-based outplacement firm, found that 88 percent of key executives, 87 percent of managers, 81 percent of supervisors, and 76 percent of administrative/technical staff got some form of severance payments. The survey found that most companies with severance policies provide one or two weeks of pay for every year an employee has worked for them. In addition, many companies provided other forms of severance compensation, such as continuation of medical insurance coverage beyond that required by federal law[64] (provided to key executives by 50 percent and to lower-level staffers by 38 percent) and life insurance (to key executives by 37 percent, to lower-level staffers by 28 percent).[65]

Outplacement services—including job search, training, and counseling for displaced workers—are an even more common feature of the modern workplace. The 1994 AMA survey on downsizing found that 84 percent of companies implementing layoffs offered some kind of outplacement assistance to at least some of their employees, with 58 percent giving assistance to all affected employees, from top executives to hourly workers.[66] Corporations choose to offer severance and outplacement services for several different reasons, including those discussed below.

Workforce Morale

Obviously, layoffs have effects not only on workers being let go but on those who remain. Retained employees wonder if they will be next. They pay attention to how their former co-workers are treated and what happens to them. Clumsily handled layoffs can decimate employee morale, harming the productivity of the firm. After the breakup of the Bell System in 1984, AT & T was forced to reduce its workforce by more than 100,000 employees. To head off potential morale problems, the company created a "safe landing" program to help laid-off employees continue their careers. In one AT & T unit that had 514 workers laid off, outplacement personnel were able to find jobs for 512 of them.[67]

Public Image

Layoffs can damage the relationship between a company and the community in which it operates, particularly if it is the major employer in a small town. When Boeing Louisiana Inc. (BLI) failed to win a government contract to maintain and overhaul KC-135 aircraft in 1991, its imminent closure threatened to devastate the economy of Lake Charles, Louisiana. BLI was the community's largest employer, providing some $30 million in payroll to 1,600 residents. But by working with employees, customers, local government, and a private outplacement firm, BLI was able to place more than half of its employees into other companies—some newly created—before its Lake Charles plant closed.[68] In a similar case, when Minneapolis-based Pillsbury Company's Green Giant division laid off 330 workers at its plant in Watsonville, California (a community with a high unemployment rate), the firm worked with a private job agency and the local Teamsters union to provide skill assessment and workshops, community referrals, and support services to the employees. Ninety-three percent of the displaced workers participated in the program, and 81 percent of those found employment at an average wage of eight dollars an hour.[69]

Cost Savings

Severance payments, while desirable in the sense that they cushion the blow to displaced workers and boost morale among retained ones, can be costly. By using outplacement services, firms can save money in severance by getting their former workers reemployed. One study by Washington State University professor Duane E. Leigh found that job-search assistance was an effective tool for reemploying people because it "allows for quick intervention before workers disperse after layoffs and plant closings; and, given their modest cost per worker, the evidence suggests that [job search] services are cost-effective" by reducing severance and unemployment insurance costs.[70] Health One Corporation discovered this fact after deciding to dismiss 1,200 employees because of the closing of Metropolitan–Mount Sinai Medical Center in Minneapolis, Minnesota. Instead of just handing out pink slips, the company found jobs for 90 percent of the laid-off workers. Health One actually saved more in forgone unemployment and severance expenses than the $500,000 spent on job training and placement for its displaced workers.[71]

Not all outplacement services are worthwhile, of course. Some firms do not retain enough counselors to adequately give outplaced workers personal attention. Other firms apply routine, standardized approaches to reemploying people that fail to take unique situations into consideration. Companies have to shop carefully for good outplacement firms, seeking out companies with good track records that specialize in their industry or worker category, just as they would any other supplier or contractor.[72] Another issue is worker preference. Many might prefer to take money rather than outplacement, then decide how best to use those resources to ease their way back into the working world. Companies could probably find a way to accommodate this need if it were not for the tax laws. Severance payments are taxable, just like wages, but in 1992 the Internal Revenue Service ruled that employer-provided outplacement services could be treated as non-taxable fringe benefits.[73]

Outplacement does, however, have its strong proponents. A magazine editor, Betsy Carter first came into contact with the Drake Beam Morin outplacement agency when a publication she started had to lay off five employees. Two years later the magazine folded, and Carter found herself "outplaced" to Drake Beam Morin. Expecting the worst, she found instead a supportive and insightful counselor who helped direct her toward a promising new job. "For the first time since the magazine folded, I felt I had sighted the other shore," she said.[74]

Another satisfied alumnus of outplacement counseling is Tom LaDore, who in 1993 was laid off a job with Baxter International in Michigan. LaDore had always wanted to open his own business, a bar and grill, but never knew how to begin. As part of his outplacement package he went through an entrepreneurial transition workshop, where staff members walked him through the process of figuring out what it was going to cost to open a bar and grill, what the financial implications were, how to market and promote the business, and how to operate it. LaDore did more research, drafted a business plan, and got a loan from a local bank. His restaurant opened in 1994 and was soon doing brisk business.[75]

CONCLUSION

A key claim of the corporate social responsibility movement is that American corporations are violating their "social contract" with workers by engaging in repeated, destructive layoffs that reduce worker earnings, limit their opportunities for advancement, rupture communities, harm the long-run interests of the firm, and generally abandon loyal employees to their fates. In reality, though, average workers have continued to see their real compensation and standard of living increase throughout the oft-criticized 1980s, and even during the painful recession of 1990–91. The social contract between workers and businesses has not eroded, because job mobility is no higher today than two or three decades ago and because the workers who have lost their jobs have, in most cases, been treated well. They have found work at other firms, opened their own businesses or franchises, started enterprises from their homes, or retired early. Most firms have helped their workers adjust to changing economic conditions, because it is hardly in their interest to treat laid-off workers shabbily.

By seeking higher profits and the most efficient use of their shareholders' resources and employees' labor, companies continue to create new opportunities in the enterprise economy of the 1990s. Looking at the various "stakeholders" involved in layoff and rightsizing decisions, one finds that most company managers, shareholders, workers, and consumers have benefited from corporate restructuring, the last because restructuring has boosted efficiency and thus lowered prices for goods and services they buy. The common good, in other words, is served.

CHAPTER 4

BUSINESS AND THE EDUCATION CHALLENGE

When Alphonso Harrell walked into Holy Cross Central School in inner-city Indianapolis in September 1991, the third grader was mad. His mother had just pulled him out of the public school where his friends were enrolled—but where he had been struggling both academically and socially—and put him in a Catholic school, run by a nun, with strict rules and a drab, three-story building. When asked if he liked Holy Cross better than the public school he left, if he liked his new teacher, and if he wanted to return to Holy Cross the following year, Alphonso responded with a simple, gruff "No." In his first year at the school, Alphonso was a behavior problem and often sat alone.

But by the time Alphonso reached the fifth grade at Holy Cross, the old Alphonso was scarcely recognizable. Consistently on the honor roll, and the first-place winner in the school's science fair, he served on the student council and won an award from a local civic club for his essay "What Freedom Means to Me." In the essay, he wrote in part that freedom meant "you can argue your disagreement. If one of us wanted to make a speech, we could say it and not be punished for it. . . . We are able to have these freedoms because we have our Bill of Rights." Sister Barbara McClelland, the enthusiastic principal of Holy Cross Central School, said that "Alphonso has made remarkable progress in two years.

He is a pleasure to have in our school and we are all very proud of him."[1] Alphonso's mother chimed in that her son had "worked hard, and Holy Cross has taught him how to be the person he should be." Alphonso described his transformation simply: "I went from being a bad person to being on the honor roll and the student council."[2]

Alphonso, like hundreds of other Indianapolis children currently enrolled in about a hundred private schools throughout the city, would never have had the chance to escape their stultifying public schools and find educational success elsewhere without the efforts of Pat Rooney, chairman of Golden Rule Insurance Company. Rooney, both a local philanthropist and an advocate of innovation in education, founded the Educational CHOICE Charitable Trust in 1991 after viewing years of failed public school reform and wasted corporate efforts at educational improvement. The last straw was the experience Rooney had with COMMIT, an organization of Indiana business leaders who tried and failed to get a school-reform package through the Indiana legislature earlier in the year. COMMIT's prescriptions for education reform in Indiana were familiar to serious students of the public schools in other areas. The group stated that public elementary and secondary schools, because they were insulated from the standards of accountability and customer service inherent in the private sector, were failing in their task of preparing young people for college, work, or citizenship. Inflexible personnel rules like tenure and uniform salary schedules hampered the effective deployment of the educational workforce. With an effective monopoly on students, public schools had no incentive to improve, to teach effectively, or to spend their money wisely. Educators were rarely judged according to results, and they viewed parents all too often as nuisances rather than customers.

COMMIT drafted a reform plan that included a controversial idea: let parents choose among public or private schools, with public dollars flowing to the school of the parents' choice. But with business executives unsure about how hard to push the package, and powerful legislators defending the state's education establishment against the prospect of competition, the bill failed. Rooney decided to take things into his own hands. On Friday, August 2, 1991, Golden Rule Insurance Company announced that it would pay half the cost of private-school tuition for up to 500 children in the Indianapolis area. Children would qualify for the Golden Rule vouchers if they met the eligibility guidelines of the federally subsidized school-lunch program—in other words, only if they came from poor families. Rooney made the student-selection process straight-forward: it would be first come, first served. By noon the following Monday, the 500 slots had been filled, and families were already being put on a waiting list. Eventually, Rooney's Educational CHOICE Charitable Trust was able to fund vouchers for 744 students in the 1991–92 academic year.

Over the next few years, the CHOICE Trust expanded steadily. Rooney and the program's executive director, Tim Ehrgott, solicited grants from other Indianapolis businesses, foundations, and individuals. There were 900 CHOICE students in 1992–93 and more than 1,000 by 1993–94. The range of participating schools included Catholic schools like Holy Cross, Lutheran schools, Montessori schools, secular schools, and many others. One small school that was struggling to survive when the program started was Capitol City Seventh Day Adventist School, located close to downtown Indianapolis in a cramped two-story building. As of 1994–95 the school was still small—only fifty-four students in eight grades—and had such a small staff that visitors were required to wait outside the locked door for the principal or a teacher to walk by. But the all-black school, founded in 1910 and supported in part by church revenues, still educates children who might otherwise fail in public schools. "The values that they teach in a private school are to respect other people, to respect the teachers and your elders no matter if they think that it's wrong or not," said one Capitol City parent. "Children are the future. If they don't get the training that the private schools are offering, then there's not going to be any other children to take over."[3]

Rooney's private voucher plan wasn't completely unprecedented. Peter M. Flanigan, a director of Dillon, Read & Company, established a similar tuition-grant program for inner-city Catholic schools in New York City in 1988. Flanigan had first gone the route pioneered by Gene Lang, a New York businessman whose "I Have A Dream" program promised some inner-city students that he would pay for their postsecondary education if they would graduate from high school. The idea got national attention and was featured in a "60 Minutes" segment. Believing that Lang had "put his money where his mouth is," Flanigan asked to sponsor a class. But he soon discovered that simply promising rewards in the future would not be enough to help most of the kids in his South Bronx public-school class. He hired tutors and a social worker to try to help the students eschew destructive behavior and focus on schoolwork, but only twelve of the forty-nine students in his class went on to higher education. The "success" rate, 25 percent, was the same percentage of students who go to college generally from the inner-city schools of New York. Flanigan decided instead to commission a Rand Corporation study of zoned public schools, public schools of choice, and Catholic schools in New York. The Rand study found that at the chosen schools, average SAT scores were 160 points higher than at the zoned schools. Based on these results, Flanigan started the Student/Sponsor Partnership, a private voucher program for Catholic schools in New York, which in 1993 had some 657 sponsors supporting a total of 647 students in fifty inner-city schools. Seventy percent of the Student/Sponsor enrollees graduate, and virtually all graduates go on to college.[4]

The strategy that businessmen Rooney and Flanigan followed for devoting resources and employees to the task of radically reforming local schools has now been emulated in other communities. As of 1994 there were sixteen other privately funded voucher programs in the United States, drawing funds from corporate, foundation, and individual sources. The largest program is in Milwaukee, where some 2,500 students used privately funded vouchers to attend private schools in the 1994–95 school year. Rooney's CHOICE Trust funded 1,010 students in that academic year. Other large programs included those in San Antonio (923 students) and Los Angeles (775 students). Overall, some 6,000 children and their families across the country obtained access to school choice that year through private vouchers—but another 13,000 were on waiting lists.[5]

Of course, millions more across the country had no voucher program for which to wait. While the efforts of Rooney, Flanigan, and other corporate leaders to direct business involvement in education reform toward substantive change have been welcome, they still represent only a drop in a much larger bucket that is corporate giving to American education. In 1993 American corporations—and thus, in effect, shareholders, employees, and consumers of the corporation's goods or services—donated more than $2.2 billion to educational institutions. Education was the largest category of corporate giving, representing about 37 percent of the total.[6] These numbers, sizable though they may be, understate the time, products, and services donated to schools, colleges, and universities by businesses. And of course, the individuals from whom corporate donations come (shareholders, employees, and consumers) also pay a high percentage of their incomes in taxes to support public schools, colleges, and universities, particularly on the state and local levels where a significant share of government budgets pays for educational institutions. Most of this tax money comes from individuals who have no immediate involvement with schools or colleges themselves; for example, only one out of every ten households has a child in public schools in a given year, and even fewer have children in higher education.[7]

Corporate involvement in education does not end there. Firms are themselves educational institutions in the sense that they educate and train their employees to perform specific tasks, to use computers and other technology, to communicate with their coworkers and customers, and in many cases to read and count. The extent of job training is difficult to quantify, because most of it occurs informally on the job rather than in classrooms with teachers and separate training budgets.[8] In 1989, though, the *Washington Post* reported an American Society for Training and Development estimate that companies spent about $30 billion on formal training programs (a low number because it does not include wages paid to employees being trained) and an astounding $180 billion on informal, on-the-job training. This represents a conservative estimate of $210 billion in corporate training expenses for 1989; by comparison, America's public schools spent about $200 billion that year, and institutions of higher education spent $133 billion.[9]

Businesses obviously have an interest in seeing Americans educated well. Today's students are tomorrow's workers and consumers. In an increasingly competitive global economy, firms cannot afford to employ people who lack basic abilities—to read and comprehend, to communicate with others, to multiply and divide. If workers do not gain these abilities through their formal schooling (paid for in large measure by corporate shareholders, employees, and consumers who do not have children currently in school), then firms must expend more resources to try to ameliorate the damage through remedial education and training. Simply as a matter of maximizing profit and return to shareholders, businesses must worry about the quality of education.[10]

CORPORATE GIVING: TURNING TOWARD RESULTS

Pat Rooney is adamant about the failure of many corporate programs to aid schools, given executives' inattention to changing the system itself.

He has reason to be skeptical. In 1991, when I analyzed business involvement in education reform for the Cato Institute, I found little evidence that simply increasing corporate giving to educational institutions or creating "partnerships" between public schools and firms had significant benefits beyond the immediate gratification of a well-publicized ribbon-cutting. Partnerships and "adopt-a-school" programs were particularly popular during the 1980s, when business leaders—convinced of the need for education reform if America were to remain competitive—nevertheless were convinced by educators that the bulk of the problem was lack of funds. By 1990 more than half of all school districts in the United States had entered into public-private partnerships, involving about 2.6 million volunteers, with an estimated value of $225 million (an increase of 125 percent just since 1986). According to the U.S. Department of Education, about half of these partnerships involved the donation of goods and services, 25 percent the donation of money, and 25 percent a combination of goods, services, and money.[11]

The problem with this rapid influx of corporate resources into public education was that there was no evidence of a proportionate increase in educational quality. This is not surprising, since careful studies have also found no statistically significant relationship between school performance and funding (within realistic bounds—naturally, a school spending $1 per student is not going to provide the quality of education available at a school spending $10,000 per student).[12] The failure of partnerships and adopt-a-school programs must be expressed on the average, however, since there are cases in which corporate support seems to have helped particular schools in measurable ways. Champion International, for example, spent $2 million to implement reform ideas from the Carnegie Council on Adolescent Development in four new middle schools in the Stamford, Connecticut, public schools. Champion, based in Stamford, hired a consultant, financed a summer school for low achievers, and sponsored biweekly training sessions for every middle-school teacher. The program seems to have worked—attendance rates for the middle-schoolers were double those of their peers in other system schools, while a majority of the low-achieving summer schoolers reached the honor roll.[13] A program created in 1989 by the Pacific Telesis Foundation has also shown some results. The Education for the Future Initiative, designed to showcase the impact of school-site empowerment, accountability, and parental involvement on school performance, includes eight elementary schools. Each has experienced an increase in attendance rates and reduced dropout rates.[14]

These specific success stories are few and far between, however, because of the relative magnitude of corporate gifts or advice on the one hand and the burgeoning budgets, rules, and bureaucratic workforces of the public schools on the other. For too long, businesses have violated common sense and market principles by giving away lots of money with little thought to the rate of return on their investment. A survey by SchoolMatch, an Ohio-based consulting firm that matches businesses with schools, shows that a majority of companies that give financial resources to schools have had little idea of the outcomes of such investments in the past.[15] Those companies that have tried to accomplish real change within the public school system have often been discouraged. In 1986, for instance, business leaders and educators created a partnership to thwart declining grades and increasing social problems in the Rochester, New York, public schools. In a much-celebrated case, the partnership raised enough money to boost teacher salaries to as much as $69,000 while giving teachers more duties to provide counseling and support services. After an initial bump in test scores, however, the effort unraveled. Student achievement gains did not correspond with the massive increase in corporate investment, businesses were dissatisfied, and teachers said they had been given unrealistic expectations.[16]

The good news about corporate giving programs, especially those directed toward elementary and secondary schools, is that managers now appear to have discovered their limitations and are beginning to rethink their strategy for effecting educational change. A recent *Fortune* magazine survey found that 55 percent of corporate leaders who have given money or in-kind contributions to schools said their involvement has made little if any difference.[17] At least they are admitting their mistakes; since corporate resources already flow to schools in massive amounts through taxation, it makes little sense to focus on supplementing budgets or operating on the margins of the school day. Instead, successful programs will take advantage of a firm's own knowledge, experience, and location to change how schools are designed and run (which is in the long-run interest of the firm) while possibly advancing other goals of the firm, such as sales, employee morale, or goodwill. Rooney's CHOICE Trust is perhaps the most radical application of these principles to corporate giving, but there are others worthy of mention.

Some companies are redirecting their efforts to take advantage of their particular expertise in curriculum or management. Delta Air Lines, for example, launched several programs in 1992 to improve geography literacy among U.S. schoolchildren. These included a national essay contest and joint publication efforts with *USA Today* and *National Geographic* for use by educators or parents. "As a global air carrier, Delta understands the importance of the geographic, economic, political, cultural, and environmental differences in our world," said Delta president and CEO Whit Hawkins.[18] The geography programs were in many ways the outgrowth of the company's Fantastic Flyer program, an outreach program to children ages two through twelve that was created in 1988. Fantastic Flyer has almost 1 million members in 150 countries, and it obviously serves as a promotional vehicle for Delta. There is nothing wrong, however, with companies advancing their own interests at the same time as they provide helpful information or publications to schools. Newspapers have done it for years by giving schools free subscriptions and encouraging teachers to use newspapers in class. In the same way television advertisers have an incentive to support programming of sufficient quality to attract significant viewership, so too corporations supporting curricular or instructional programs with donations—and, increasingly, with advertising[19]—have an incentive to make sure the programs are sound and will pass muster with parents and educators.

Just as Delta used its expertise with travel and geography to create an educational program, McDonnell Douglas has created programs to encourage its employees to volunteer with schoolchildren in its home city of St. Louis to improve science education. McDonnell Douglas workers can judge science fairs, work with Young Astronaut Clubs, design computer programs, or take students to work to show them how science can lead to challenging and rewarding careers. The company has also created a "Homework Control Center" where math, chemistry, and physics textbooks are kept and company employees volunteer to answer science-related questions from students on weeknights.[20] Numerous other companies have applied the principle of expertise to their education efforts in recent years. American Express created an Academy of Travel and Tourism to provide courses and summer internships at tourism-based companies across the United States. AT & T established a Teachers and Technology Institute to train educators about the real-world impact of technology. Dow Chemical and Du Pont both help train science teachers.

Electronic Data Systems spent $250,000 to create ten computer centers in Dallas and Detroit public housing projects, while Apple Computer has long donated equipment to schools and provided training to help teachers integrate computers into the curriculum. Ford Motor's Academy of Manufacturing Sciences prepares students in five states for careers in manufacturing, engineering, and skilled trades. E.W. Scripps in Cincinnati has created student journalism programs and paid for the broadcast of student-produced cable programming.[21]

A related idea is for companies to target their efforts toward "market testing" new ideas for organizing and operating schools. The Golden Rule, Champion, and Pacific Telesis cases cited above typify this approach. Another good example of the market-test strategy is the Corporate/Community School of America, Inc., created in 1988 by Chicago businessman Joe Kellman and Baxter International Inc. CEO Vernon R. Loucks. The school, funded by corporations, foundations, and individuals, offered tuition-free early childhood and elementary education to inner-city kids in Chicago. The school stayed open twelve hours a day, eleven months a year and maintained constant relationships with about eighty community-service organizations in the city to help children and their families receive health and social services. Teachers and principals were well-paid but not tenured—a crucial deviation from standard public-school practice. Parents were more heavily involved than in most public schools, volunteering for a minimum of ten days for the early childhood program or five days for elementary school. The school even sent letters to parents' employers to inform them of the school's expectations regarding parental involvement. After four years of operation, the school's attendance rate averaged 97 percent, parental participation in teacher-parent conferences was better than 95 percent, and 88 percent of six-year-olds who began in the preschool program tested at or above grade level in reading (64 percent did so in vocabulary, and 56 percent in math)—all this in a city whose public schools are widely viewed as among the worst in the nation. What is more, the school spent no more than the average per-pupil cost of Chicago public schools.[22]

By 1994 the business leaders who began the Corporate/Community School, feeling that they had proved the effectiveness of their education model, sought to expand it. As part of that process, the private school joined the Chicago public system in August 1994. Businesses and foundations continued to pay for the early childhood, technology, and family-outreach programs that were the hallmark of the school, while its other innovations, including the lack of tenure, were maintained. "The public schools have had a change of heart," Kellman said. "That's what leads me to believe this merger will maybe make a difference in education in this whole country."[23]

Other corporations have helped to establish schools or separate academic programs to test various educational strategies. The Public School Academy in Minnesota, created in part by General Mills, removed all supplementary and compensatory programs and equipped its rooms with phones for parent-teacher contact. The focus of the school is basic education rather than drug rehabilitation, social work, and the like. "There are three givens in a classroom: students, teachers, and time," said Larry Sawyer of General Mills. "There are three things that need to be done: education, remediation, and socialization discipline. If the majority of teachers' time is spent on remediation and socialization discipline, the school is failing in its primary function—education."[24] In 1989 Boeing helped redesign Washington State's "tech-prep" courses to give high-school students not bound for college a more realistic notion of what the world of work was all about. Boeing gave grants to schools to implement the new "applied academic" model. Enrollment in tech-prep courses grew, and average science test scores increased by 50 percent following completion of the new curriculum.[25] San Francisco–based Chevron and Stanford University helped create accelerated classes for at-risk students in Los Angeles who might otherwise be put in slower, remedial classes. At the participating 99th Street Accelerated School, average reading scores on the California Test of Basic Skills rose from the 16th percentile to the 23rd percentile in three years. RJR Nabisco makes grants of up to $250,000 for three years for its Next Century Schools project, created in 1990 as a $30 million program over five years to support innovation and reengineering efforts.[26]

Another way to target education programs is to focus on a firm's employees or immediate neighborhood. Two Minneapolis-based companies, Northern States Power Company and IDS Financial Services, contributed $300,000 each over three years to lease space for and operate a new school that would primarily serve the children of the two companies' employees. The Downtown Open School opened in 1991 in an office building two blocks from Northern States and one block from IDS. Opening the new school allowed the companies' employees to interact more with their children and schools. "We've brought the school to where the parents are," said Dick Stanford, Northern States' education coordinator. "Mom and Dad are just a few blocks away. They know the teachers by their first names and even have lunch with them occasionally. The parents are totally involved in their children's education."[27]

RJR Nabisco has chosen to create several programs aimed at helping employees educate their children. The company allows a lot of time off to participate in school activities and provides a Scholastic Saving Plan, which allows employees to save money tax-free (matched by corporate money) for postsecondary education.[28] The Bank of Boston started a work-study program for kids in nearby Hyde Park High School in the mid-1970s. Participating students are hired full-time during summer vacation; in 1993 one hundred students worked at the bank. Colgate-Palmolive in New York invites local seventh graders to accompany Colgate employees to work to see how they use communication and math skills in their jobs.[29]

The fact that American businesses have been rethinking their "shower the money" strategy for addressing educational woes should not invalidate the value of some donations, partnerships, and mentoring programs. Like the programs described above, these endeavors can confer some specific benefits on individual schools and students while advancing the general reform cause and, not unimportantly, advancing other goals of the profit-seeking firm. Firms do have expertise in their own fields of production or service that can be valuable in developing curriculum or preparing students for the working world. Firms also have the freedom to test new ideas on their own, using the results to push for substantive change of the public system. And it makes sense to focus limited resources on a firm's immediate neighborhood, employees, or customers, since the investment can pay off in greater worker or consumer loyalty and good public relations. "We didn't [start CHOICE Trust] for public relations purposes," Pat Rooney said, "but if we had done so it would have been justified."[30]

As corporate giving continues to become more strategically or bottom-line oriented (a trend discussed in Chapter 2), firms will increasingly think through the real costs and benefits of investing time and money in educational programs. This is most welcome. Like Rooney's CHOICE program or some of the less ambitious but still worthwhile experiments discussed here, these programs should ultimately have as their goal changing the way in which public education is provided and public dollars spent.

TRAINING: THE COMPANY AS SCHOOL

While education reform has been an interest of businesses, and indeed remains a worthy cause for business managers to support and advance, the education and training that occur at the workplace are obviously more under firms' direct control. As stated above, workplace training is hardly a minor enterprise in the educational scheme of things; in dollars spent, it probably rivals or exceeds either the public schools or higher education. Workers learn new skills, information, or problem-solving strategies virtually every day, sometimes in formal programs but more often in the process of performing their jobs. While there is certainly room for improvement, the evidence shows that American businesses are doing a great deal to raise or maintain the productivity of their workers through training programs, resulting in the long run in higher profits, better products, and higher compensation levels for workers. This record clearly differs from that of government-sponsored job training programs, which have consistently posted mediocre or even negative returns on billions of dollars in public money.[31]

Let's take a closer look at employee training programs, using data gathered by *Training* magazine for its annual survey of training in the United States.[32] In 1994 more than 47 million workers received some kind of formal training, up 15 percent since 1992. Employers spent more than $50 billion on formal training in 1994; if the same ratio of formal to informal training existed as was reported by the *Washington Post* in 1989, then employers spent as much as $300 billion in informal training costs, including cost of supervision, publications and materials, and lost production time. (Of course, when you say "employers spent" you might really be saying that "employees spent," since at least a part of the training cost would come out of a worker's prospective salary as a cost of labor to the firm.[33])

The most popular types of formal training among companies with more than one hundred employees were management skills (offered by 89 percent of firms) and basic computer skills (offered by 88 percent). Other common training areas were communication skills, supervisory skills, executive development, customer relations, and clerical or secretarial skills. The two categories of workers who were most likely to be trained were middle managers and executives, with 72 percent and 70 percent of employers providing training, respectively. Administrative employees, first-line supervisors, senior managers, and customer service employees were also more likely than not to be working for firms with formal training programs. Less than half of employers provided training to salespeople (42 percent) and production workers (40 percent); however, these are precisely the workers most likely to receive significant on-the-job training, which is not represented in these statistics. Remedial education—defined in its broadest sense, including a host of academic skills—was offered by fully 45 percent of firms in the *Training* survey. Limiting the definition just to reading, writing, arithmetic, and English as a second language, the magazine found that 22 percent of employers provided these services to their employees. This is an astounding number, and it is sobering to think that in the firms providing remedial education, 67 percent of participants are actually graduates of American high schools.

One way to gauge the value of workplace training to employees is to look at survey data about how many workers needed training to qualify for the jobs they currently hold. A U.S. Bureau of Labor Statistics (BLS) study in 1991 found that 57 percent of workers said they needed training to qualify for their current jobs. About half of those workers received the training they needed through informal, on-the-job training. Another 21 percent received their training from formal company programs. Much smaller percentages said they got necessary training from high school or postsecondary vocational programs. Similarly, when the BLS asked workers where they had received training to improve their skills (not necessarily to qualify for employment in the first place), formal and informal company programs again accounted for about three-quarters of the training provided. One interesting finding of the study was that many workers with college degrees earn less than workers with less formal education who nevertheless have obtained specific training, often through formal or informal company programs, for their jobs. In terms of the cost-effectiveness of various public or private means of delivering training, BLS economist Alan Eck wrote that company-provided training programs, particularly formal ones, "have more of an impact on increasing those workers' earnings than does any other source of training."[34]

Corporate training programs run the gamut from high-tech free-standing training centers to informal instruction in word processing or directions on how to operate presses or rollers on a factory floor. Motorola, the manufacturer of cellular and paging devices, is often identified as a model company for its variety of training programs. The company gives all employees at least forty hours of training a year, one of the heaviest commitments of time in U.S. industry. Much of this training goes on at Motorola University, its $120 million, fourteen-branch teaching center. The firm's training is frequently job specific; indeed, there is often a direct connection between skills learned and business targets. For example, the company will set a goal to reduce the cycle time for product development, then design a course to accomplish that. In 1985, though, Motorola discovered that its employees lacked even the basic skills to perform many of the functions the fast-growing manufacturer needed performed. About 60 percent of its workforce had trouble with seventh-grade math, a necessity for workers needing to track error rates, compute percentages, and solve other daily problems. Bob Galvin, then chairman of the company, decided to devote at least 1.5 percent of payroll to training (this figure has since risen to 4 percent). All employees must have at least seventh-grade math proficiency, and Motorola has even begun training its *suppliers* in statistical process control to reduce errors and the number of bad parts it receives.[35]

Few firms dedicate as much time and resources to training as Motorola does—and, in fact, there is little evidence to suggest that Motorola's huge investment necessarily gives it a competitive advantage over firms with less ambitious training programs[36]—but corporate training is nonetheless an enormous enterprise that employs thousands of Americans. One company with a substantial investment in training is Manpower Inc., the largest temporary agency in the United States. About 1 million people get job assignments from Manpower in a given year, and many of those workers go through a company-run training program emphasizing technical and computer skills, communication, customer service, and quality control. In addition to preparing temps for the job market, Manpower vends its training expertise directly to employers. Almost 90 percent of all Fortune 500 companies have at one time or another called on Manpower to help train their employees, and as of 1995 some 500,000 workers in thousands of companies had benefited from the company's computer-assisted training program, called Skillware.[37]

Some firms, especially medium-sized and small ones, contract out their training needs to consultants or rely on employee volunteers. Avco Financial Services of Irvine, California, asked a local nonprofit organization, the South Coast Literacy Council, to help start a program in English as a second language (ESL) for its employees. The literacy council has trained dozens of Avco employees to serve as tutors for their English-deficient coworkers, many of whom were recent immigrants from Mexico, Vietnam, Cambodia, Russia, and Romania. While the program has been successful in improving the communication skills of many Avco employees since its inception in 1993, it costs the company relatively little because both tutors and students work on language instruction on their own time. Avco President Warren Lyons said that the modest company investment has more than paid for itself: "Those individuals who have a need or desire to become more literate do so, but this process offers much more. Respect for each other, improved self-esteem, and greater workplace efficiency translate into a better total workplace environment."[38] William Dudek, president of William Dudek Manufacturing Co. in Chicago, created a similar ESL instruction program as well as basic math classes for his employees. "We're not saints here," he said. "We're in business to make money. We just thought this was the best way to do it."[39]

Other companies pay for classes for their employees at community colleges or cover tuition for students in night school or even universities. The Hampden Papers factory in Holyoke, Massachusetts, encourages every employee to go to school and spends about 1.5 percent of its payroll to pay their way. Some have learned English or received their high school equivalency diplomas. Some are in college, and the company's president, Robert Fowler, is almost halfway through law school. "The success or failure of this company depends on the quality of the decisions made by every employee here, every day," Fowler said. "Our philosophy of education is simple—everybody should get more."[40]

It would be a mistake to view job training by businesses as directed only to higher-skill, higher-wage occupations. Firms and trade associations play a major role in training hourly workers in many fields. Carolinas Associated General Contractors, for example, offers classes in construction fundamentals, math, carpentry, electrical work, plumbing, sheet metal, and mechanical courses to prospective construction workers in North and South Carolina. Many of these classes are taught at company offices, high schools and community colleges, and the trade association's own offices, and they are combined with on-the-job apprenticeships with sponsoring contractors. Members of the association offer training to workers because they desperately need skilled individuals to hire: "Contractors feel it directly when there's a shortage of labor," says Carolinas AGC building director Dave Simpson.[41]

On a much larger scale, McDonald's trains many thousands of young people each year in its nearly nine thousand restaurants across the United States. "Sending a kid to the army used to be the standard way to teach kids values, discipline, respect for authority, to be a member of a team, get to work on time, brush your teeth, comb your hair, clean your fingernails," said Edward H. Rensi, president and CEO. "Now, somehow, McDonald's has become the new entry-level job-training institution in America. We find ourselves doing things in that role that we would never imagine we would do." Two specific programs deserve special mention. The McJobs program has trained thousands of disabled people to function as restaurant employees; meanwhile, the McPride program emphasizes education for young employees, with incentives for those who stay in school and achieve. Some restaurants pay employees to study an hour before or after work. Bob Charles, a franchisee in Boulder, Colorado, explained his restaurant's participation in the program by comparing the attitude and work habits of his employees before and after McPride: "You'd almost never believe the change in these kids."[42]

Of course, in the competitive economy of the 1990s, companies must subject even the most innocuous-sounding expenditures to a rigorous cost-benefit test. In some cases, training expenses will be more appropriately paid by employees rather than employers, particularly when the training is of a general nature that is easily portable to other companies in the future. The *Training* magazine survey for 1994 found that business managers actually do scrutinize training expenses to evaluate their impact on productivity. Almost two-thirds of the employers surveyed said they evaluated trainees' behavior after they return to the job (including testing workers to find out what they have learned), while about half of employers look for quantifiable changes in business results (such as sales, labor costs, or error rates).[43]

APPRENTICESHIP AND THE GERMAN MODEL

One cannot talk about business involvement in American education without delving into the issue of apprenticeships. One charge often lobbed both at business leaders and educators is that the United States has serious competitiveness problem with countries like Germany and Japan that have much larger, more integrated systems for moving non-college-bound youngsters from school to work. The fact that, according to the Office of

Technology Assessment, 20 to 30 percent of U.S. workers remain deficient in the basic skills they need to work effectively in their current jobs helps to underline the need for worker education to improve.[44]

Critics often point to the example of Germany when discussing how apprenticeships should be structured.[45] Germany, like Japan, has a much more extensive system of tracking elementary and secondary students than does the United States. By the sixth grade, German students are sorted into three types of schools: *Hauptschule*, where they continue until grade nine or ten; *Realschule*, where they continue until grade ten; and *Gymnasium*, where they continue until grade thirteen. Both *Hauptschule* and *Realschule* route their students into formal apprenticeships, which typically last up to three years. Students are paid about a quarter of the standard full-time wage for their apprenticeship work—an exception to Germany's minimum wage laws similar to proposals in America for a sub-minimum "training wage."

The German apprenticeship system, with its government planning and formal structure, is viewed as crucial to the country's high rates of productivity. Yet when researchers have attempted to quantify how much better the German system is than the less formal, more chaotic and company-driven American system, they have failed. One study of the real economic returns of the German system found that they are quite low. Another study revealed that the rate of growth of earnings for workers *with experience* is the same for German and American youths. In reality, as James J. Heckman argued in *The Public Interest* in 1994, the German apprenticeship system is an elaborate escape mechanism from the country's oppressive wage and employment regulations. In an economy with an almost totally unionized labor force, German firms rely on apprentices for flexible, low-cost work. Because the American labor market is less regulated and unionized, no such safety valve is needed. To the extent that the German system suggests anything to American business leaders and policymakers, it is the value of choice—one real benefit to German youth from the system is that they can choose both the company and the school at which they will work and study, creating a competitive market for secondary education. German high schoolers do tend to outscore their American counterparts in international tests of academic knowledge, but there is no evidence that apprenticeships or job training programs themselves are more successfully carried out by German firms than by U.S. firms.[46]

Apprenticeship programs are already quite common in the American workplace. In Rockford, Illinois, a coalition of six industrial firms has helped to design a local apprenticeship program that seems to work well, with students going through academic coursework while working at participating businesses.[47] In Addison, Illinois, Sears, Roebuck & Co. and a local vocational school started a program in which apprentices work a total of thirty hours per semester at a Sears Service Center, working one-on-one with mentors who are regular Sears technicians. In south-central Los Angeles, Hyundai Motor America started a six-month apprenticeship program that includes eight automotive classes and one life-skills class. Graduates from the program find jobs at one of eleven southern California Hyundai dealerships.[48] In Louisville, Kentucky, KFC Corporation gives students from a local high school the opportunity to run their own Kentucky Fried Chicken restaurant. KFC provides the $225,000 trailer, a "restaurant on wheels" that is parked on the school's campus. The profits from sales to students and other customers go to a college scholarship fund from which participating students can draw after graduation.[49]

The German model for apprenticeships, relying as it does on government planning and strict tracking practices likely to prove unpopular in America, offers us few lessons. Ironically, it was the American business sector emulating Germany during a previous century that led to the establishment of public education monopolies across the United States. The nineteenth-century system of both public and private schools, attended by choice, was viewed as uncompetitive with Otto von Bismarck's German system of public trade schools that were "at once the admiration and fear of all countries," according to one excitable observer. During the late 1800s and early 1900s, U.S. industry support was crucial to the establishment of public school districts and state and federal funding for public education.[50] Now, as serious school reformers seek to move back toward a more locally controlled, privatized, and competitive model for education, business leaders should eschew misleading international comparisons and play a more constructive role in the process.

CONCLUSION

American business is heavily involved both in donating to all levels of education and in providing education and training directly to workers. Recognizing the incredible waste of resources on inefficient and unaccountable public schools, corporate leaders are beginning to target their educational programs to test new ideas and change the public debate over school reform, rather than simply showering more money onto a monopolistic, bureaucratic system. In the training area, companies spend hundreds of billions of dollars on formal and informal training, helping to improve their bottom lines while giving workers more skills and prospects for advancement. While training provided by employers, no matter how extensive, cannot substitute for a solid elementary or secondary education, it at least helps to ameliorate the economic problems caused by the public school monopoly.

Education, unlike other areas discussed in his book, will require public policy intervention for sizable gains to be made. But businesses have an important role to play on several levels, even assuming that deregulation, competition, and choice are introduced into the public schools. For one thing, if education dollars are eventually doled out in a more efficient manner—for example, in the form of vouchers or tuition tax credits— then many firms should consider expanding their current training programs into legitimate education enterprises and entering the market. "The most obvious question," stated Bernard Avishai in a much-discussed 1994 essay in *Harvard Business Review*, "is why businesses, which need to spend so much of their energy on training in any case, should not simply organize some of the elements of primary and secondary education themselves."[51] Just as American Airlines spun off its popular reservation system into a separate and profitable enterprise selling its services to all comers, why shouldn't a Motorola or other firms with particular expertise at teaching science, or training computer technicians, or teaching recent immigrants English not market that expertise?

For-profit companies have already proven themselves to be excellent providers of educational services, whether it be Sylvan Learning Centers contracting with public schools to tutor slow learners in reading or DeVry Institute of Technology preparing tens of thousands of young people for high-skill, high-paying jobs each year at its eleven campuses in the United States and Canada.[52] And company training already extends beyond just the ranks of employees. For example, many private firms spend a lot of time and money educating consumers about their products or services, for the obvious reason that it increases sales. Home-improvement stores such as Home Depot and Lowe's hold classes for consumers on how to build decks, lay brick, install windows, and hang doors. Many of their stores include bleachers and display areas for classroom visuals.

"The reason why any retailer does it is to get more people to come to the store more often and to make more purchases while they're in the store for the classes," said Ellen Hackney, communications director with the National Retail Hardware Association. "It ties the consumer to the store that's offering the classes."[53]

Competing for education dollars against public and private schools—with the promise of superior job preparation and access to mentors, apprenticeships, and constantly changing technology—businesses could help drive American education toward a system in which all students, regardless of their capabilities or plans for the future, can obtain a rigorous and worthwhile education. Of course, there will be resistance to the expansion of for-profit enterprise in education, as evidenced by the extreme reaction of many observers to such current practices as contracting out and corporate advertising on school buses and in school buildings.[54]

Secondly, while most of the discussion of education in this chapter has focused on K–12 schools, the majority of business donations to education flow into colleges and universities. American higher education is vastly superior in quality to American elementary and secondary education—since it operates in a competitive, if not free, market—but business leaders should still be more active in combating problems such as waste, corruption, falling academic standards, and grade inflation. Martin Anderson, a fellow at the Hoover Institution and a former domestic policy advisor to President Ronald Reagan, wrote a revealing book in 1993 entitled *Imposters at the Temple* about the problems of higher education. He exhorts college and university trustees, alumni, and major corporate donors to demand more accountability from institutions and more of a focus on undergraduate education.[55]

Lastly, businesses should continue to evaluate their own training programs to determine exactly what returns they generate. While private firms seeking to maximize profit are much less likely to waste money on unnecessary programs and unproved techniques than are public schools or colleges, they must still be careful not to treat good public notices or testimonials from their workers as final proof of the efficacy of any program. The good news is that there is no need for federal or state governments to spend a great deal more money trying to improve worker training, as has often been suggested. Most firms train their employees inexpensively and informally, and even those who pay for formal training programs do not end up spending that much on the margin. One study found that firms in four major states spent an average of six hundred dollars per worker for formal training programs. The fixed costs of training have often already been paid for, by public support for community college construction and curriculum development.[56] No new infusion of public money is required.

As many thoughtful observers of school reform have pointed out, business leaders in the past played only a marginal—and sometimes even destructive—role in the education debate. Ted Kolderie, a senior associate at the Center for Policy Studies in Minnesota, has pointed out that too many business executives have traditionally shied away from challenging the education establishment on basic issues. "Educators understand and exploit this position," Kolderie said. "They use business's political influence to get taxes raised, and they use business's contributions to finance the facade of activity that protects the system from having to change in unwelcome ways."[57] If the efforts of Pat Rooney's Golden Rule Insurance Company and other innovative businesses become the norm, corporate America will finally be playing a constructive role in the education reform debate of the 1990s. It is impossible to overstate the importance of this debate to the future of American enterprise.

CHAPTER 5

REVITALIZING AMERICA'S CITIES

When the Lucky Stores chain opened its new supermarket in south-central Los Angeles in the spring of 1992, it knew it was gambling that the potential payoffs of moving into a sorely underserved market would outweigh the risk of locating in a crime-ridden, devastated urban neighborhood. What Lucky officials could not know was that only weeks after the store opened, the Rodney King verdict would set off a disastrous riot that would wreak havoc (at least $750 million worth) on businesses and homes throughout the Los Angeles area.[1]

The new Lucky supermarket in the Baldwin Hills neighborhood escaped damage, however, in large part because it was protected by a wrought-iron fence and a nearby police substation. And early reports show that, in fact, the store has prospered despite the devastation around it. Just during the year after the riot, the store's sales put it among the chain's best performers in its southern division. "We think the inner city is a viable market," said Judy Decker, communications manager for the Lucky chain, based in Dublin, California. The store has generated community enthusiasm not only for selling groceries but also for creating a mentoring program, "Partners in Youth," for local high school students who have grade-point averages of 3.0 or better and 90 percent school attendance. The students come to work at the supermarket. Lucky, aided by co-sponsor Pepsi, assigns an adult mentor to each new hire to provide job training and advice. "It's to reward kids who already work hard,"

78

Decker said. "It takes kids who are doing well and who want to succeed, and it helps them see how they can fit into the process."[2]

And, of course, the program also serves as an enticement for high-achieving, motivated teenagers to become store employees, while generating goodwill in a community where goodwill is a particularly valuable commodity. Lucky had spent four years developing its plans for the Baldwin Hills market, including extensive discussions with community leaders and potential consumers and workers to determine exactly what their expectations were. The Vons supermarket chain, based in Arcadia, California, pursued a similar strategy when planning its new stores in inner-city Los Angeles. The company held a series of focus group discussions with urban consumers on such issues as design features, security, product lines, and employment possibilities. "Consumers want very much a voice in the store and their community," said Bill Davila, Vons president emeritus.[3] Based on these discussions, Vons developed a training program for new employees (including both job training and remedial education). Company officials view these investments as bottom-line issues. "This is a public company," said Vons vice president Mary McAboy. "There are many people we look to serve. Our shareholders expect a financial return. Employees expect growth and career opportunities. And the community expects to be served. We think we can serve all three constituencies very well."[4]

The blight, hopelessness, and despair that plague many urban communities across the United States have multiple causes and will not be easy for any social institution to address. But as the experiences of many companies that still operate successfully in inner cities demonstrate, the solution lies in solving practical problems and looking at cities as underserved markets, as economic opportunities—not as charity cases or destinations for government aid. American cities have lost residents and businesses over the past few decades mostly due to public policy, rather than corporate decisions. That does not mean, however, that there are not ways businesses can cope with urban decay and find profits in unlikely places. It may be challenging, but as an increasing number of companies can attest, it may also be highly rewarding.

THE DECLINE OF THE CITY

Public policy analysts have a host of explanations for the state of American cities, some more plausible than others. But no one disputes the notion that, particularly as centers of commerce and employment, central cities have declined. While suburbs have been a part of America's metropolitan areas since the middle of the nineteenth century, the most sizable movement of people and jobs away from central cities to suburbs and new "edge cities" began after World War II. By the mid-1960s, some 30 percent of Americans lived in suburbs. That figure rose to 45 percent by the mid-1980s and broke the 50 percent mark in the early 1990s. Central cities, by comparison, house only 25 percent of Americans today.[5] Business investment has also shifted. By 1980 central business districts could claim only 7 percent of employment in the country's ten largest metropolitan areas, and by 1990 more than 60 percent of U.S. employment and two-thirds of U.S. office space were in suburban areas.[6] In 1994 the unemployment rate stood at 7.8 percent in the nation's twenty-five largest cities, compared with 6.4 percent for the nation as a whole. Some cities, such as Detroit, Cleveland, and Los Angeles, posted double-digit jobless rates.[7]

Part of this movement can be attributable to the normal ebb and flow of real estate prices and economic growth. When a central business district is bustling, its land prices tend to rise with demand, encouraging some prospective tenants or entrepreneurs to seek out cheaper land in outlying areas of the city or nearby towns. In time, buildings in the business district age and become more expensive to maintain. That encourages further flight to newer locations. This explanation, however, is not necessarily bad news for cities. As the demand for land or office space in central cities falls, prices eventually will become competitive with those available in suburban or edge-city locations, allowing business districts to recover. After all, these districts represent a huge past investment in infrastructure that (assuming competent management) retains its value. And even though there has been a great deal of out-migration, many potential workers still live in cities and greatly desire job opportunities close to where they live.

Unfortunately, neither the initial move out of central cities nor the potential for businesses to move back into them can be understood solely as normal market fluctuations. The fact of the matter is that government policies provided a great deal of the impetus for both residential and commercial flight from cities, and the failure of local governments to provide quality services at reasonable prices (in the form of taxes and fees) continues to deter business investment in cities today.

The post–World War II movement into American suburbia was partly financed by government subsidies. Prompted by programs for new home buyers such as the Federal Housing Authority and the Farmers Home Administration, consumers could buy more land and housing for less of a down payment and at lower interest rates. Federally subsidized interstate highways helped redirect residential and commercial investment into suburban neighborhoods and new clusters of development (edge cities) along highway exits. Along with these carrots, government at all levels added some sticks: higher city taxes, more onerous land-use and business regulations, misguided "urban renewal" policies that ignored the dynamics of neighborhoods and local markets, busing and other failed attempts to improve public education, and less confidence in the ability of city police to protect residents and businesses against crime. Many of these carrots and sticks remain in place today, creating substantial barriers to successful business investment in downtowns and inner cities.[8]

Most analysts of urban economics and demographics believe that even if governments had not intervened, there would have been a significant amount of out-migration and shifting of investment from central cities into surrounding areas over the past half-century. After all, these changes can be seen across American communities with varying degrees of government taxation and interference, as well as in other countries with different national policies. Many families desire larger houses, more land, less traffic congestion, and other amenities, and they often find them by leaving the city.[9] But without the public policy mistakes of past decades, these changes in urban life would not have been so massive and abrupt, would have reflected economic rather than politically generated incentives, and would have left central cities more competitive with their suburbs and adjoining towns.

PRIVATE-SECTOR INITIATIVE

So, given that many urban problems were created by governments and cannot be completely solved except through public policy decisions, where does that leave American business? With many opportunities to prosper by rejuvenating cities and tapping unserved markets. An appropriate analogy might be to hurdles: Bad political decisions may have raised their height, but innovative companies that find ways to clear them will often find tremendous rewards at the finish line.

The supermarket industry is one that seems intent on reentering urban areas and establishing profitable operations. In addition to the Lucky and Vons investments in Los Angeles, forays by major chains into urban markets include the 1990 opening of a Pathmark store in Newark, New Jersey, by Supermarkets General Corporation, First National Supermarkets' reentry into Northeast and Midwest cities in the late 1980s and early 1990s, Finast's moves into predominantly black and Hispanic neighborhoods in Cleveland, and a successful Tops store in East Harlem, New York. The clean, well-stocked Tops store was packed for months after it opened in April 1991, in a neighborhood where major supermarkets had been an unfamiliar sight. "Quality retailers will always do well here," said one developer of the mall where Tops serves as an anchor tenant, "because their competition is shoddy, overpriced merchandisers."[10] Supermarket chains still find government-imposed impediments in urban areas. Many of New York's potential sites, for example, are off-limits because of zoning laws that require special permits to build non-manufacturing stores occupying more than 10,000 square feet.[11] "It is much more complicated in an underserved area—zoning restrictions, transportation issues, all kinds of license fees," said Karen Brown, senior vice president for the Food Marketing Institute, a supermarket trade association. "Just to get the land parcels together is an issue."[12] Nevertheless, many chains see urban markets as potentially solid performers. And the success of supermarkets can have important ancillary effects. "Supermarkets send a message of vitality to the local governments, the residents, and other entrepreneurs," said Paul Grogan, president of New York City's Local Initiatives Support Corporation.[13]

Franchisers represent another industry with an interest in capturing more of the urban market. KFC Corporation, based in Louisville, Kentucky, has a program to increase franchises in inner-city areas. In 1981 it began financing up to 95 percent of the cost of franchises in such areas, reducing the cash requirement for franchisees and waiving net worth requirements. The gamble paid off. Originally planning to have at least 88 new franchises in the program by 1986, KFC reached and exceeded its goal, and the firm now claims 175 new restaurants from the program. Sales at each of these stores averaged about $50,000 more than the rest of the franchise system in 1993. "This type of program makes not only social, but financial, sense," said KFC vice president for business development Walter Simon. "These are untapped markets."[14]

The KFC strategy of "up-fronting" money for inner-city franchises points to one of the most frequently noted problems with urban economies today: lack of access to capital and credit. Many aspiring entrepreneurs in cities have a hard time securing loans from financial institutions or insurance from traditional underwriters. While many politicians and activists have blamed these problems on racial discrimination or "redlining" (which, in actuality, is rare or nonexistent; see Chapter 9), the real reason is that an assortment of factors—crime and regulatory costs chief among them—have kept many lenders and insurers out of urban residential and commercial markets.

But not all. After taking the helm of American Savings Bank (based in Irvine, California) in 1989, Mario J. Antoci began increasing the thrift's lending in inner cities. By 1992 loans in low-income neighborhoods made up about 20 percent of American's loan originations and more than 10 percent of its total loans. American found that it could still identify good credit risks in inner cities by using alternatives to its standard formulas, such as substituting timely payment of utility bills for more familiar evidence of creditworthiness. In 1993 American's loan delinquencies in Los Angeles low-income neighborhoods were less than 35 percent of those on loans in affluent areas. "It's a great niche," Antoci said.[15]

LEAPING THE HURDLES

In spite of all the risks and problems of inner-city enterprise, many business owners still manage to find financing and success, with resulting benefits for themselves, their employees, their customers, and the communities at large. They have found ways to reduce the disadvantages and prosper from the advantages of their urban location. Some problems urban enterprisers are working to solve are discussed below.

Crime

In 1992 the crime rate in America's twenty-five largest cities was 60 percent higher than the national average.[16] The higher crime rates and, more importantly, the more widespread fear of crime in central cities can be seen as the most important barriers to business success because they drive up insurance and lending costs while scaring away potential customers or workers. But there are many strategies companies are using to reduce their crime-related costs. Smart & Final, a West Coast food wholesaler with outlets in poor Los Angeles neighborhoods, goes out of its way to protect customers and employees. "We don't want to open ourselves up to robberies, so we're very careful about receiving shipments late at night," said company chairman Robert Emmons. "We won't do it if there's just one or two people in the store." Store managers deposit receipts several times a day, instead of just once, to minimize the amount of cash that can be stolen.[17]

There is no escaping the fact that coping with crime represents added costs for inner-city businesses. Each Finast's supermarket in downtown Cleveland employs two full-time security guards and sometimes a vehicle to patrol the parking lot, at a total cost of as much as $12,000 per month at each location. On the plus side, though, the company has found that inner-city shoppers load up on fresh produce, fish, and meat, which carry higher margins than nonperishable packaged foods bought at higher rates in suburban stores. Despite the higher security costs, two-thirds of Finast's inner-city supermarkets were profitable in 1995, and their sales were growing faster than those in suburban stores.[18]

Many businesses, frustrated with the slow response and lack of effectiveness of many urban police departments, have turned to alternative ways (like Finast's in-house security force) of guaranteeing worker and consumer safety. Indeed, the private security industry has grown dramatically since the mid-1980s. By 1990 private security guards outnumbered public law enforcement officers by nearly three to one, while private businesses, neighborhoods, and individuals spent $52 billion on private security protection, almost twice the amount collected in taxes for police expenses. These private security personnel are directly accountable for what they do, unlike the police, and are responsive to what businesses specifically need. There is evidence to suggest that the boom in private security may well be paying off. "Since burglary rates (unlike most felony crimes reported to the police) have declined over the last decade, alarm systems and other private measures appear to have deterred burglaries," noted criminal policy analyst Morgan Reynolds.[19] The Pathmark supermarket in downtown Newark, New Jersey, mentioned earlier may well owe its success to the fact that, located behind a barbed-wire fence with a single entrance manned by security guards, it is frequently referred to as "the safest place in Newark."[20] Customers feel secure, and they view Pathmark as interested in their well-being—a view that translates into loyalty. "We're taking care of customers, we're doing the right thing, and we're making money," said Jack Futterman, chairman of the company. "It's a win-win-win situation."[21]

Another interesting development has been the role insurance companies are playing in reducing crime and apprehending criminals. Both insurers and residents of inner-city communities have incentives to create anti-crime programs. "Neighborhood watches make neighborhoods safer and hopefully [facilitate] enhanced insurance availability in those markets," said Richard Berstein, vice president and general counsel for Metropolitan P&C.[22] Insurers also frequently offer rewards for information leading to conviction in arson cases, which cost subscribers about $1 billion in losses each year. Reynolds points out that insurers could institute similar bounties for the apprehension and arrest of those who harm or steal from commercial policyholders, a move that would "raise the arrest rate sharply and boost the recovery rate of stolen property."[23]

Blight and Abandonment

Businesses have begun to take the lead in renovating downtown areas and fostering new business development. After all, existing businesses have a tremendous incentive to attract new firms to the area, because the newcomers expand the tax base and stimulate customer flow through central business districts. In virtually every city in the United States, banks, insurance companies, and utilities themselves employ thousands of economic developers whose job it is to convince existing companies to move into their areas or to help new companies get started.

Many analysts, beginning with Dr. Martin Anderson in the 1960s with his book *The Federal Bulldozer,* have noted that government-driven urban renewal programs decimated existing neighborhoods and business districts in many cities in an ill-fated attempt to stimulate development mainly through infrastructure improvements and beautification.[24] The good news is that since the late 1970s and continuing into the 1990s, downtown development has become more of a business-led rather than government-led enterprise. Private developers, though usually with local or state tax abatements and subsidies (and sometimes federal money through such programs as Urban Development Action Grants, or UDAGs), have constructed numerous shopping, office, and residential projects in downtowns. These projects—including major downtown malls like Faneuil Hall Marketplace in Boston, Pike Place Market in

Seattle, and Horton Plaza in San Diego—have had varying degrees of success, but at least they have not been as disastrous as previous urban renewal programs designed almost totally by government planners.[25] Indeed, Boston's Faneuil Hall, opening to great fanfare in 1976, made a profit for developer Frank Rouse after six years and continues to be a modest downtown success. Other Rouse projects in Norfolk, Toledo, and Richmond, however, have been flops.[26]

In the Bronx, the Concourse Plaza Shopping Center, a $150 million project, opened in May of 1991. The first day of operation, the shopping center's anchor tenant (a Waldbaum's supermarket) sold more than $250,000 of groceries to 10,000 customers. "Until recently, most retailers have been too scared to go into inner-city areas," said Bernard Rosenshein, developer of Concourse Plaza. "But now that the suburbs are saturated, the greatest opportunities are in the inner cities."[27]

The key to success for downtown redevelopment appears to be the degree of leadership and risk-taking provided by businesses. When significant amounts of public money are involved, developers tend to ignore customer demand and market analysis, to the detriment of the project's ultimate viability. "The government can't create a viable business when the market won't support it," said Bill Stern, a former chairman of the Urban Development Corporation and a vocal critic of big-government projects in downtowns.[28] Dolores Palma, an Alexandria, Virginia-based consultant to businesses and local governments, concurs. In downtown development, "use of the physical 'Field of Dream' approach . . . will continue to wane as the limits of its success become more and more apparent," she said.[29] Another key to redevelopment success is to avoid the trap of focusing on big business at the expense of small business. A 1987 study of firms in the Dayton, Ohio, "enterprise zone" revealed that small businesses were actually more likely than big businesses to cite revitalization as an important reason for locating in the inner city.[30]

One trend to watch is the appearance of business improvement districts (BIDs). In cities like New York and Philadelphia, business leaders and landlords—fed up with deteriorating infrastructure and high crime rates—have gotten together to pool their resources to hire security guards, clean up streets and sidewalks, renovate buildings, promote office sites, and expand parking spaces. By 1992 there were some nine hundred of these efforts under way in cities across the country.[31] At New York's

Grand Central Station, a BID installed new signs, streetlights, and shrub-
bery to make local retail establishments more attractive. Its private security force keeps petty crime to a minimum (reported crime fell more than
a third during the first four years of the BID's operation, which began in
1988).[32]

Financing

Would-be entrepreneurs in the inner city find that lack of access to capital
and insurance are serious barriers to entry. But there are ways to find
financing, and a growing number of large and small financial institutions
who are actively seeking business in inner cities.

As in the American Savings Bank example described above, lenders
and insurers looking for opportunities in cities must often find innovative
ways of locating good risks, relying on evidence of regular bill payments,
longtime residency, and good character. In this effort, financial institutions are not exactly reinventing the wheel. One of the nation's largest
banks, San Francisco–based Bank of America, owes its existence in part
to founder Amadeo Peter Giannini's willingness to advance money to
Italian and other immigrants in northern California in what Giannini
called "character loans"—backed by an individual's reputation more than
his documented track record. His Bank of Italy, founded in 1904, grew on
the strength of small accounts that other institutions wouldn't touch, and
he even solicited depositors and loan applicants door-to-door. By 1945
the renamed Bank of America was the largest bank in the world.[33]

Today immigrants remain the driving entrepreneurial force in many
American cities, and they often get financing in untraditional ways.
Korean grocers get much of their startup capital from revolving private
credit associations. West Indians rely on group savings plans called *sou
sou*, in which members make periodic donations but then get a turn at
receiving large loans. "Microlending" by banks, credits unions, and
small nonprofit agencies has become a popular means of obtaining loans
ranging from $1,000 to $50,000 to finance new enterprises.[34] Microlenders often use peer pressure to ensure payment. For example, Working
Capital Inc., of Cambridge, Massachusetts, has its borrowers form
"business loan groups" of four to ten people. The group members act as
informal advisors to one another and approve one another's loans, but

the group also serves to reduce defaults. Unless all group members are current on their microloans, none is eligible for more. Working Capital's default rate is 2 percent.[35]

Community banks, such as South Shore Bank in inner-city Chicago and Mutual Savings and Loan in Durham, North Carolina, have enjoyed profitability by seeking out investments in downtown businesses and residential developments.[36] American Savings opened a branch in the Watts neighborhood of Los Angeles to drum up more business.[37] By buying up faltering savings and loans, First National Bank of Chicago grew from five to seventy-seven branches from 1986 to 1994, taking the bank into ethnically diverse neighborhoods. First Chicago evolved new business strategies to serve their new customers. For inner-city entrepreneurs, the bank works with and helps to fund the Women's Self-Employment Project, a nonprofit microlender, to channel funds into promising small start-ups.[38]

But even big banks are finding that a focus on multimillion-dollar loans to large corporations is no longer a promising financial strategy, because such corporations increasingly have direct access to capital markets. Banks are now entering the market for smaller loans in cities from Washington, D.C., to San Francisco, sponsoring conferences and mentoring programs to help small businesses find a footing. "We think small businesses are looking for a partner, not a lender," said Sandra Maltby, senior vice president for small business services at KeyCorp., based in Cleveland. "Money isn't always the answer. It often is, but not always." Banks such as North Carolina–based First Union Corporation and Richmond-based Crestar have had to revise their management practices and underwriting deals to efficiently handle smaller loans, but many financial executives believe the risk will be worth the effort.[39]

Insurers have also begun to identify money-making opportunities in inner cities. One problem is that many urban entrepreneurs, immigrants and nonimmigrants alike, are unfamiliar with basic insurance concepts and may not realize they should purchase insurance to operate a business, a decision that can be disastrous for a start-up firm. In inner-city Milwaukee, the Community Insurance Information Center, founded by state and national underwriters, helps inform potential customers about insurance needs. The center refers individuals and businesses to potential insurers—and also, when necessary, helps explain why an applicant was rejected for coverage and what to do to become eligible.[40]

Insurance companies have many financial incentives to make sure that urban communities where they already have substantial investments succeed and prosper. A healthy downtown means fewer business failures, lower crime, and increased underwriting opportunities. After the riots, State Farm insurance invested a total of $1.2 million in three Los Angeles inner-city banks to stimulate business growth, and in 1994 it opened an additional office in Brooklyn to generate new business.[41] In Newark, Prudential Insurance Company has invested hundreds of millions of dollars in downtown retail stores, recreation and entertainment complexes, and child care facilities.[42] Protective Life Insurance of Birmingham, Alabama, has made inner-city development a corporate goal since 1987. So far it has made loans to thirteen shopping centers and business ventures; one $4.8 million loan turned a group of vacant lots into an 84,000-square-foot shopping center, with a supermarket, a drugstore, and the state's first black-owned McDonald's franchise.[43] In Washington, D.C., Consumers United Insurance Company has made a major effort to invest in new businesses and residential developments. It has financed either the start-up or the survival of at least a dozen minority-owned businesses in the inner city, as well as low-income housing developments and a college scholarship program for local teens. "We want to bring these communities into the developed world," said Jim Gibbons, founder and president of Consumers United. "We want to create opportunities for full participation in the American dream for all citizens. Our goal is to change the cycle of dependency and depression, and create a cycle of hope and renewal."[44]

Some insurance professionals have proposed more ways that underwriters can foster greater development and opportunities in inner cities. For example, Charles L. Young, a California risk management consultant, argues that one of the biggest challenges facing urban families or businesses is saving enough money to move to a new location or make a needed investment. Insurers can alleviate that problem by issuing low-cost, small-payment bonds to guarantee credit at low interest rates. These bonds would be underwritten by local insurance agents, who would gauge the trustworthiness of applicants in their communities. Eventually banks, landlords, and retail establishments with store credit programs could all benefit by participating in small-payment bond programs. "It doesn't take much to realize," Young said, "that any vehicle that guarantees small sums of money can help" inner-city communities develop.[45]

Another way to increase available financial resources in cities is for existing manufacturers or service industries to loan money directly to new start-ups, much like KFC provided up-front costs for its new franchisees. Harlem resident George Rowan secured financing to start his own franchise after convincing an official from Pak Mail, the national chain of mailing and business-support offices, to visit his proposed site. "We walked around the neighborhood and talked about demographics," Rowan said. They visited Harlem's one post office, a small and dingy place where you can "go in for stamps and be there for half an hour." Recognizing a good business opportunity, the company not only financed half of Rowan's franchise fee but reduced the fee itself.[46]

After the Los Angeles riots, the Walt Disney Company established a $1 million loan fund program to help small, locally owned businesses reestablish themselves. The loan fund, administered by the city's First African Methodist Episcopal Church, offered as much as $20,000 in loans to businesses that could not qualify for bank loans.[47] The money has been used by both entrepreneurs and existing businesses seeking financing for renovation. "Spiritual development cannot take place without economic development," said Rev. Cecil Murray, explaining his church's participation in the program.[48]

While the financing challenges faced by inner-city businesses are very real, it would be a mistake to exaggerate the barrier this creates to successful start-ups. Many profitable companies have been started with little more than credit cards, family funds, and faith. The Subway restaurant chain, for example, is now one of the largest fast-food franchise operations in the United States, with $2.2 billion in systemwide sales in 1994 and $170 million in royalties to the corporate headquarters. But when Fred DeLuca and Peter Buck founded the first Subway restaurant in Milford, Connecticut, in 1965, all they had was $1,000 in personal savings; their initial salary was $14 a week. Similarly, John Egart and David Soderquist started First Team Sports in 1985 with $1,000 and an idea for roller skates that would have only one row of wheels and feel like ice skates. With $35.5 million in revenues in 1994 and a major share of the in-line roller skate market, First Team's founders demonstrated how hard work and salesmanship could lead to huge success.[49]

Job Training

As discussed in the previous chapter, many firms spend significant funds training employees and potential employees to perform jobs. In inner cities, companies have found that training expenditures can serve their own interests as well as those of urban residents. Dallas-based SER–Jobs for Progress Inc. offers job-skills training to Hispanics in ninety cities around the United States. In exchange, companies involved as partners get information about the best prospective recruits—and demographic information for marketing their goods and services to Hispanics. In St. Louis, K-Mart has a partnership with a local university and local high schools to hire, train, and even transport inner-city kids to local K-Mart stores. The new hires receive ten weeks of training in "life and retail skills," including how to follow instructions and get along with coworkers and customers. K-Mart began the program after finding that some of its stores lacked access to good employees.[50]

In south-central Los Angeles, Pioneer Electronics USA created Pioneer Academy in 1993 to train promising high-school juniors and seniors in electronics. These students learn not only hands-on skills but also scientific concepts and even life skills (such as stress management and how to establish credit). If they perform well, students get a paying summer internship at a Pioneer plant, and some graduates have already gotten jobs there. A similar effort in the same neighborhood is the Toyota–Urban League Auto Training Center, sponsored by Toyota Motor Sales USA. The program has placed three-fourths of its graduates in auto-service jobs around the city.[51]

Transportation

One of the greatest catastrophes of urban policy in American has been wasteful public transportation systems. Billions of federal, state, and local tax dollars have been poured into public rail or bus transit systems that have been poorly designed or poorly run. During the 1980s more than $20 billion was spent to build and expand urban rail systems in fourteen cities, yet the market share of work trips accounted for by public transit actually declined in all but one of these cities.[52]

Fortunately, employers and private transportation companies in many cities are working to improve urban transportation offerings. In some central cities where highways are chronically congested and transit options unattractive, companies have adopted four-day weeks with longer workdays or flextime strategies to reduce work trips. Others have allowed some workers to telecommute (that is, to work from home or another site by computer rather than come into a downtown office), thus reducing transportation costs and hassles. The federal government predicts that telecommuting salaried employees could number 15 million by 2002, which by itself would divert nearly as many annual passenger miles from automobiles as public transit carries today, but without any public subsidies (a more extensive discussion of telecommuting can be found in Chapter 10).[53]

Private transportation companies are much more efficient than their public-sector counterparts. Miami's unsubsidized private vans (or jitneys) carry more riders than its expensive rail transit system. Privately operated express buses operate at speeds competitive or superior to rail.[54] In some cases, private employers have begun their own shuttle services to transport workers from suburbs to downtown business sites, or vice versa. Preferred Products Inc. (PPI), a division of SuperValue Inc. located in Chaska, Minnesota, created its own van service to bring workers from downtown Minneapolis to its Chaska plant, which manufactures and packages candy, peanut butter, and mixed nuts. This program solved the company's chronic labor shortage while giving inner-city residents access to good jobs. "It's a project that gives me a feeling of fulfillment," said Art Timp, operations manager for the PPI plant. "I feel good about working with people who have a difficult time getting back into the workforce and about giving them an opportunity to rebound."[55]

Social Ills

Many downtown businesses have discovered that it is in their financial interests to pitch in and help ameliorate social problems like homelessness, poverty, hunger, and drug abuse. Their efforts range from simple and inexpensive programs to ambitious projects requiring a substantial investment in time and money. One item in the first category would be an interesting idea from Prestige Cleaners, a small business with stores in Aliso Viejo and La Palma, California. Prestige offers job seekers free dry cleaning of suits, dress shirts, and blouses so they can make a good impression on a potential employer; all the individual needs to do is show the cleaners a recent unemployment check stub. Besides generating good feelings, why offer such a service? "We want to do our share to help people find work," said Prestige owner Rod McDermott. "Our business comes from people with jobs."[56]

Many retailers donate food, clothing, and other goods to inner-city homeless shelters, soup kitchens, and charities. Major grocery chains such as A & P, Acme, Pathmark, and Thriftway are a common participant in these programs. Raley's, a grocery chain based in West Sacramento, began its Food for Families program in 1988 to collect and distribute food and money. Local television stations promote the program in public-service announcements, and Raley's advertises it on grocery bags. Cash contributions alone from shoppers and vendors have topped a half-million dollars per year.[57] Marriott Corporation, based in Washington, donates nonperishable food, personal care products, and other nonfood items to a national food bank and allows catering clients to ask the company to donate the cost of unserved hotel banquet meals to the food bank.[58] Harper/Connecting Point Computer Center in Portland, Maine, donates machines and training time to urban schools, arts organizations, and local firms.[59]

Businesses cannot afford to be social services agencies for distressed urban communities, except in the important sense that employment represents the best antipoverty program. Nevertheless, imaginative ways to serve the needs of these communities can justify themselves (if they are modest in cost) by improving a company's environment and creating a more stable, prosperous population of potential workers or consumers. Arby's restaurants found a low-cost way to help the needy while promoting its own food: its Neighbors in Need program, launched in 1992, has participating restaurants ally with local charitable organizations to find homeless families in their communities and issue weekly meal cards to them for lunch or dinner. The restaurants assist a different family each month. "We in the food business can—and should—play a role in alleviating hunger," said Gaylon Smith, vice president of franchising.[60]

Community Support

Businesses operating in inner-city areas have found that earning the trust of consumers and community leaders can be crucial to enjoying long-term success. Indeed, in the case of McDonald's franchises in the Los Angeles area, community support and respect may well have saved businesses from destruction during the riots. There are some thirty McDonald's restaurants in south-central Los Angeles, but none was torched and few were damaged at all that fateful week in April 1992. Rioters avoided the restaurants, except perhaps to eat in them (along with police officers and firefighters) every day after curfew was lifted. "We were spared—if we can use that term—because of our involvement in the community," says franchisee Leighton Hull. "The folks know we're involved in the community. To them, we aren't the guys who just take the money and leave town."[61]

Community involvement has long been the corporate policy at McDonald's. Operators are encouraged to support schools, sponsor Little League teams, be involved in local chambers of commerce and community organizations, and hire and train local youths. Would-be managers take courses in community involvement and responsible management practices, featuring interactive video programs and discussion sessions, at Hamburger University, the chain's training center. "We're constantly providing franchisees with tools they can use to help them work with their local communities," said Stephanie Skurdy, director of communications at McDonald's headquarters in Oakbrook, Illinois.[62] Hitachi America is another company that encourages employee involvement in community projects, through the company's Community Action Committees. Employees organize themselves to volunteer in the communities where Hitachi plants are located. The company, in turn, provides funds to some of the organizations with which employees are working, and it holds an annual conference for employee volunteers.[63]

Community involvement is not just a public relations tool or, in extreme cases, a way to avoid vandalism. It can be a marketing and research tool. Getting to know the communities in which a business operates can help that business tailor its offerings to meet the needs of potential customers or workers. Lenny Brown, a former owner of a chain of inner-city supermarkets in New Jersey, believes that to be successful "you have to give your inner-city customers a nice store. Their money is just as green, and the profit margins are there." That means, for example, varying the products available to reflect ethnic or cultural preferences and selecting advertising media with the greatest appeal to customers. Brown found, for example, that community circulars and radio were much more effective than newspapers in advertising his grocery offerings in inner-city areas.[64] Americas' Food Basket, a Cuban-owned supermarket based in inner-city Boston, had $8 million in sales after only two years of operation by developing a mix of products that satisfied local demand for Latin American foods.[65] Thirman Miller of First National Supermarkets agrees that community involvement can be the key to understanding urban consumers and is simply a "cost of doing business" in inner cities.[66]

CONCLUSION

Cities have traditionally been centers of commerce, culture, and civilization. Most appeared and grew around trading routes and marketplaces; they reflected a deeply felt need for people to congregate, to exchange products and ideas, and to find economic opportunities for themselves and their families. While American cities retain these functions for millions of citizens, particularly those who have recently immigrated to the United States, they have in many cases also become crime-ridden, blighted, devoid of enterprise, and costly places to live or work.

For traditional American downtowns to regain their standing and compete for people and investment with suburbs and new edge cities, public policymakers on the local, state, and national levels will have to change destructive policies like overtaxation, overregulation, and bureaucratic bloat.[67] But responsible businesses will play an important role, as well, to the extent that their financial interest in selling their goods or services and making profits are in line with the social interest of rebuilding distressed communities. "Jobs, investment, and businesses in our inner cities will materialize only as they have elsewhere—as the result of private, for-profit initiatives and investment based on economic self-interest and true competitive advantage," said Michael E. Porter, the management consultant and author.[68] As one perceptive *Fortune* magazine essayist wrote, inner cities "won't revive until they rejoin the national economy. That means empowerment of the residents as consumers, workers, and entrepreneurs—with help from businesses that can make money as they create wealth. Look at these places not as pits of despair but as regions of opportunity."[69]

CHAPTER 6

PROMOTING HEALTH
AND WEALTH

At the sprawling 312-acre campus of the National Institutes of Health in Bethesda, Maryland, the federal government has long showcased its commitment to medical research. The history of the NIH dates back to 1887, with the founding of the Laboratory of Bacteriology. In the mid-1990s the various labs that make up the NIH are working on AIDS, cancer, heart disease, and other illnesses. NIH grants flow from Washington to university campuses across the country, funding research into the complex interaction of chemicals in the human brain and the medical applications of rare tropical plants. For many, the NIH shows that the much-maligned federal government can be effective and even noble. Republican Newt Gingrich, writing shortly after taking office as Speaker of the House in a Congress full of new members seeking places to cut spending, noted that "government does some things very well" and gave as an example its role in enabling "valuable research, like discovering the cure for polio."[1]

What is often forgotten is that the NIH and other U.S. government research agencies play at best a minor role in developing new drugs, therapies, and medical devices to alleviate pain and suffering. Fully 90 percent of useful new drugs come from corporate research.[2] For every polio vaccine developed by federally funded scientists, profit-seeking business has generated many more medical breakthroughs that have benefited millions of people. During the 1930s a private pharmaceutical company, Merck & Co., did pioneering work on vitamin B-12 and developed the first steroid (cortisone) in its company research lab. Five Merck scientists received Nobel prizes in the 1940s and 1950s.[3] Another private company, medical-device manufacturer Baxter International, developed the first sterilized vacuum-type blood collection device in 1939, allowing blood to be stored for weeks rather than a few hours and revolutionizing American medicine as a result. Decades later Baxter introduced the first portable kidney dialysis machine (1978), advancing patient welfare and comfort immeasurably.[4] Overall, according to a study by the Battelle Medical Technology and Policy Research Center, private pharmaceutical advances in just two fields—coronary artery disease and strokes—will save about 5.5 million American lives from 1990 to 2010.[5]

In recent years, private industry has become the largest source of funding for medical research, accounting for more than half of all expenditures, compared with the NIH's 32 percent.[6] In just one area, biotechnology, private investors spent more than $10 billion during the 1980s bankrolling thousands of new companies working on everything from AIDS cures to bovine growth hormones. In the coming years, the social benefits of one of the biotechnology industry's most eagerly awaited innovations—monoclonal antibodies to treat everything from arthritis to cancer—will likely be staggering.[7] These investments were not made philanthropically; they were made in an attempt to realize big profits from promising new technologies. They were also made with an eye to the long term, since the vast majority of these new biotech firms have yet to make money. "No other nation on Earth could have generated so much capital to launch biotechnology companies," said James Vincent, chairman and CEO of Biogen, Inc. "No other nation has the scientific base on which to draw. And it's because no other nation has the free-market system of risk and reward that America does."[8]

Too often, discussions of corporate social responsibility in the area of health care have focused on whether firms offer health insurance to their employees, or whether profit-seeking business has a place in providing the medical services that Americans need. In a broader context, American business is already playing a substantial and largely unappreciated role in making individuals and families healthier—by pursuing market opportunities, taking risks, and valuing the health and well-being of employees and consumers in economic decisions. Indeed, the health care field contains some of the most socially responsible corporations in America, when responsibility is understood as conferring great benefits on society.

RESPONSIBILITY AND MEDICAL PRODUCTS

For many observers, the paragon of corporate social irresponsibility is the greedy drug company that profits at the expense of human suffering. During the national debate on health care reform in 1993 and 1994, advocates of greater federal involvement in the regulation and delivery of medical services cited the high profits of pharmaceutical companies as proof of the incompatibility of profits and health concerns. Commenting on the fact that average drug prices rose six times faster than the general inflation rate during the 1980s, then-Sen. Howard Metzenbaum remarked that it was "hard to believe that a company could charge so much for such a tiny pill."[9] Only a month after taking office in 1993, President Bill Clinton called drug prices "shocking" and stated that "we cannot have profits at the expense of our children."[10] But when you consider that the profits of drug and medical product manufacturers help underwrite most health research in the United States and are responsible for the discovery of the vast majority of useful therapies for life-threatening or painful diseases, this often-asserted incompatibility of profits and health seems doubtful. And when you consider the role of profit-seeking companies in the efficient and effective delivery of medical services today, health and wealth start to look almost inseparable.

In many cases, perceptions of drug companies as socially irresponsible can be attributed to ignorance about how the pharmaceutical industry operates. Take the case of Ergamisol, produced by New Jersey–based Johnson & Johnson. It was originally developed as a drug for deworming animals. Later, though, researchers discovered a more valuable use of the drug: it helped cure colon cancer in some humans. Testifying before a U.S. House Committee in 1993, First Lady Hillary Rodham Clinton pointed to Johnson & Johnson's marketing of Ergamisol as a case of corporate greed. "You had a drug being charged at six cents a pill for use in sheep," she said. "When it came on the market [for humans], the drug manufacturer started charging $6 a pill. . . . There was no justification whatsoever for that difference in cost."[11]

But that simple explanation of the Ergamisol case is misleading. "We didn't just take a sheep pill and start feeding it to people saying, 'Hey, look! It works,'" said Robert Kniffin of Johnson & Johnson. Before releasing the drug for use in humans, the company conducted 1,400 studies involving 40,000 patients over the course of thirty years. The total price tag for the research was about $60 million and encompassed not only colon cancer trials but also experiments into lupus, rheumatoid arthritis, and other varieties of cancer. Finally, after the company had enough evidence to suggest that Ergamisol could lead to a 50 percent higher survival rate among colon cancer patients, it received approval from the U.S. Food and Drug Administration for domestic distribution in 1990 under the name Levamisole. But the company's patent for Ergamisol (obtained many years before) expired in 1994, giving Johnson & Johnson only four years to recoup its research investment. So for cancer patients, the drug was priced at $1,250 for a year's supply—higher, certainly, than the price of Ergamisol bound for sheep ranches but actually lower than many comparable cancer drugs.[12]

The Ergamisol case is one of many where companies have plowed millions into research and development, waited for government approval, and found themselves with only a few years of patent protection left in which to recoup their investment before generic brands could enter the market.[13] This happens because drug companies must apply for a patent early in the development process of a new compound in order to protect proprietary research and permit publication of research findings in medical journals; otherwise, competitors could simply copy down formulas and research notes and start their own production lines. But patent protection is granted for only seventeen years (twenty-two years in rare instances). Given the fact that it takes twelve or more years on average to conduct the necessary animal and human tests to obtain FDA approval, that leaves a scant few years of sales before the patent expires.[14] Moreover, companies must also recoup enough from the sale of successful drugs to pay for R & D on drugs that did not pan out. Incredibly, for every drug ultimately approved by the FDA, companies test some five thousand other compounds and find nothing of value.[15] Tim Rothwell, chief executive of Sandoz Pharmaceuticals, notes that "it takes on average $350 million to bring a new drug to market, and only 3 out of 10 medicines recover that average cost. So the successes have to cover the cost of those failures."[16]

Maybe patent protection itself is the problem, some critics assert. They ask why companies should enjoy what amount to monopolies on the production of a drug or medical device that patients desperately need. But these critics probably have not heard of Dr. Raymond Damadian, inventor of the magnetic resonance imaging (MRI) device that has become one of the most important medical advances of the past few decades. The primary use of MRI technology is to find cancers that otherwise might go undiagnosed for years. Damadian began working on the idea in 1970 and, with a colleague, began testing the technology on rats at a private research lab in Pittsburgh. Proving the concept to be workable, Damadian obtained a patent in 1974 and by 1977 had tested an MRI scanner on a human being. The following year, Damadian and his coworkers started FONAR Corporation to manufacture MRI scanners. By 1982 large domestic and foreign companies decided the concept made sense and began introducing their own MRI products despite Damadian's patent. Over the next few years, even as FONAR pursued legal action, the company continued to refine MRI technology, generating more than 80 percent of all the innovations in the industry and securing another twenty patents. But every innovation the company introduced was promptly copied by its largest competitors.[17]

Damadian's company survived with the help of some limited success in the legal arena and because it continued to be the most innovative; most domestic competitors eventually tired of the chase. But what if innovators couldn't patent their discoveries? What if Damadian's even limited patent protection had been nonexistent? "I once thought that the patent was one of many elements of our economy," Damadian said. "I recently realized that it is our economy." Since winning recognition and numerous awards, including the prestigious National Medal of Technology, for his work during the 1980s, Damadian has worked tirelessly to defend the rights of inventors against patent infringement.[18]

Patent protection is important, but by no means is it the end of the story when discussing the prices of drugs and medical devices. Even though patents protect innovative companies from having their ideas stolen by others, they do not protect these firms from competition. In virtually every case where a drug has been introduced to treat a medical condition, alternative treatments for that condition exist, sometimes including other patented drugs. Physicians and their patients often have numerous choices among drug therapies, radiation, and surgery, and each choice has its costs and benefits. So the only way to interpret whether the price of a particular drug is "fair" or "responsible" is to compare the cost of the drug to the cost of alternative treatments. For example, the cost of treating ulcers with H-2 antagonist drug therapy runs about $900 a year. To a patient with a serious ulcer condition, spending $75 a month on drugs would seem to be an expensive proposition; however, the average cost of ulcer surgery is $28,900.[19] Similarly, despite its high cost, Merck's drug Mevacor reduced hospitalization to treat high cholesterol by 30 percent, thus reducing the overall cost of treating the disease.[20] Even for so-called orphan drugs— designed to treat relatively rare illnesses in only a few thousand potential customers from which to recoup a company's investment—seemingly high prices have arisen out of competition. Genzyme Corporation, for example, produces the drug Ceredase to treat Gaucher's disease, a crippling and sometimes fatal illness affecting an estimated eleven thousand people in the United States. Ceredase treatment is expensive, costing tens of thousands of dollars a year, but the company faces competition from copycat drug therapies and other forms of treatment.[21] "Critics focus only on a particular drug's price when, in fact, it must be looked at in the context of all health costs," said Gerald Mossinghoff, president of the Pharmaceutical Manufacturers Association. "Pharmaceutical therapy is the least expensive way to treat many illnesses."[22]

But the debate over responsible pricing of drugs and medical devices is about more than trying to explain high prices for these goods. The fact is, the statistics used to advance the proposition that prices have been rising for decades are flawed. As I have argued in previous chapters, these sorts of numbers often ignore the role of quality in pricing, instead assuming that the same level of quality in medical treatment is being sold at higher prices. The federal government's price statistics, for example, do not account for quality at all. A 1992 Massachusetts Institute of Technology study of blood pressure medications found that from 1986 to 1991 more than half of the reported price increase (54 percent) was actually due to improvements in quality. A University of Michigan study of anti-ulcer drugs reached similar conclusions.[23]

PRIVATE-SECTOR INNOVATIONS

Accusations of corporate irresponsibility on the part of medical manufacturers are particularly misplaced when you consider that the cost of medications is a surprisingly small part (about 7 percent) of total health care expenditures and has stayed the same or actually declined relative to total health spending every year since the early 1960s. Expenditures on medical devices from syringes to multimillion-dollar scanners are a more significant part of the health care pie, but in many cases they are caused more by distortions in medical markets than by the costs of the devices themselves, at least when compared to the benefits new technologies offer patients.[24] Consider just a few examples of how private firms and individuals have enriched people's lives by developing and marketing medical innovations:

- The Upjohn Company was formed in 1886 with a patent to produce "friable" pills that disintegrated readily after being swallowed. Until that time, many medications came in pills so hard that they would not disintegrate even after being struck by a hammer. Seventy years later the same company introduced Orinase, the first oral agent to treat diabetes.[25]

- Human insulin, interferon, and the hepatitis B vaccine all derived directly from industry-funded research at universities.[26]

- In 1963 Leon Hirsch, a would-be inventor and dry-cleaning equipment salesman, was lounging around a New York patent broker's office when he noticed an ungainly Eastern European surgical stapler invented in 1908. Seeing the potential for the device, Hirsch bought the licensing rights and founded U.S. Surgical Corporation to market the staples. They close wounds more quickly, safely, and comfortably than traditional needle and thread sutures, reducing blood loss, tissue trauma, and operating time. A 1984 study by the Health Research and Educational Trust of New Jersey found that the use of staples rather than sutures on surgical patients reduced hospital costs by as much as $1,700 per patient and reduced hospital stays by up to 7.5 days.[27] Later U.S. Surgical introduced devices to allow for increased use of laparoscopy, in which surgeons use tools and cameras snaked into the body to perform gallbladder, uterus, and hernia operations more efficiently and less painfully than traditional methods.[28] Just in the case of gallbladder surgery, the *Wall Street Journal* estimates the savings at more than $1 billion a year.[29]

- Genentech, one of the largest U.S. biotechnology firms, began in 1994 to market a drug it developed called Dnase that is considered the first big advance in treating cystic fibrosis in thirty years.[30]

- Dr. Wallace Abbott founded a company in 1888 to sell his improved form of the dosimetric granule, a pill that supplied uniform quantities of drugs. Abbott faced criticism from established medical associations for his aggressive marketing, but he successfully defended himself and rallied many doctors to embrace the role of private enterprise in serving the interests of patients. Later Abbott Laboratories Inc. discovered techniques for synthesizing anesthetics and sedatives during World War I—a crucial discovery, since these had previously been available only from some German companies. During the 1930s the company created its own magazine, *What's New*, to keep doctors and patients up-to-date about the latest company-generated innovations. After World War II, the company introduced new forms of penicillin. More recently it developed the LifeShield infection control system to protect health care workers from needle sticks.[31]
- Researchers at W. R. Grace and Company, an established manufacturer of many chemical and medical products, are creating an artificial pancreas for diabetics. Implanted in the hip, it senses blood sugar levels and pumps out insulin to keep levels in the safe range, thus reducing the need for constant checks and injections as well as decreasing the damage done to a diabetic's system over time.[32]
- David Schick, an electrical engineer and founder of Schick Technologies of Long Island City, New York, invented and in 1994 began selling a new device to take dental X-rays that eliminates film altogether—thus saving time, reducing the bother to dental patients, and eliminating hazardous silver waste from the film.[33]
- Dr. Edward Squibb founded a company in 1858 to develop techniques for making pure ether and chloroform, some of the most widely used compounds in medicine at the time. More than a century later Bristol-Myers-Squibb was the first to introduce a cardiovascular drug, Capoten, specifically developed to attack a disease-causing mechanism rather than simply discovered by trial and error.[34]

The last point above is important to understanding why private industry has become the largest funder of medical research in the United States today. Until the 1970s, most drug discoveries were made essentially by trial and error—both public and private laboratories would test thousands of compounds and hope that one would turn out to be useful in the area in which they were working at the time. In many cases, their only clues that

a substance might be useful came from folk tales or apocryphal anec-
dotes. But advances in microbiology, anatomy, and genetic engineering
have given researchers much more information about how specific systems of the body work and how disease-causing organisms or substances
affect those systems, as well as a whole new set of tools for arresting or
reversing disease. Also, computer modeling now allows drug researchers
to diagnose problems more accurately and predict what sorts of medi-
cines might address them.

In the wake of these scientific and technological advances, *Scientific
American* pointed out, "the biotechnology boom that followed transformed
a good deal more than the techniques used in laboratories. It also changed
fundamentally the financial environment and the culture of biological
research."[35] Private companies are now interested not only in clinical trials
of potentially useful drugs but also in basic research into how diseases and
illnesses occur. Until the early 1980s, most health care research funding
came from the federal government. But in the middle of the decade, the
graph lines crossed, and by 1993 private health research spending had
reached $16 billion. Private firms funnel much of this money to public and
private universities in the form of general grants for biological or chemical
research as well as contractual agreements with professors that include royalties and equity options in finished products. "Industry realizes that the
more classical way of discovering pharmaceuticals is not going to lead to
the breakthrough drugs of tomorrow," said Gary A. Wilson, director of science and technology at the Miles Inc. Pharmaceutical Division's research
center in West Haven, Connecticut. "That's why we're funding more
research in disease mechanisms now." Examples of this phenomenon in
1993 would include a $1 million grant to Rutgers University from Hoechst-
Rousel Pharmaceuticals Inc. to fund neuroscience programs and North
Carolina-based Burroughs Wellcome Co.'s $5 million in research and
travel grants to researchers in such fields as toxicology or molecular para-
sitology.[36] Other pharmaceutical firms, such as Merck, SmithKline
Beecham PLC, and Pfizer Inc., have spent millions of dollars on private
efforts to map and study human genes, despite the existence of the govern-
ment-funded Human Genome Project.[37]

The role of private industry in funding medical research and basic science will only increase in the future, say many observers.[38] One sign of
the times is that the number of biologists under age thirty-seven applying
for independent government grants plummeted by more than 50 percent

from 1986 to 1994. These younger scientists know that they can earn bigger salaries and face fewer bureaucratic hurdles in industry than in academia, even with NIH grants.[39]

RESPONSIBILITY AND THE HEALTH CARE INDUSTRY

The role of profit-seeking companies in the provision of health care services has also often been criticized as greedy and capricious. These critics often ask: Should private firms prosper because of the suffering of others? Health insurers, investor-owned hospital chains, and private managed-care companies have all come under fire for their alleged tendency to put profits ahead of serving patients. Particularly during the national health care debate that followed the election of President Clinton in 1992, news reports, commentators, and congressional debates all focused attention on industry practices (such as insurance underwriting, exclusive contracts, and utilization reviews) that seemed to deny medical services to patients, waste money through bureaucracy and red tape, and put the interests of providers above those of consumers. The problem in trying to analyze these complaints is that they do not distinguish between decisions made by private firms on the basis on market incentives and decisions made because of government intervention in those medical markets. Two forms of government intervention have such a significant impact on the provision of medical services that it is impossible to evaluate the responsibility of health care companies without recognizing them: the role of the federal income tax system in subsidizing health insurance, and the role of the government itself in funding medical care.

Until the 1940s most medical services were purchased directly by families, who paid cash or obtained credit with doctors and hospitals. Some families had health insurance—obtained on their own or through their employers—to pay for catastrophic events that required expensive hospital stays or ongoing care. During World War II, however, the role of health insurance in paying for care began to grow in part because of wartime regulations on the wages companies could pay their employees. Because fringe benefits such as health insurance were not being regulated by the federal government, many firms who were competing for workers in a particularly tight labor market resorted to increasing the value of fringe benefits they would offer potential employees in lieu of extra salary. Another factor that helped to spread health insurance coverage among the population was that the premiums companies paid were not taxed by the federal government, while the wages they paid were. As the income tax burden grew more onerous, this tax break became more valuable to employers and their employees.

By 1960 private insurance was paying 22 percent of all health care bills, but patients were still paying the largest share of their bills out of their own pocket. In 1965, however, another third-party payer entered the picture in a big way with the creation of the federal government's Medicare program for older Americans and Medicaid program for poor Americans. In just two years, federal spending on health care more than doubled, and state and local government payments for medical services also increased. Over the next three decades, both private and government insurance supplanted individual consumers to fund the vast majority of health care expenses. By the year 2000, out-of-pocket expenditures are predicted to account for less than a fifth of medical consumption, with government insurance paying for a third of it and private insurance paying for almost 30 percent.[40]

So what does it matter whether individual patients or third parties like private insurers or governments pay for health care? Economists say it matters a great deal, even though third-party expenditures are eventually paid for by employees through lower wages, or by taxpayers. Consumers spending money out of their own pockets tend to be more efficient than consumers who file insurance forms. One study by the Rand Corporation found that patients whose health care bills were paid totally by insurers consumed 50 percent more medical services than patients who had to pay some of their bills out-of-pocket.[41] Also, it is interesting that in two familiar segments of the health care industry where private or public insurance plays a relatively small role—dental care and eye care—costs have not exploded, and patients generally report a great deal of satisfaction with the services they receive. Certainly there is one straightforward way in which third-party payment affects health care cost: It is much more expensive for providers to administer insurance claims than it is to receive cash, checks, or credit card payments from patients.

Health care researchers have traced many of the problems average citizens perceive in the health care system today to the ways in which government tax policy and programs like Medicare and Medicaid affect the decisions of medical providers and patients. Indeed, what is striking is that the good news about cost savings and improved care for patients in recent years has come almost entirely from the private sector, where for-profit companies have introduced innovative new ways to organize and deliver medical care. The benefits of many of these innovations have been ignored by critics of corporate health care and purveyors of the notion of a "health care crisis."

One development that has been hard to miss is the growing investment of profit-seeking companies in American hospitals. For-profit hospitals are not new; in the early 1900s more than half of all U.S. hospitals were proprietary rather than owned by governments, churches, or nonprofit organizations. But during the twentieth century, the percentage of proprietary hospitals fell as federal, state, and local governments expanded their roles in the delivery of health care services. Since 1970, however, for-profit hospitals have retained and even expanded their share of the medical marketplace. More importantly, the past two decades have seen the dramatic growth of a new form of hospital organization, as large national chains have supplanted independent proprietors.[42]

Investor-owned hospitals have grown at the same time that the need for hospitals in the health care system has shrunk. In 1985 hospitals accounted for 40 percent of national health care expenditures but stood about one-third empty. A key reason for dropping hospital occupancy was the development of new technologies, often by private firms, that allowed surgeries to be performed on an outpatient basis or with a short rather than a long hospital stay. "The heart surgeries that once required sawing open the chest bones could now be performed through small openings into which a catheter is inserted," wrote Regina Herzlinger in *The Public Interest*. "Similarly, knee surgeries and the removal of gall bladders and hernias are now commonly performed through small holes rather than major incisions. As a result, patients spent less time in the hospital, if they went at all." This led not only to slumping business but also declining quality of care in hospitals, since medical personnel tend to perfect their techniques through repetition. One way for investor-owned hospitals to cope with these changes was to specialize in particular forms of surgery and treatment and to invest in outpatient clinics and home-based services. Home-care companies saw their revenues grow from $1.3 billion in 1980 to $8.5 billion in 1991; new free-standing and hospital-based ambulatory surgery centers performed 13 million surgeries, more than half of all those performed in the United States, in 1990.[43] Private hospital companies have invested in these operations for the straightforward reason that customers demand it. "Everyone is complaining about high hospital charges and room rates," said David Colby, chief financial officer of Columbia/HCA Healthcare Corporation. By using new technologies and organizational strategies, hospital chains like Columbia/HCA have cut prices and improved service.[44]

At the same time, other companies began to market drugs, devices, and services directly to patients. Medco Containment Services, for example, distributes pharmaceuticals directly through the mail to patients, bypassing pharmacies. Its Prescriber's Choice program, introduced in 1991, tracks client prescriptions and alerts physicians when a cheaper equivalent is available. Medco's success led to its purchase by Merck & Co. in 1993.[45] Similarly, California-based Access Health Marketing operates telephone services in conjunction with hospitals to provide consumers with information about treating cancer, choosing doctors, and caring for their own health care problems. Its Personal Health Advisor system serves thousands of patients in several states by giving them useful information and reducing their or their company's health care expenses (by avoiding costly unnecessary hospital or doctor visits). "Well-informed individuals are more conservative about their own treatment than doctors," said Kenneth Plumlee, CEO of Access, "and that translates into lower costs."[46]

Another development likely to increase the number of informed patients is the growth of computer and information systems providing health care information. Commercial on-line services such as CompuServe and America Online offer health reference databases and the opportunity to discuss health issues with fellow patients or health professionals. Already, these new communication technologies have yielded results. Jeff Newman, a commodities trader on the Chicago Board of Trade, used a CompuServe forum to request information after he developed polyps in his throat caused by a papilloma virus. Newman's own doctor said that the only treatment was to keep having the recurring polyps removed by surgery. But Newman, whose ability to do his job was obviously compromised by the inability to shout, wanted an alternative. He got one from a CompuServe user in Seattle, who suggested that a compound in cabbage juice might slow the growth of polyps. "It's been thirteen months since my last operation," Newman proudly told *USA Today* in early 1995. "If it were not for e-mail and CompuServe, I believe my life would have regressed along with my hope." When Madeline

Shea's young son woke up in the middle of the night, congested and cranky, the Iowa City biochemist wrote an e-mail message to her child's doctor. Though it did not seem like an emergency situation, Shea asked, should she be worried about her son's condition? The doctor, George Bergus, replied early the following morning that the condition was normal and nothing to worry about. "I feel like I have a direct line to my doctor at any time day or night, but without annoying him or interrupting him," said the grateful mother.[47]

Jerome P. Kassirer, editor-in-chief of the *New England Journal of Medicine*, editorialized that "on-line computer-assisted communication between patients and medical databases—and between patients and physicians—promises to replace a substantial amount of the care now delivered in person." That means not only cost savings but, Kassirer argued, improvement in the quality of health care. "The interaction with an on-line computer system can be quite comfortable," he wrote. "Studies show that many patients feel even less discomfort 'talking' to a computer about personal matters than to a physician."[48]

In a medical marketplace dominated by third-party payers, some analysts believe that vertical and horizontal integration of health care institutions offers the prospect of both lower costs and better care for patients. That explains the phenomenal growth of hospital chains and managed-care networks such as health maintenance organizations (HMOs).[49] Certainly the introduction of these profit-seeking enterprises seems to have at least temporarily arrested growth in health care costs. One of the largest of the hospital chains, Columbia/HCA, has saved customers money by acquiring and closing redundant hospitals in many markets and buying supplies and equipment in bulk. Regional mergers in places like Massachusetts and Louisiana have allowed smaller hospitals to lower per-patient costs by economizing on equipment and specialized personnel and to provide fixed-priced coverage for larger groups of patients.[50] Humana, another national chain of some eighty hospitals, seems to have reduced costs and improved service by installing a sophisticated information system to manage patient and provider data more efficiently. HMOs like Kaiser Permanente System offer low prices in many markets.[51]

It may be impossible to evaluate the social benefits of mergers and managed-care arrangements on their own terms, because of the way government policies have distorted medical markets. But certainly one can point to many cases in which private-sector innovators have found ways to improve health care delivery in the United States, and these improvements rarely make it into official tallies of the cost and effectiveness of medical care. The standard measurement of medical price inflation computed by the federal government, for example, does not capture the many ways in which recent changes in medical care have reduced costs. The inflation measurement counts only "list" prices, even though most third-party payers negotiate contracts with providers that discount these prices up front. Similarly, the government numbers for hospital expenses do not adequately track services that were once provided on an inpatient basis but are now, due to innovation, provided on an outpatient basis. Most outpatient services cost dramatically less than their inpatient predecessors. "This measurement problem tends to lead officials to overestimate price changes in the industry, creating the appearance of a 'crisis' where perhaps one does not exist," wrote Suzanne Tregarthen in the *Wall Street Journal*.[52]

HEALTH AND RESPONSIBLE EMPLOYERS

Even if we had a freer, more competitive marketplace for funding and delivering health care, it is likely that health insurance obtained at the workplace would remain an option for many employees. They might choose employer-provided plans as a convenience, or because employers have set up plans that serve their particular needs. Employers, at the same time, would continue to have an incentive to make sure that their employees are healthy. That incentive, of course, is productivity: Good employee health gives you more of it for a longer period of time, while poor employee health gives you less.[53]

Buying health insurance for workers is not the only way companies seek to improve their workers' health. To save on health and workers' compensation insurance costs and to maximize productivity, many employers offer wellness programs to their employees or at least encourage them to stay fit. A recent study conducted by Hewitt Associates, a benefits consulting firm, found that 76 percent of employers surveyed offered some type of initiative to encourage healthy lifestyles among their employees.[54] In the early 1990s Dow Corning Corporation of Midland, Michigan, created a health care task force to provide management with a plan to reduce insurance costs and improve the health of its 8,600 employees. The task force came up with programs such as sending health and safety magazines to employees and retirees, opening a health library, offering smoking-cessation and nutrition classes, and screening high blood pressure on-site. The company gives a free car seat to all expectant mothers who visit their physician within the first trimester of a pregnancy.[55] North Carolina–based Sara Lee Knit Products opened its own fitness center complete with cardiovascular equipment, weight room, and aerobics classes. Northwestern Mutual Life Insurance has offered reimbursements to its employees who join local YMCAs.[56] Hershey Foods Corporation takes wellness incentives a step further: Employees who fall within an acceptable range in five risk factors—tobacco use, blood pressure, weight, exercise habits, and cholesterol—receive credits toward their flexible spending accounts or receive extra cash in their pay. "Rewarding healthy behaviors is a concept employees agree with," said David S. Pratt, director of corporate medical affairs at Hershey.[57]

Helping employees obtain the information they need to be better health care consumers is a reasonable service companies can provide. The St. Paul Companies Inc. in Minnesota works with health insurers to provide health education for its workers through toll-free numbers and publications. "The premise of our activities is employees don't have enough tools to be good health care purchasers, and employers, along with their health plan administrators, have a role in trying to get that information available," said the company's group benefits manager, Todd Connerson.[58]

In many cases, corporate wellness and health promotion programs save more money in lower health or life insurance premiums than they cost.[59] Of course, if health insurance and other fringe benefits were treated the same as wages for tax purposes, many employers and employees might negotiate different arrangements about health care than they do now. Even today, a surprisingly small percentage of people make decisions about where they work based solely on health insurance offerings. One careful study by a Syracuse University researcher found that only those with chronic ailments, about 3 percent of his sample group, were truly fearful about moving to jobs where they could not get insurance.[60] In a negotiation largely free from government-introduced distortions, many more employees would probably purchase health plans and life insurance on their own or as part of networks not based around the workplace. That is why it does not make a lot of sense to rate the social responsibility of companies on the basis of whether they offer insurance to their employees.

CONCLUSION

The rhetoric of political fights over health care reform notwithstanding, the history of medical care in America is filled with examples of private innovation leading to great benefits for patients and society as a whole. Because health is a universally sought-after good, there are huge profits to be made by inventing new products or techniques for delivering care more effectively as well as less expensively. Profits are no more incompatible with the interests of patients than they are with the interests of consumers regarding food, clothing, or shelter—other necessities that virtually everyone recognizes are successfully provided, by and large, in the private sector. Indeed, medical-products manufacturers and health care providers have strong incentives to guarantee the safety and effectiveness of their products or care. For pharmaceuticals, for example, the "negative fallout of dangerous drugs is much worse in many cases than not getting the drug approved to begin with," said Dr. Kenneth Kaitin, assistant director of the Center for the Study of Drug Development at Tufts University. "If a drug has to be pulled from the market, it's very bad for public relations, financially, and in every possible way."[61]

While Americans spend a great deal of their income to purchase health care services, this may well be a sign more of affluence than of waste or greed. Because the U.S. economy provides other goods and services at relatively low cost, families can afford to spend more of their resources to improve their lives. Health care has not been the only beneficiary of this development. The share of income devoted to airline travel, for example, increased faster from 1965 to 1990 than did health care expenditures. So did spending on clubs and fraternal organizations, televisions and video equipment, computer equipment, and general recreation. "In a free marketplace such as ours, allocation of resources primarily reflects consumer preferences," said former Congressional Budget Office director Robert Reischauer. "And not surprisingly, in this rich country, people place a high value on good health and high-quality medical care."[62] To a degree not adequately realized by critics of American business, the search for profit has led to the astounding advances in drugs, medical devices, surgical techniques, and delivery of care that American consumers have enjoyed.

CHAPTER 7

SELLING SAFETY

It was a horrible tragedy, as much for the mental images it generated as for the death toll. On September 3, 1991, at around 8 A.M., a grease fire broke out at a chicken processing plant in Hamlet, North Carolina. As the fire (which started on a chicken fryer) spread quickly inside the Imperial Foods Products building, workers tried desperately to escape the smoke and flames, clawing at locked exit doors in panic. Twenty-five Imperial employees died; fifty-six more were injured in the blaze. The event made national headlines and attracted everyone from network news reporters to Rev. Jesse Jackson, who visited Hamlet several times in an attempt to link the chicken plant tragedy to the national civil rights movement. "I see the same faces here that I saw in Memphis, Tennessee, with Dr. [Martin Luther] King," he said. "Just basic, humble people who want to work and get a fair day's wages for a fair day's work."[1]

Furious voices were raised against state and federal safety inspectors, as well as the state's business community. The Hamlet fire became the cause célèbre of politicians and activists seeking tougher workplace-safety laws in Congress, including a greatly expanded Occupational Safety and Health Administration and new mandates on businesses down to the smallest family firms.[2] "We want action now. We want to know this catastrophe will not be repeated," said Mark Schulz, executive director of the North Carolina Occupational Safety and Health Project. "We want respect for workers, safe and healthy jobs, not locked doors and industrial genocide."[3] As Hamlet became the national symbol for corporate irre-

113

sponsibility in workplace safety, one small but significant detail escaped the notice of many in Congress and the media: The exit doors that sealed the plant had been ordered closed and locked by the federal government.

The problem with the Imperial Plant, a U.S. Department of Agriculture poultry inspector had said the previous June, was flies. "Both doors at the [trash] compactor was [sic] open when I arrived at 8:45 P.M.," the inspector wrote in a deficiency report. "Several flies [were] observed in all areas of the plant." Imperial's response, also written into the deficiency report, was to promise that the outside doors "will be kept locked." The inspector verified that corrective action had taken place and signed his name. The doors were locked, and a horrible chain of events set in motion.[4] Imperial Foods was hardly blameless in the tragedy—various safety problems existed at the time of the fire—but the role of heavy-handed government regulation cannot be discounted. The chicken plant was one of the few employers in a poor, rural community. It ran on a very thin margin, using an old building and struggling every week to keep production going. Installing state-of-the-art alarm doors at the side and rear of the plant was an expensive proposition. When forced by federal edict to make a trade-off between food quality and worker safety, plant managers chose the former, with disastrous results.

THE SAFETY SUCCESS STORY

The Hamlet chicken plant fire was one of the worst workplace accidents in recent memory, but despite the heated rhetoric of activists and union organizers it can hardly be viewed as representative of the attitudes or conduct of modern American business toward safety. Government regulators were at least as culpable as corporate managers in the case. Even if isolated tragedies were a useful guide to evaluating corporate responsibility to workers or customers, the Hamlet case would not tell us much.

The reality is that, as in so many other measures of economic or social progress, safety has been improving on average in the United States for decades. Companies have undertaken massive campaigns of training, coordination, technological investment, and management innovation to realize tremendous safety gains. Private laboratories test consumer products for safety, and private insurers and consultants redesign industrial plants to reduce accidents. Entrepreneurs find and market new products that are safer and easier to use than the products they replace. Businesses have huge incentives to promote safety (such as lost productivity and worker's compensation or liability insurance costs) that swamp the prospect of regulatory violations. They know that consumers value safety and will reward producers who deliver it. They have also found that safe workers are happy workers, and happy workers are productive ones.

Far more typical of American businesses' record on safety than Imperial Foods would be Northern Indiana Public Service Company's Dean H. Mitchell Generating Station. Each year, all employees must attend two safety-education classes; in addition, the plant holds weekly "safety tailgate sessions" with all its workers to discuss specific safety topics. Accidents and "near misses" lead to an intensive incident review, with the results discussed at weekly safety sessions. Workers and managers alike think of safety not as a program but as a process. The plant's motto ("Safety, Pride, Teamwork") typifies everyone's commitment. "We were able to make significant strides by having our employees buy into our cause," said J. N. Kocsis, personnel and safety supervisor at the Mitchell station. Between 1982 and 1992, the incidence rate of accidents at the plant fell by 57 percent.[5]

Nationally, the number of people injured annually (at work and home combined) fell by 15 percent from 1970 to 1990, with most of the decrease occurring during the 1980s.[6] Accidental deaths show an even steeper decline, with both the rate and the actual number of deaths falling for more than sixty years. In 1930 there were about 30,000 accidental deaths at home, but in 1993 there were 22,500. For workplace accidental deaths, the actual number fell from about 20,000 to less than 10,000. Factoring in population growth, the National Safety Council reports that accidental death rates at home fell from 24.9 per 100,000 Americans in 1928 to 8.7 in 1993 (a 65 percent drop) and accidental death rates at work fell from 15.8 to 3.5 (a 78 percent drop).[7] Accidental death rates may well be a better overall guide of safety trends than reports of all injuries and illnesses; the latter may understate safety gains, as companies, workers, and individuals have become more likely to report accidents and injuries over time.[8]

Measures of specific hazards also show a steady downward trend. Between 1983 and 1992 alone, the number of firefighters and civilians killed by smoke and flames fell by 34 percent and 20 percent, respectively. Highway fatalities, the biggest killer of Americans aged five to thirty-two, fell from 2.6 per 100 million miles driven a decade ago to 1.8 in 1993, the lowest rate ever recorded. Drunk driving, still a major hazard, nevertheless caused fewer fatalities per miles driven in 1993 than ever before. That same year, the rate of aircraft fatalities hit its lowest point since 1980. "It may not feel like it because of all the coverage disasters get," said Richard Mintz of the U.S. Department of Transportation, "but things are improving in almost every category." Similarly, Gus Toscano of the U.S. Bureau of Labor Statistics remarked that "most people don't know it because the media usually concentrate on the bad news, [but] life in the United States, in and out of work, really is safer."[9]

These safety gains cannot be attributed to regulatory effort on the part of federal, state, and local governments. Accidental deaths at work, adjusted by population, declined at roughly the same rate before and after the passage of the 1970 Occupational Health and Safety Act.[10] W. Kip Viscusi, an economist at Duke University and a leading scholar of safety regulation and risk, found in a study of the Consumer Product Safety Commission's record that available data provide no "clear-cut evidence of a significant beneficial effect on product safety from CPSC actions. If there is a beneficial effect of these regulations, then it is too small to estimate reliably."[11] Indeed, some product regulations have been counterproductive: "child safety caps" required for aspirin and other medicine bottles have actually led to more poisonings—because adults have left the hard-to-open caps off—and carpet-related injuries rose after the CPSC required new flammability standards that resulted in slippery carpets.[12]

One way to think about the relative efforts of government and business in the safety arena is this: on any given day in America, thousands of local, state, and national safety regulators are inspecting businesses, studying test data, issuing regulations, and adjudicating violations. But on that same day there are literally millions of American workers, managers, designers, and engineers working to make their workplaces and products safer in the interests of maximizing sales and revenues, minimizing losses, and maintaining good long-term relationships with productive employees and satisfied customers. The magnitude of private-sector safety efforts, both in time and money spent, far exceeds that of even today's bloated regulatory bureaucracy.

IMPROVING WORKPLACE SAFETY

It is at the workplace, over which businesses have greater direct control, where the safety gains have been the largest. While accidents still happen and some jobs remain more dangerous than others, there have been very few years since the mid-1930s in which workplace accidental deaths have risen rather than fallen. To understand why firms might spend a great deal of time and money improving worker safety, you must first get a clear picture of how costly it is to have a serious accident in a workplace.

Two main private-sector "regulators" affect occupational safety. The first is the labor market itself. In the market for workers, perceptions of risk have a significant impact on the wages employees demand. If a profession or individual business is known to be unsafe, potential workers will want more salary or benefits to compensate for the higher risk. Even if workers do not know going in how dangerous a particular workplace is, their subsequent discovery can cost firms a bundle. For example, when a business loses a proficient worker in an accident, even for a relatively short time, that worker must be replaced with a new one, often needing training. The injured employees' coworkers also reappraise their own job risks, sometimes resulting in higher wage demands. The firm's hiring and training costs rise again if disaffected workers quit. The resulting turmoil can wreak havoc on production, costing the firm sales. The safety risks posed by businesses differ dramatically, but studies have estimated that the labor market adds an average risk premium of about $1,000 to each worker's salary (meaning that on average, workers demand $1,000 more in salary than they otherwise would to compensate them for the workplace risks they perceive).[13] Finding ways to reduce that cost is clearly a desirable goal for any business, large or small—and keep in mind that this is only the mean. Some firms face very high risk premiums and save a lot of money from even modest safety improvements. Working in occupations such as logging, meat-packing, mining, and construction continues to pose a higher-than-average risk of injury. For these occupations, says Duke University's Kip Viscusi, "the marketplace generates enormous wage premiums for risk on the order of $80 billion a year in terms of higher wages for risk—and that's where firms get their financial incentive for safety."[14]

In the search for safety gains, employers have a strong ally: the insurance industry. By law, most employers must have worker's compensation insurance for their employees, but they can purchase their coverage from the private insurer of their choice. The "worker's comp" system is at least partially experience rated; that is, the premiums businesses pay bear some relationship to their rate of accidents. Firms that find ways to cut their accident rates pay correspondingly lower insurance premiums. Insurers who help their subscribers cut accident rates and costs will prosper and are more likely to keep their customers in the future. So both business managers and insurance underwriters have huge financial incentives to improve workplace safety (although unwise state regulation still keeps the system less efficient and safety-promoting than it could be).[15] "If you're a good company with a good safety record, insurance companies are knocking on your door for your business," said Steve Reynolds, safety supervisor at Crowder Construction Company in Charlotte, North Carolina.[16] Many worker's comp insurers employ armies of consultants, engineers, and designers to help their subscribers reduce accident rates and cut claims costs, which totaled $70 billion in 1994.[17]

Compared with the risk premium imposed on firms by the labor market and worker's comp premiums imposed by insurers, the prospect of being fined by OSHA is almost laughably tiny in dollar value. Average OSHA fines per worker were about 50 cents in the early 1990s, up from 35 cents in 1983 but below the peak of 65 cents in 1978. Considering that the likelihood of being inspected, much less found in violation, is low in a given year, these fines obviously play little to no role in business decisions about safety. Increasing OSHA inspection and increasing fines are not likely to change that underlying economic calculation very much.[18]

Innovative companies and insurers have spent years or even decades learning how to reduce safety-related costs by reengineering workplaces, training employees, managing better, and using new technologies. Even small changes can reap big rewards. Take Rosendin Electric, Inc., an electrical contractor based in San Jose, California. Linda Johnson, Rosendin's benefits administrator, said that when she first came to the company in 1991, it was not tracking worker's compensation costs in an efficient manner. Rates of accident frequency and severity were soaring to worrisome levels. Teaming up with the firm's safety director and risk manager, Johnson employed a new computer software package to track the type and total number of injuries, as well as dollars being spent on premiums. She found that approximately 50 percent of total claim costs were for back- and eye-related injuries; back injuries alone were costing the company an average of $15,000 to $20,000 for each instance. "Many of the injuries could have been prevented if they'd been tracked effectively," Johnson said.[19]

Supplied with up-to-date reports on how and where accidents were happening, Rosendin managers were able to find their biggest risks and address them. The company started a program to train workers about the importance of back-support belts (providing them to the workers free of charge) and how to work with the least amount of stress on the back. Rosendin managers also found that a major cause of eye injuries was that workers were not wearing their safety glasses when they needed to. Much of the company's work was done on high ladders, but safety glasses were needed only some of the time. Workers ended up leaving the glasses at the bottom of the ladder rather than balance them precariously at the top, but then failed to retrieve the glasses when their use was warranted. "Employees needed something to keep their glasses around their necks when they weren't wearing them," Johnson explained. A simple solution followed: each pair of glasses was equipped with a cord to go around a worker's neck. That one seemingly minor action reduced eye injuries by 20 percent. Between October 1992 and October 1993, Rosendin worker's compensation claims decreased in frequency by 35 percent. The severity rate fell by 10 percent, and the company saved 27 percent in claims dollars.[20]

Subaru-Isuzu Automotive found another simple way to achieve safety gains at its Lafayette, Indiana, plant. Twice a day for five minutes, all employees are encouraged to participate in group exercise workouts. Twisting to workout standards like the theme from *Rocky,* employees stretch their arms, legs, necks, and backs before beginning work assembling cars, moving materials, or even typing on computers. New employees also learn about exercise and physical exertion during their two-week orientations. Of eighty hours of orientation, forty-five hours are devoted to physical training. Employees participate in various exercises depending upon their upcoming responsibilities in the plant. In-house physical therapists coordinate these programs, which more than pay for themselves in reduced worker's compensation costs, according to Subaru-Isuzu officials. "Our goal is to prevent injuries," said Mark Siwiec, manager of safety and environmental compliance. "If injuries do occur, however, they should be less severe."[21]

Other companies have found similar results from modest changes in operation or training. When too many AT & T workers were getting injured working on telephone poles, the company started a "pole-climbing school" to teach the three-point contact method (meaning that workers should keep three limbs touching the pole at all times). Once AT & T workers mastered the method, accident rates fell. Similarly, Coca-Cola

Bottling Group cut accident rates among its truck operators by instituting warm-up exercises, improving interior lighting in company trailers, adding more trailer hand grips, and lowering the trailers two inches to make it easier for workers to pull out cases of drinks.[22]

LSG/Sky Chefs, an in-flight caterer based in Arlington, Texas, has realized significant safety gains by experimenting with financial incentives. In the late 1980s the firm was logging 1,000 injuries a year and losing more than 18,000 workdays—a huge number for a company with 8,000 employees. Sky Chefs kitchen workers were constantly straining their backs lifting heavy objects, an injury that costs an average of $25,000 in worker's compensation claims. New president Michael Kay introduced a safety program in 1991 to address the problem. Employees were taught how to lift objects without back strain; kitchen workers got a weekly five-minute "safety short" taught by one of their coworkers. The firm also began offering financial rewards to workers with good safety habits, as supervisors passed out $20 Sears gift certificates to employees who lifted or cut in an exemplary way or who took the initiative to clean up a spill. Supervisors, in turn, saw a quarter of their annual bonus tied to their unit's safety record. These and other changes helped reduce lost workdays at Sky Chefs to 8,500 in 1993 and about 5,000 in 1994. Focusing on rewards rather than punishments was the key to the new program's success, said Kay: "Our old approach was called the Stop program. It was designed to catch employees doing something wrong. This one's had a remarkably better effect."[23] Construction firm McDevitt Street Bovis Inc. in Charlotte, North Carolina, established a similar system that rewards hourly employees for avoiding accidents. The company provides a gift worth up to $25 for each three-month period without an incident requiring a doctor's attention. Hourly employees can save their "safety bucks" and trade them in later for more valuable gifts.[24]

Some of the most sizable gains in workplace safety have taken place in recent years under the tutelage of insurance companies. Insurance broker Johnson & Higgins, for example, helped one of its clients, a book publisher, set up a worker safety program that included routine monitoring, goal setting, active involvement by management, strategic planning, and bonuses tied to safety performance. The publisher had seen its accident rate rise and its worker's compensation costs shoot up by 41 percent from 1987 to 1990. After Johnson & Higgins helped the company install its new safety program, worker's comp claims dropped by 35 percent (and dollar losses by 63 percent) the first year. Georgia-Pacific Corporation, the wood-product company, worked with insurers in Georgia to reduce accidents by 31 percent in 1991 and 1992, with Georgia-Pacific's sawmills experiencing only one half of the industry's average number of incidents.[25]

Hartford Steam Boiler Inspection & Insurance Company in Connecticut has made a $562 million business out of reducing workplace accidents. The firm is now the leading provider of boiler and machinery insurance in the United States. "Our interests and our customers' interests are aligned," said Wilson Wilde, president of Hartford Steam Boiler. "Both of us are going to be hurt financially if an accident occurs, so we can justify investing time and money in loss prevention." Most of the company's four thousand employees are scientists, engineers, and technicians who work with electric utilities, chemical plants, and paper manufacturers. They have developed an array of devices, processes, and designs to enhance safety, including a device introduced in 1990 to examine hard-to-reach boiler tubes for corrosion. The company has worked with utilities to detect problems with steam turbine rotors so as to head off high replacement costs. It used new sensor technology to diagnose a turbine's vibrations and signal when to weld cracks shut. Fixing rather than replacing rotors saved millions for the insurer's utility subscribers while reducing the danger of faulty rotors coming apart in generators.[26]

Reengineering workplaces according to principles of ergonomics has become a common strategy for businesses and insurers to reduce worker injuries, particularly cumulative trauma disorders (CTDs) such as wrist strain, elbow strain, or carpal tunnel syndrome. CTDs are a fast-growing category of both occupational illnesses and worker's compensation claims, but the severity of the injuries has been exaggerated significantly by the media (carpal tunnel syndrome, a seriously debilitating illness that is often mentioned, accounts for only 1.4 percent of all injury or illness cases according to the Bureau of Labor Statistics).[27] Nevertheless, muscle strains caused by repetitive motions or poor posture do cause discomfort and pain, limit mobility, and reduce worker productivity. To address the problem, companies consult ergonomics experts and buy redesigned office furniture and machinery from manufacturers such as Michigan's Haworth Inc. (which makes motorized tables that adjust height during the course of a working day) and Nova Office Furniture of Effingham, Illinois (which sells desks with computer monitors built into them, so workers peer down at them like newspapers rather than up at them like televisions).[28]

OshKosh B'Gosh, a Wisconsin-based manufacturer of children's clothing, used several strategies to reduce CTDs at its main plant in Oshkosh. The company's employees were performing numerous tasks involving small, awkward motions that require force. Inspectors checked the snap crotch of each pair of pants, pinching six hundred snaps per hour; machine operators developed back trauma from twisting and turning heavy garments, and they sustained shoulder and hand problems from bending over to reach different-sized clothing. The company's safety team decided to purchase seven thousand padded, adjustable chairs at $100 each and to redesign many of the firm's machines. Company engineers devised an air-driven, automatic "crotch snapper," and mechanical "feed dogs" were installed to pull fabric through sewing machines. Plant workers were encouraged to report minor pain or discomfort so company engineers could find ways to address the problems; they were also rotated through several different jobs within plants to reduce constant stress on one part of the body. After an initial surge in reported injuries (workers were being told, after all, to report even minor problems more often), worker's compensation claims fell, as did the severity of reported injuries. From 1992 to 1993, worker's compensation costs at OshKosh B'Gosh fell by a third, more than paying for the company's safety innovations.[29]

In the search for workplace safety, even industries considered to be "dangerous" have made great strides. In 1976 the mining industry had the third highest rate of all injury cases and the highest rates of any industry division for injuries with lost workdays. By 1992, however, its rate of all injuries and of injuries involving lost workdays had dropped below the rates not only for all the other goods-producing industries but also for parts of the service sector.[30] The efforts of enterprises like Kerr-McGee Coal Corporation's Jacob's Ranch Mine in Gillette, Wyoming, have contributed to this impressive record. The mine's incentive program for zero accidents is a quarterly award of $100 in gift certificates from local merchants. For every accident, each of the mine's four hundred workers loses $10 from his award. "Everyone gets penalized so there's a real incentive to wear safety glasses and do the right things," said safety supervisor Lenny Altenburg. The company spends $205,000 a year on the gift certificates, but the investment has paid off: the company had lost no work time due to accidents at all from 1991 to 1994.[31] Other mining firms have introduced new technologies, begun safety training programs, and used similar financial-incentive systems to minimize accidents. Compare the mining industry's typical death toll today (97 in 1992, for example) to the 3,500 annual deaths typical in the first part of the century, and you have some idea of the progress that has been made.[32]

The efforts of these and many other American companies to reduce accidents and injuries are ongoing and massive. But conscious decisions by corporate managers and workers to address safety are not the only causes of safety gains. Larger trends in the economy, reflecting innovation and productivity gains linked to goals other than safety per se, have also contributed to lower rates of accidental deaths and to safer workplaces. For example, it now takes fewer employees to manufacture goods in America—and that means fewer chances for injuries, illnesses, and accidental deaths as more workers move into services. Also, the quality of medical care provided both at the workplace itself and in hospitals and urgent-care centers has steadily improved, reducing the severity of injuries and the risk of death from accidents. Furthermore, a great deal of recent job growth has occurred among the smallest businesses in the country, which also have tended to post the best safety records (large businesses post the second-best safety records, while medium-sized firms have traditionally reported the most accidents).[33] Finally, and perhaps least recognized of all, is that the very act of employing a person makes that person safer. Unemployment, because of its effects on stress levels and standard of living, is more hazardous than employment; it is estimated that a 1 percent increase in U.S. unemployment for one year results in 37,000 deaths (plus 4,200 admissions to mental hospitals and 3,300 admissions to prisons)."[34]

That corporate decisions made for bottom-line reasons nonetheless have advanced the cause of safety should not surprise us. As the preceding discussion shows, accidental injuries and illnesses are themselves economic costs to firms, and they show up on balance sheets as losses to be mitigated or eliminated.

CONSUMER PRODUCT SAFETY

While it is easier to see the financial incentives for corporate responsibility in occupational safety, corporate responsibility toward the safety of consumers is also rewarded in the marketplace. That is one reason why consumer products have gotten safer during the past few decades, while injuries and illnesses in the home have dropped. Maximizing consumer safety is an important goal for companies on several levels. First and most obvious is the fact that a consumer who gets sick or injured while using a product is less likely to buy from its manufacturer in the future. Also, negative publicity about faulty or dangerous products can turn off first-time consumers as well as potential workers or investors. Studies show that consumers rate safety concerns at or near the top of the list of factors they consider when choosing among products. In one study for the Whirlpool Corporation, some 80 percent of Americans named safety as an always-important indicator, compared with workmanship (74 percent) and materials (66 percent).[35] The safety of products can also significantly affect a manufacturer's stock price.[36]

Safety improvements often cost more up front, of course, and the price of products can reflect that. But that does not deter companies from introducing new, safer products; they have found that consumers will often pay for the safety gain. Medtronic, a medical-products manufacturer based in Minneapolis, has found that buyers at hospitals and doctor's offices will pay higher prices for products when the safety gains are clear. "The medical community typically buys the better product because doing so is in its interest," said Winston R. Wallin, the chairman and CEO of Medtronic.[37] For some products it is more difficult to pass along the costs of safety gains, but even at lower prices companies benefit from manufacturing and selling them, especially by generating customer loyalty and subsequent purchases. Searching for safety improvements can be an excellent way for a company to increase market share and establish the foundation for long-term success. "The free-market system rewards innovation," said N. Craig Smith, associate professor at Georgetown University's School of Business Administration. "In fact, the market system permits wasteful duplication of R & D efforts because of the importance of creating incentives to innovate." After a company adopts an innovation, competitors are spurred to improve on it, and society stands to benefit from the competition.[38]

One test of how intent many businesses are to market safe products is the success of private product testing operations such as ETL Testing Laboratories in Cortland, New York, MET Electrical Testing Laboratories in Baltimore, and the granddaddy of them all, Underwriters Laboratories (UL) of Northbrook, Illinois. Product testing is now a multibillion-dollar industry; from 1988 to 1992, UL's revenues alone rose about 50 percent. Formed by insurance companies in 1894 to provide risk data for the new crop of products using electricity as a power source, UL has become a tester of products ranging from toasters and televisions to toilet paper brands, and companies pay a stiff fee for the UL seal of approval.[39] Of course, most also do their own in-house testing; American firms spend hundreds of millions of dollars testing each of the twenty thousand new products that make it to the marketplace each year.[40]

Product liability costs also play a role in product safety decisions, but this role is not always clearly understood or friendly to consumers. Liability litigation has been exploding for at least two decades, with the number of cases increasing more than fivefold and insurance premiums rising more than sixfold since 1975.[41] The adoption of strict liability and broader burdens for design defects and hazard warnings by most jurisdictions has contributed to this increase in liability litigation and cost. While some form of legal responsibility for product safety is clearly necessary, one can argue that lawmakers have pushed liability law too far in an attempt to shift the costs of virtually all injuries or illnesses, even those due mostly to consumer negligence or uncontrollable fate, to firms.[42] The result might well have been to actually reduce the level of product safety below that which would exist under a more entrepreneur-friendly regime. The Monsanto Company, for example, decided not to market an asbestos substitute made of phosphate fibers because it was not prepared to accept the potential liability risk.[43] Similar cases in the pharmaceutical and aircraft industries have demonstrated that discouraging companies from introducing new products can have the perverse effect of keeping less-safe products on the market. An interesting study by Duke University's Kip Viscusi and Michael Moore found that changes in liability law in recent years have had the effect of reducing research and development spending and product innovation.[44]

Innovation is the name of the game when it comes to enhancing consumer safety. Some gains are made by companies and entrepreneurs consciously seeking to design and sell safer products. Remember the "Baby on Board" fad? In 1984 former executive recruiter Michael Lerner started a firm at age thirty to distribute the distinctive black-and-yellow signs for car windows, based on an idea he heard about from Germany. By 1985 he was selling about five hundred thousand signs per month, and by 1987 he had made millions of dollars. He began to think about more substantial ways to market safety to young families. His company, Safety 1st Inc., introduced a line of safety products for babies, including stove-knob covers, better-fitting outlet plugs, and an inflatable bathtub spout to keep kids from hitting their heads on hard metal spouts. After securing an exclusive contract with Toys 'R' Us, he introduced a series of other safety products: a $13 baby bath seat that swivels 360 degrees for better and safer washing in the tub, a high-tech baby monitor, and a bedrail with a built-in night-light. To say these efforts at household safety have paid off would be an understatement: Lerner and his partner, Michael Bernstein, sold 31 percent of Safety 1st Inc. to investors in 1993 for $24 million.[45]

Millie Thomas, founder of RGT Enterprises Inc., got the idea for her safety-product line from her one-year-old son, who came toddling toward her one day with a toothbrush in his mouth. Thomas had nightmarish visions of her child being impaled on the long handle (children under five are a high-risk group for choking) and instinctively bent the toothbrush handle into a ring shape. Soon thereafter, she began to consider the possibility of making safer dining and bathroom utensils for kids. "After visiting two or three specialty stores and seeing nothing remotely like it, I knew I was onto something," she said. Her Kindertools, each featuring triangular easy-grip handles, went on the market in late 1993.[46] Other products peddling safety to parents of young children sell like hotcakes. The Travel Safety Car Seat made by Brooklyn-based Babystar uses air cushions to protect small passengers; it weighs only five pounds (a third the weight of regular child seats) and collapses into a package about the size of a briefcase—making it easier for parents, siblings, or baby-sitters to carry around and use in different vehicles.[47] The simple invention and cheap installation of household detectors of smoke and carbon monoxide has saved countless lives, many more than any government regulatory standards or interventions have.[48]

Product safety innovations also occur as a side benefit from economic decisions made for other reasons, as in the case for occupational safety. Advances in solid-state electronics, for example, have improved controls in appliances and reduced fires and electric-shock hazards.[49] Advances in information and communications technology also have reduced the need for business travel, thus cutting the risk of auto or other accidents.

TRANSPORTATION SAFETY: A CLOSER LOOK

An important subset of both workplace and consumer safety is the area of transportation safety. A significant number of occupational injuries involve some kind of vehicle, be it a car, truck, forklift, or tractor. For individuals and families, auto accidents still present one of the biggest risks of injury and death, while rare accidents involving other forms of transportation such as airplanes are heavily reported in the media. Rates of transportation accidents and accidental deaths consist of particularly complex data. A variety of factors—including demographics, alcohol and drug use, changes in reporting and definitions, and changes in the urban landscape—interact with product design and business decisions to determine the likelihood of accidents. Nevertheless, the available data show a downward trend for transportation-related accidents similar to the larger downward trends in work and home accidents.

Again, the measure likely to show the least bias due to changes in data-reporting and gathering is unintentional-injury deaths. For motor vehicles, the death rate fell overall during the 1930s, 1940s, and 1950s, rose during the 1960s, and then fell again during the 1970s, 1980s, and early 1990s. The death rate for other transportation types showed the same pattern: dropping until the 1960s, rising a bit, then dropping again in later decades. Increased government regulation, instigated during the 1960s and 1970s, exhibits no obvious relationship with these long-term trends.[50] Indeed, for one celebrated act of deregulation—that of airlines—the record on safety is, on balance, positive. Fatal accidents per 100,000 departures have trended downward (albeit with significant variation) since 1950, and the advent of greater market competition in the mid-1970s has not appreciably affected that trend, despite the occasional tragedy reported in the news media.[51] The real story is that deregulation, by attracting more travelers onto planes and away from highways through lower prices, has resulted in net safety gains. Between 1978 and 1986, for example, the increased airline ridership brought about by deregulated fares reduced passenger-car travel by an average of 4 percent a year, resulting in 600,000 fewer highway accidents, 65,000 fewer highway injuries, and 1,700 fewer highway deaths each year.[52]

Attributing these safety improvements to any particular cause or set of causes is a tricky business. It is undeniably true that automobiles, buses, and airplanes have been redesigned to reduce the possibility of accidents and deaths, but it is not clear what market incentives and government regulations have each contributed to this success. Auto companies, for example, have introduced new designs for windshields and seats, seat belts, passive restraints, air bags, anti-lock brakes, and a host of other changes. Some have a clear safety benefit, but others, surprisingly, do not. A 1994 study by the Highway Loss Data Institute, representing insurance companies, found that computer-assisted braking systems are not, as might be predicted, "reducing either the frequency or the cost of crashes that result in insurance claims for vehicle damage."[53] A similar study found uncertain safety gains from the introduction of air bags.[54] A possible reason for these findings (which have been hotly disputed among automakers, insurers, and government regulators) is that drivers compensate for the existence of new safety devices by taking more risks in driving. Their sense of increased safety, in other words, lulls them into paying less attention to road hazards.[55]

A related issue in transportation safety is whether the public sector or the private sector has the stronger motivation to promote safety. In the case of rail safety, for one, private operators seem to be more safety conscious. The E. H. Harriman Memorial Awards, given for railroad safety since 1913, helped to illustrate this point in 1994, as privately owned railroads took prizes and publicly owned or publicly subsidized railroads posted mediocre or poor safety records. Among the largest railroads in the country, Norfolk Southern took first place while Amtrak, the federally subsidized national passenger rail system, came in last. Similarly, among nine medium-sized railroads, the three publicly owned lines ranked fifth, seventh, and ninth. Guilford Transportation Industries Inc., which operates lines in New England, won its category (small railroads) despite run-ins over the past few years with labor unions and federal regulators (whose ranks are dominated by union veterans). Colin Pease, executive vice president at Guilford, explains that while many publicly owned or subsidized railroads rely on "feel-good programs" to promote safety, private lines must operate safely or go out of business. Insurance costs, replacement costs, and disruption of freight deliveries all skyrocket when lines are unsafe. "There is a major economic impact to whether your workers perform their jobs the right way or not," he said. "But the motive breaks down in the public sector." Pease believes that when workers are working safely, they are working productively—and in a competitive enterprise like transportation, productivity gains are the only way to stay ahead of competing rail or trucking firms. Guilford supervisors provide daily safety instruction and perform "test and observation" procedures twenty-four hours a day, seven days a week.[56]

CONCLUSION

While interpreting safety data and identifying causes and effects of particular trends can sometimes be challenging, the overall message about corporate responsibility in this area should not be obscured. Driven by the pressures of the market to lower costs, keep skilled workers, attract and retain customers, minimize legal and insurance costs, and avoid bad publicity, American businesses have toiled endlessly to make their workplaces and products safer. To a large extent, they have done so. In a real sense, the tremendous reduction in accidental deaths accomplished since the 1930s represents an advance in the quality of life of workers and consumers no less significant than pay raises or price reductions. (Nor has it been just since accident data were gathered that companies have exhibited a commitment to safety. The Hartford Steam Boiler Inspection & Insurance Company, for example, has been working on ways to decrease boiler accidents since its founding in 1866!) As Viscusi, the safety researcher, puts it: "The main reason we're getting safer is [that] we're a richer society and we demand greater safety."[57]

Responding to this powerful demand for safety, communicated through worker and consumer demands in the marketplace, involves integrating the search for safety and quality into virtually every aspect of corporate decision-making. Managers have to remember that they set an example for their workers, and that the short-term costs of stopping production to fix safety problems can easily be far outweighed by the costs of accidents later on.[58] New monitoring and computer technologies can help companies track their safety records and target their efforts to reduce risk.[59] For consumers, making safety gains often means taking a long-term view of the company's best interests—investing in research and development, for example, or sacrificing immediate market share—and thinking of consumer education as just as important a part of the safety process as good design. Horrible accidents such as the Hamlet chicken-plant fire are human tragedies, but in the context of corporate decision-making in a market economy they are also economic disasters. That is why responsible firms today are investing so much time and money trying to avoid them.

CHAPTER 8

NURTURING NATURE

Profit and the environment are supposed to be enemies. Remember that the next time you visit Yellowstone National Park, one of the crown jewels of the National Park System and a popular attraction for tourists, backpackers, and amateur botanists, zoologists, and geologists. Yellowstone boasts some of the most breathtaking sights in all of North America—but it also boasts an interesting, capitalistic pedigree. It was the Northern Pacific Railroad, a private corporation, that funded early expeditions to the Yellowstone region and helped establish the Yellowstone National Park in 1872. "Because it provided the main form of transportation to the region," report economists Terry Anderson and Donald Leal, "the railroad could profit from preservation of this scenic wonder and therefore had an incentive to preserve it." Many other Western parks were promoted and protected by private railroad and development companies for the same reason.[1]

More recently, some private timber companies have found that by exploring other uses of the forest lands they own, they can increase their profits. In International Paper's commercial forests in Texas, Louisiana, and Arkansas, company biologist Tom Bourland implemented a fee-based recreation program to make money from *not* harvesting trees. His program charged sportsmen for hunting access and leased small tracts of land on which families could park their motor homes and enjoy the woods. After three years, International Paper saw its revenues from the program triple and the resulting profits grow to 25 percent of total profits from the area. Since this valuable use of private land relied on beauty and wildlife variation rather than ease of harvest, the company had an incentive to preserve habitat for white-tailed deer, wild turkey, fox, squirrel, quail, bald eagles, and red-cockaded woodpeckers.[2] Deseret Land and Livestock pursued a similar strategy after its Nevada cattle ranch began to fall on hard times. Deseret managers decided to diverge from standard ranging and invest in wildlife habitat, charging hunters for the right to hunt elk and other animals. Herds of elk and mule deer on Deseret land actually grew (since they were now a valuable commodity), and the company became a thriving business.[3] Other ranchers have had similar experiences in diversification. One of the most famous, the 1,289-square-mile King Ranch in South Texas, now makes 60 percent of its income from business activities other than cattle—including revenues from hunters and nature lovers. The King Ranch can afford to do this in part because it has pioneered and implemented new ways of breeding cattle at lower costs, in shorter time, using less land and feed. As the percentage of total ranch land needed for raising cattle profitably has been reduced, letting more land be used to harbor wildlife has become economically viable.[4]

ENVIRONMENTALISM AND CORPORATE RESPONSIBILITY

Within the corporate social responsibility movement, there is no more important issue than environmentalism. Often the call for corporate responsibility and the exhortation to "save the planet" from a host of environmental problems seem to be the same thing. The firms most often honored for their responsibility—such as the Body Shop, Patagonia, and Ben and Jerry's—usually exhibit some sort of (highly publicized) commitment to environmental goals. "Corporations, because they are the dominant institution on the planet, must squarely face the social and environmental problems that afflict humankind," said Paul Hawken, a founder of eco-conscious catalog company Smith and Hawken. "The ethical dilemma that confronts business begins with the acknowledgment that a commercial system that functions well by its own definitions unavoidably defies the greater and more profound ethic of biology. Specifically, how does business face the prospect that creating a profitable, growing company requires an intolerable abuse of the natural world?"[5]

The notion that profit and ecology are at inevitable loggerheads, thus requiring businesses to put environment obligations over economic ones, is but one take on the issue among corporate social responsibility advocates. A different notion, championed most famously by Vice President Al Gore, is that doing business in an environmentally friendly way is also a way to increase the profitability of firms. "We can prosper," he wrote in his book *Earth in the Balance,* "by leading the environmental revolution and producing for the world marketplace the new products and technologies that foster economic progress without environmental destruction." This is the idea, currently much in vogue among business executives and activists alike, that environmentalism in the business world might be a series of "win-win" scenarios in which companies adopt new practices or develop new products that increase profitability and enhance ecological goals.[6]

When you begin to think through the complex issue of corporate environmental responsibility, however, neither Hawken's win-or-lose proposition nor Gore's win-win proposition ultimately satisfies. Both have some merit, but they ignore the most important characteristic of environmental ethics: uncertainty. For Hawken, the fact that the world is headed for environmental catastrophe is scarcely debatable. Only if you buy his apocalyptic predictions about overpopulation, global climate change, deforestation, and depletion of natural resources does his recipe for a low-growth, heavily regulated, "sustainable" economy make any sense. Gore, meanwhile, makes no conceptual distinction between profiting from innovation and profiting from regulation. Throughout much of his book, he argues that governments should make environmental regulations more strict, repeating many of the doomsday scenarios of which Hawken is fond, but then concludes that American firms can make money designing technologies to meet the higher standards.[7] This is no doubt true, but it ignores the firms—or, to be more accurate, shareholders, workers, and consumers—who clearly lose when regulatory standards change.

Innovative compliance might reduce the cost of regulation, but it does not eliminate it. For example, a state might decide to require that only cars fueled by electric batteries will be sold within its borders. This might well lead to the development of better, cheaper electric cars as firms struggle to capture as much as they can of the new automobile market, but that is not the only consideration. Such a mandate would be necessary only if electric cars remained uncompetitive with gasoline-powered cars in terms of price, performance, reliability, and aesthetics. Under the mandate, then, consumers would lose access to the products they prefer; some individuals and businesses would leave the state entirely. The resulting costs and dislocations would far exceed the environmental benefits of lower auto emissions, which are questionable in any event (the electricity, for example, would still have to be generated somehow, no doubt producing some air or water pollution).[8]

Gore, in other words, is essentially arguing that it is worthwhile to build a better mousetrap, regardless of how many mice you think may be actually running around in your house. Perhaps the more pressing problem you face in your home is termite infestation (about which the mousetrap can do nothing), or even a shortage of food for your family (a problem the cheese-baited mousetrap might make marginally worse).

In a different sense, though, Gore is on exactly the right track in charting a course for corporate responsibility on environmental matters. Corporations are not governments, nor are they charities. They are unlikely to be successful if they pursue the same sorts of strategies that governments and philanthropic organizations use to protect wildlife habitats and promote clean air and water, such as setting and enforcing standards of health and safety for the public.[9] As with so many other areas of concern addressed in this book, corporate America's unique contribution to solving real environmental problems will come from innovation—finding new ways to produce goods and services, package and deliver them to consumers, and dispose of or recycle the wastes generated by their own production or by consumption.

POLLUTION AND PROFITS

Corporate innovation in the pollution-reduction area is already widespread. The Pollution Prevention Pays program begun by Minnesota-based 3M in 1975 has reduced the company's emissions by more than 1 billion pounds while simultaneously saving $500 million. "At our company, we view a good portion of the environmental problems most talked about today as symptoms of an underlying disease," said 3M chairman Livio D. DeSimone. "That disease is waste—the wasteful and inefficient utilization of our resources."[10] Similarly, Dow Chemical and Westinghouse have implemented waste reduction strategies that have saved millions of dollars since the mid-1980s. One Westinghouse plant in Puerto Rico reduced dragout (the contamination accidentally carried as chemicals flow from one tank to another) by 75 percent by shaking the tank to remove solids before releasing the chemical on to the next tank. Chevron saved $10 million in waste disposal costs and reduced hazardous waste by 60 percent in the first three years of its Save Money and Reduce Toxics (SMART) program.[11]

Over the past few decades, timber companies have found that by adopting *sustainable yield forestry*—including practices like preventing fires, spraying for pests, and quickly replanting harvested areas—they would produce less waste and higher profits while also preserving habitat for wildlife. "Probably there is no area where the potential for compatible economic and environmental benefits can be more easily found than in the forestry world," said Tom Massengale, president of Forestland Group LLC, an investment firm based in North Carolina. "Good forest management need not sacrifice either financial return or ecological integration of the forestry landscape."[12] In addition, forestry companies have reformed their manufacturing processes: for example, by using leftovers from lumbering to make paper pulp and to generate steam for paper mills. International Paper saved about $100 million in disposal expenses between 1988 and 1995 by recycling and reusing its manufacturing wastes.[13]

To be successful at both saving money and "saving the planet," however, corporate waste reduction programs cannot be based on rhetoric or ideology or guesswork about what is or is not environmentally friendly. One of the greatest myths perpetrated by the corporate social responsibility movement is that the most environmentally friendly way to produce goods and services is already known; all corporate executives need do is embrace the environmental ethic. This is untrue. Often the consequences of corporate decisions are ambiguous in terms of overall effect on health, air and water quality, species survival, and the global environment. In some cases, the very practices or policies advocated by environmental activists could very well worsen the environment, albeit in less obvious ways or over a long period of time.

Consider the historical example of the automobile. Given the problems of air pollution and oil spills grabbing headlines today, one might well believe that the environment would be better off if cars had never been invented and, through the genius of American entrepreneurs such as Henry Ford, mass produced for widespread use. But such a judgment would be hasty. While cars created a new source of air pollution, they also virtually eliminated one of the oldest sources of air and water pollution known to man: animal dung. A horse, for instance, produces about forty-five pounds of manure each day. In American cities before the advent of automobiles, massive amounts of horse manure collected daily on streets, sidewalks, and public property. The resulting mess fouled the air, water, and sometimes food. It had to be collected and dumped or buried, often at great expense. Then the horses died; in New York City during the late nineteenth century, some fifteen thousand dead horses had to be disposed of each year. Sometimes this difficult task was not performed as quickly as it should have been, resulting in outbreaks of disease. In 1885 a British writer described London in the supposedly pristine days before the car: "It is a vast stagnant swamp, which no man dare enter, since death would be his inevitable fate. There exhales from this oozy mass so fatal a vapour that no animal can endure it. The black water bears a greenish-brown floating scum, which forever bubbles up from the putrid mud of the bottom. . . . It is dead."[14]

Fred Smith, president of the Competitive Enterprise Institute in Washington, D.C., and a former environmental regulator, explained that the automobile swept away many of these environmental problems. Besides reducing the need to deal with horse and draft-animal wastes and corpses, the car "encouraged developments that reduce air pollution," he observed. Before the automobile, most urban homes and businesses were heated with coal, an extremely dirty source of energy that spewed sulfur dioxide, particulates, and toxic ash into the air. As the demand for gasoline stimulated oil exploration, heating oil and natural gas became cheaper and more readily available. "Cars create pollution. This most common indictment of the automobile is, of course, true," he pointed out. "But it's also true that cars may well have dramatically decreased overall pollution."[15] And by no means is the automobile emissions problem of the twentieth century an intractable one. Indeed, as manufacturers have worked to increase the efficiency of gasoline-burning engines—specifically, to increase the percentage of the fuel that is burned—air pollution generated by cars has been drastically reduced. Research by Donald Stedman, a chemistry professor at the University of Denver, has found that about 90 percent of the cars operating in the United States today generate very little pollution. The remaining 10 percent of all cars, typically poorly maintained and constantly driven cars such as taxicabs and delivery trucks, generate fully 50 percent of all auto pollution. Nor has the reduction in air pollution occurred primarily because of federal auto emissions standards. The latter were adopted in 1975, but Stedman shows that even among cars manufactured before 1975, three-quarters run cleanly.[16]

Did the inventors and early manufacturers of the automobile perceive its potential environmental benefits? Have General Motors, Ford Motor Company, and Chrysler been run by environmental activists for the past half-century? Hardly. Their environmental records are mixed. Nor have all the environmental problems created by the human need for transportation and fuel been solved—particularly in those unique areas, such as southern California, where topography and climate make auto emissions a continuing problem. The automobile example shows only that economic decisions, motivated by an insatiable demand for higher productivity, lower costs, and bigger profit margins, can have unforeseen benefits for third parties and the environment.

IT'S NOT EASY BEING GREEN

One problem for corporate managers is that years of apocalyptic rhetoric and breathless media coverage have created environmental illiteracy among many Americans, including potential consumers and employees. When McDonald's first began to research whether its plastic "clamshell" hamburger boxes posted a significant waste disposal problem, company scientists came to the conclusion that paper wrappers would actually be harder to recycle. But in a well-publicized 1990 decision, the restaurant chain nevertheless switched to paper. The reason was not sound environmental policymaking but public relations: A letter-writing campaign organized by environmental activists and teachers had schoolchildren across the country telling their favorite fast-food outlet (and their parents) that they wanted paper rather than plastic to "save the planet." McDonald's complied. Subsequently, a study in the journal *Science* concluded that the plastic alternative was less environmentally harmful once all the relevant costs—such as the energy expended to make the paper wrappings—were factored in.[17] Not only did McDonald's appear to make the wrong decision from an environmental standpoint, but the company also nipped a promising business venture in the bud. Before the paper packaging decision was announced, Dow Chemical and seven other plastic manufacturers had formed the National Polystyrene Recycling Company to recycle polystyrene from 450 McDonald's restaurants. The switch to paper nixed the deal, which would have advanced plastics recycling to an unprecedented level.[18]

The effects of corporate decisions on the environment are extremely difficult to predict with accuracy. Self-styled environmentalists focus almost exclusively on intention rather than result, even though many business decisions based on other criteria have the side effect of reducing pollution. Corporations pursuing profit (within the bounds of contracts, of course, as discussed in Chapter 1) have as much of a chance of generating environmental benefits as regulators or environmental activists do—particularly when they are faced with prices for waste disposal that are as close to cost as possible. For natural resources over which property rights are relatively easy to establish (such as oil, minerals, or timber), prices serve as an early warning signal to companies about scarcity. A rising price suggests more demand for the resource than can be met by available supply; companies then have a financial incentive either to find new supplies or to reduce the need for the resource by developing alternatives or ferreting out waste.[19] This market process amounts to a sort of ongoing environment research project seeking an answer to this question: What is the most efficient and least resource-depleting method of producing the goods and services people need? A good example of how this process works can be found in the development by Bristol-Myers-Squibb of a new way to make Taxol, a treatment for ovarian and breast cancer. Taxol had been made from the bark of the endangered Pacific yew tree, but the process killed the tree. Responding to the mounting cost and difficulty of obtaining Pacific yew bark, the company found a way to make Taxol from the needles and twigs of the more common Himalayan yew tree, thus assuring a continued supply of reasonably priced Taxol while at the same time reducing the need to harvest the endangered yew species.[20]

For resources over which property rights have not been established, either because of technical difficulty or because of bad public policy decisions, the pricing system does not work as well. When governments relieve corporations of the need to pay the full cost of disposing of waste, for example, by operating and subsidizing waste collection, landfills, incinerators, and recycling programs, they reduce the incentive for those corporations to find alternative methods that produce less waste (or waste that is more easily disposed of). Air pollution is a harder case, because there is no obvious way to communicate true costs to corporations except through the regulatory process (this is less true for waterways, over which various sorts of ownership or stewardship arrangements can be extended).[21]

Nevertheless, even for the difficult cases, an economy based on the search for profit and market prices will often find solutions to environmental challenges, especially those that involve industrial waste, land use, and human health. Many innovations with ecological value have been motivated by purposes far afield from concern about pollution. In the area of corporate responsibility and the environment can be found perhaps one of the clearest examples of Adam Smith's invisible hand at work, as millions of American workers and entrepreneurs—looking for ways to make more with less—are generating both ecologically valuable innovation and the wealth required to clean up and protect environmentally sensitive areas.

ENVIRONMENTAL SURPRISES

Some ecological benefits come from surprising places. Man-made pesticides and the companies that produce them, for example, are often reviled for the risks they supposedly pose to humans and habitats.[22] But as Dennis Avery, director of global food issues for the Hudson Institute, has exhaustively demonstrated, the Herculean efforts by American companies and researchers to make farming more productive over the past few decades (by introducing insecticides, herbicides, crop breeding, and genetic engineering) have resulted in a reduced need for farmland in the United States and other countries. Besides reducing the real price and improving the quality of the foods consumers buy, this happy result has had the side effect of protecting forests and other sensitive habitats from being cleared for agriculture. "Today's typical environmentalist worries about how many spiders and pigweeds survive in an acre of monoculture corn without giving environmental credit for the millions of organisms thriving on the two acres that didn't have to be plowed because we tripled crop yields," Avery commented.[23]

Reducing the price and improving the quality of agricultural produce has had its own salutary effects on human health. Throughout human history, most people in most societies have had little to eat; starvation has until recently been the typical state of much of the world's population. Only within the past century has agricultural productivity increased rapidly enough to guarantee a plentiful supply of food at affordable prices in developed countries.[24] Much of this productivity is due to the invention and production of agricultural chemicals and the development of new farming practices by American entrepreneurs. Even today, herbicides and pesticides help make fruits and vegetables cheaper and more attractive, enticing consumers to buy more of them. One study by Texas A & M University researchers found that without pesticides, potato yields would drop 50 percent, orange yields by 55 percent, and corn yields by 78 percent. Prices for these commodities would therefore rise tremendously without pesticides. Since consumption of fruits and vegetables is crucial to good health (and in particular to reducing rates of cancer, heart disease, and immune dysfunction), the progress made in agricultural productivity and availability has huge implications for human well-being. Carotene, for example—found in carrots, broccoli, and many other orange and dark-green leafy vegetables—is converted in humans to retinols. These retinols reduce risks of skin, breast, bladder, esophagus, colon, pancreas, lung, and prostate cancer. By comparison, the cancer risk posted by pesticide residues on agricultural produce is almost immeasurably small.[25]

Companies introducing these agricultural innovations have clearly advanced the interests of their shareholders as well. The Monsanto Company, founded in 1901 to produce saccharin in competition with German firms, has diversified throughout the century into chemicals, fibers, plastics, and pharmaceuticals, but two of its most profitable recent products have been the popular herbicides Lasso (introduced in 1969) and Roundup (1973). Roundup is one of the best-selling agricultural products of all time, bought by commercial farmers and household gardeners alike. Monsanto continues to introduce new products to increase agricultural productivity, such as Posilac, which boosts milk production in cows and thus reduces per-unit consumption of feed grains.

Genetic engineering offers tantalizing opportunities for increasing productivity, reducing waste and land use, and improving the availability and quality of food. California-based Calgene Inc. introduced its Flavr-Savr tomato, the first genetically engineered food product, in 1994. By engineering a tomato that can ripen longer on the vine without decay or rot, and that retains its freshness weeks after being picked, Calgene has increased the quality of tomatoes available to consumers.[26] In 1995 the federal government approved the sale by Mycogen Corp. and Ciba-Geigy Ltd. of a genetically engineered corn seed. The corn generates its own proteins to fight the European corn borer, which causes more than $1 billion in crop damage in the United States alone. By using the engineered seed, farmers can save money on chemical sprays and yield a healthier, higher-quality crop.[27] Less well known are the economic as well as ecological benefits introduced into agriculture by American computer and software companies. Computers help dairy and hog farms, for example, carefully monitor feed, water, temperature, and ventilation. Farms save money from this system by consuming less feed and energy while reducing the amount of waste products they generate.[28]

If anything symbolizes the irresponsible corporation in the minds of many theorists, it is the manufacturer of that epitome of twentieth-century wastefulness, plastic. Typically made from a nonrenewable resource—oil—plastic has come to represent everything that is wrong with American commercial life and our "throwaway culture." But once again, it is important to look carefully at both sides of the equation. Is plastic really a significant environmental problem? And, on the other side, does it provide any benefits to human health and safety or the environment that need to be weighed? Dr. William Rathje, a professor of archeology at the University of Arizona, has spent years studying solid-waste disposal patterns. His excavations of landfills have found that plastic of all kinds makes up about 7 percent by weight and 16 percent by volume of the typical landfill—much less than paper or yard waste. Polystyrene plastic, the substance used in drinking cups and those "clamshell" hamburger containers McDonald's abandoned, makes up only 1 percent of landfill volume; fast-food packaging amounts to no more than one-third of 1 percent. Of course, environmentalists fault plastic for much more than taking up space in landfills, pointing out that plastic manufacturing relies on extracting and transporting oil. But since less than 2 percent of the world's petroleum in used to produce petrochemicals of all kinds, from fertilizers to plastics, the impact on the need for oil of using plastic to make consumer products is negligible.[29]

Consider, on the other hand, the benefits of plastic. Even something as banal as plastic wrap has had a tremendous positive impact on Americans' health and safety. A hundred years ago, grocery stores had little in the way of prepackaged foods. At the turn of the century, paper packaging began to enter food retailing, but it had limitations. Meat, for example, was still often shipped in the form of whole carcasses as late as the 1940s. Consumers would request particular cuts of meat from butchers, who kept carcasses until they were all sold or completely spoiled. The meat was expensive, particularly because butchers had to spend so much time carving it. Much of the meat was barely edible, particularly in poorer neighborhoods where consumers could not afford to pay butchers to constantly bring in new meat.[30]

During the 1950s, however, the advent of plastic packaging began to change food delivery. Dow Chemical of Midland, Michigan, was an industry leader during this period, not only in supplying plastic products to businesses but also by introducing its first major consumer product, Saran Wrap, in 1953.[31] Plastic packaging made it possible for grocers to sell smaller portions at lower prices, and for consumers to store food more efficiently and effectively. Instead of being transported solely in whole carcasses, meat could be shipped as "boxed meat," which was less expensive. Moreover, clear plastic wraps allowed consumers to see the meat they were buying, reducing the consumption of rancid or spoiled food. One study estimates that the modern system of packaging lowers the price of beef by about forty cents a pound while also improving its quality and safety.[32] Furthermore, the use of plastic and other types of packaging for foods seems to have reduced, not increased, total household waste. When Rathje took his garbage-archaeology team to Mexico City in 1990, they found that the average household there discarded 40 percent more refuse each day than the average U.S. household, because the Mexicans used more whole fruits and vegetables and thus had more rinds, peelings, and other food debris to throw away. In America, food processors sell prepackaged fruits and vegetables in cans, bags, or microwaveable plastic containers. From an environmental standpoint, this has the effect of accumulating the food debris in a central location, thus making it easier to dispose of in the form of compost, animal feed, and other products.[33]

Today the American plastics industry is one of the most innovative in the world. By finding new ways to manufacture, package, and store products that cost less, last longer, require fewer resources, and reduce harm to the environment, the industry is constantly changing the way we live, work, and consume for the better. Since World War II, innovations in the manufacture, design, and use of plastics have yielded tremendous benefits for the public in terms of safety, health, economy, and quality of life. Consider the following examples:[34]

- Plastic tubing made possible the first disposable, ready-to-use hypodermic needles. Initially introduced for combat use in the 1940s, the disposable needle soon made it possible to conduct safe and effective mass inoculations against disease in America and throughout the world.

- In 1945 Earl Tupper introduced the first flexible plastic storage containers to replace glass, earthenware, and metal containers for storing food and other perishables. His product, Tupperware, vastly improved the freshness and quality of stored food, making it easier to prepare food before mealtime and save leftovers. This seemingly banal contribution to the American kitchen let families plan their time better to maximize work or leisure. By 1991 there was a Tupperware sales party every 2.7 seconds somewhere in the world.

- Plastic siphon tubing made mass irrigation possible in the 1940s and 1950s, thus contributing to the "green revolution" that increased agricultural productivity and eliminated famine in much of the world. In the 1960s plastic pipes began to replace other forms of piping for water distribution and drainage, because plastic resisted corrosion better, was lighter, and was easier to install and use than were alternatives.

- Plastic parts and casings made electrical appliances and commercial machinery safer by insulating users from current and by reducing corrosion. Eventually, as companies like Du Pont developed stronger polyester films and epoxies, electrical devices got progressively smaller, safer, and more powerful.

- In the early 1960s a research effort by Amoco Chemicals Corp. yielded plastic coatings for underground storage tanks, reducing the likelihood of oil spills.

- Plastic innovations during the past three decades by such companies as Phillips Petroleum, Union Carbide, and Shell Chemical have made possible such lifesaving and life-enhancing products as artificial organs, comfortable prosthetics, body armor for law enforcement personnel, unbreakable but light children's toys, and many automotive body parts.

- Cheap, all-temperature-performance, flame-retardant, high-impact resistant plastic parts made the first home computers (manufactured by Apple Computer and Tandy) viable products.

Lingering environmental controversies such as the risks of dioxin—which many view as a potent human carcinogen—are being resolved by plastic designers who, just in the past few years, have developed products that reduce or eliminate these real or perceived environmental problems. GE Plastics, for example, developed a new flame-retardant product that does not produce dioxin; it is also easier to make and costs no more than the plastic it replaces. Apple Computer is using the product in its Macintosh line of personal computers.[35] Waste-to-energy plants, which dispose of about sixty thousand tons of refuse each day and supply electricity to nearly a million Americans, also employ a series of technologies that reduce dioxin emissions to almost immeasurable levels. One such technology is carbon injection, in which a charcoal powder that acts as a dioxin sponge is blown into the exhaust.[36]

THE RECYCLING CONUNDRUM

An article of faith among environmental advocates is that by increasing its commitment to recycling, American business will help conserve natural resources and demonstrate its environmental responsibility. This assumption does not account for the potential costs, including environmental costs, of pursuing recycling regardless of whether it is truly profitable. For example, curbside recycling programs usually require more collection trucks than simply taking everything to the dump; that means more fuel consumption and engine emissions. Some recycling programs produce high volumes of wastewater and use large amounts of energy. When researchers have tried to examine every aspect of the recycling equation—from energy use to production costs—they have found that sometimes recycling makes sense from an economic and environmental standpoint, while other times it does not.[37]

The aluminum can is a clear example of a commercial package that should be recycled. It takes 10 percent less energy to recycle aluminum than it does to make it from mined bauxite, so aluminum recycling is profitable—and commonplace. Steel is also relatively economical to recycle; virtually all products made with steel contain at least 25 percent reclaimed steel.[38] In contrast, recycling juice containers probably does not make economic or ecological sense. Filling disposable cardboard boxes takes half as much energy as filling recyclable glass bottles. For a given beverage volume, transporting the empty glass bottles requires fifteen times as many trucks as does transporting disposable boxes. Transporting the containers once they are filled also costs less when using disposable boxes. And on the other side of the issue, juice boxes do not break like glass bottles can, they are easily packed or frozen, and they seem to encourage juice consumption among the young, with whom they are popular.[39] Similarly, disposable diapers are clearly popular and convenient, and they are not necessarily more environmentally destructive than cloth diapers. The latter must be collected, cleaned, and returned to households on a regular basis, necessitating significant consumption of energy.[40]

For some commodities, such as newsprint, it seems that the only way to make recycling profitable is to force manufacturers to use them. Many states have passed laws requiring that newspapers contain a certain percentage of recycled paper, thus artificially creating a demand for newsprint that would not otherwise exist.[41] Similarly, most observers of the plastic recycling industry believe that legislation, not market demand, will drive most of its growth over the 1990s.[42] Even mandates sometimes fail to make recycling work: in Germany, laws requiring plastics recycling have resulted in a glut of collected plastics with few economical uses.[43] Advocates for such laws argue that market prices do not capture all the costs of alternatives to recycling, and this is no doubt true.[44] But prices nevertheless contain important information. When forest stocks become scarcer, for example, the price of virgin timber will rise, thus making recyclables more attractive. Similarly, as long as landfills are run to at least break even if not make a profit, then as they fill up their tipping fees will rise, again encouraging diversion of waste products into recycling or reuse. These price mechanisms already exist to a significant degree, and yet paper and plastic recycling often makes no sense absent government mandates.

For corporate managers trying to make heads or tails of the economic and environmental issues surrounding recycling, the answer may well be to trust an imperfect system of market prices over an even more imperfect attempt to guess at the ecological impact of the various waste reduction and recycling strategies peddled by environmental activists. In everyday decision-making, this means weighing costs and benefits with an eye to maximizing shareholder return. Bi-Lo, a chain of 188 supermarkets based in South Carolina, recycles plastic stretch film for storing food in its warehouses. The company generates an average of six to eight 800-pound bales of used stretch film for shipment to its recycling plant each week. The labor cost of baling the used plastic is about the same as putting it into a trash compactor, but the company saves thousands of dollars by not having to pay hauling and landfill fees.[45] Du Pont found a lucrative commercial market for one by-product, gypsum, that had previously just been discarded. The market was so lucrative, in fact, that plant managers began to dig up previously buried gypsum to keep up with demand.[46] Ford Motor Co. saved millions in 1994 when it converted several components of its automobiles into 100 percent recycled plastic, and Chrysler is using completely recycled plastic in the interior trim of its popular minivans. Both car companies have been increasing use of these recycled plastics, made by companies such as Washington Penn Plastics and AlliedSignal, because of their cost and performance advantages over "virgin" plastic, not because of an attempt to meet some vague environmental goal. The savings "go straight to the bottom line," said Tony Brooks, Ford's special recycling coordinator. "Ford's position is that we will do everything we can to use recycled materials in our cars, but they can't cost more than virgin and they must perform at least as well as virgin."[47]

PROBLEM, INNOVATION, SOLUTION

Most environmental issues in America today represent not only public-sector controversies but also private-sector opportunities. For companies that can identify a problem and devise a solution, the potential profits are significant. In the case of plastics, for example, one can make a strong defense of plastic food packaging as having health, safety, and cost benefits for consumers while contributing little to the waste stream. Others will challenge this proposition, suggesting instead that food be packaged with paper or even carried in burlap bags. But profit-seeking corporations are not accepting the forced choice among these alternatives. Instead, they are experimenting with *edible* food packaging that offers better protection, lower cost, and few environmental considerations. ConAgra Inc., the processed-food giant, is working on an edible bag in which to package products (such as frozen entrees) that currently use plastic bags. "If you could make a boilable, edible bag, you could replace the plastic with something that is part of the food—ultimately eliminating a source of package waste," said the company's packaging director, Brian Hopkins. Other companies are working along similar lines. Quaker Oats is testing edible coating for breakfast cereals, and RJR Nabisco is working on a film made from milk protein that could potentially be used to coat frozen fish products and baked goods.[48]

These innovations are not being pursued simply to reduce package waste; food manufacturers also want to improve food preservation to enhance the taste and freshness of their products. One possible application would be to fresh produce. Instead of having consumers buy whole fruits and vegetables and then slice or dice them at home, manufacturers could prepare large quantities of fresh produce—such as presliced onions or oranges—and then preserve them with edible coatings. The cost of the foods would be lower, consumers could enjoy greater convenience, and waste peelings (currently spread out over the entire population of homes) would be centralized in manufacturing facilities and thus easier to dispose of. Once again, the resulting impact on human health would be significant. "Consumption of fresh fruits and vegetables could be higher if this service were provided," said Attila E. Pavlath, a food scientist with the U.S. Department of Agriculture.[49]

A more serious problem than food packaging is the question of hazardous waste spills. Whether it is the *Exxon Valdez* oil spill of 1989 or Superfund sites or underground leakage of cancer-causing chemicals, the topic of hazardous waste often generates passionate feelings and great concern about environmental damage. But is the answer to spills to be found in banning substances or jawboning industry to reduce its dependency on them? Many entrepreneurial U.S. companies say no. The answer, they suggest, is to find new ways to clean up spills quickly, easily, and effectively. Bioremediation—using bacteria or fungi either found in nature or engineered in laboratories to clean up hazardous wastes—is a promising technology that offers the prospect of a cleaner economy without sacrificing the modern industrial processes than make our economy so productive. In downtown Seattle, Unocal Corporation is using petroleum-eating bacteria to clean a six-acre patch of dirt where an oily residue of gasoline and diesel fuels had accumulated over sixty-five years of leaks from its Seattle Marketing Fuel Terminal. Once the site is clean, Unocal expects to sell it for a significant price to commercial or residential developers.[50]

Cyto Culture International Inc., a California-based firm, has adopted a similar approach. At an Emeryville, California, truck terminal, oil and fuel leaking from underground tanks over several decades severely contaminated the groundwater and surrounding soil. Cyto used specialized bacteria to eliminate virtually all the pollution. Now the bankrupt truck terminal is gone and a new shopping center occupies the site. "Hydrocarbons serve as perfectly good food for [the microbes]," said Cyto founder

Randall von Wedel. "Bacteria metabolize motor oil in much the same way you metabolize vegetable oil."[51]

Bioremediation is not exactly a new idea—municipal water systems have long used bacteria to purify sewage, and paper companies have used them to remove organic matter from industrial sludge—but a bustling new industry of bioremediation enterprises promises to clean up such hazardous materials as DDT, wood preservatives, toxic petrochemicals (including benzene), and radioactive waste.[52] Corporate pioneers in the area include Amoco Corporation and Du Pont, but most of the new technologies are coming from small, start-up firms such as Remediation Technologies of Concord, Massachusetts, Alpha Environmental in Austin, Texas, and Envirogen Inc. of Lawrenceville, New Jersey. Ironically, many bioremediation approaches have come from a close observation of how Mother Nature herself deals with waste. In searching for microbes to clean up oil spills, Alpha Environmental president Eugene Douglas said, "we went to where there are natural oil seeps in the Mediterranean, Central Asia, and North America, but where there isn't what you'd call pollution. Over time, microbes at these sites have evolved the ability to ingest that oil."[53]

Bioremediation is not the only solution profit-seeking corporations are working on. For the problem of oil spills, for example, Sea Sweep Inc. of Denver, Colorado, has developed an oil-absorbing, floating material (made from heating sawdust and woodchips) that will absorb 3.5 times its weight in oil. If administered to a spill, Sea Sweep will absorb the oil and then float to the surface for easy collection, after which it can be burned as fuel. Wyoming-based Centech has developed a centrifuge that generates relatively clean water and marketable oil from oil sludge, which is a serious problem around crude oil storage tanks and pipelines.[54] In the area of industrial wastes, Tennessee's Olin Corporation has developed a process for dramatically reducing absorbable organic halides (such as dioxin) from the paper pulp-bleaching process. Martin Marietta Energy Systems Inc. has a process for dechlorinating wastewater streams.[55] Pittsburgh Mineral and Environmental Technology has a technology for extracting residual mercury from contaminated soil and industrial waste, generating 99 percent pure metallic mercury suitable for reuse as well as no secondary wastes.[56] Catalytica Inc. of Mountain View, California, is developing a series of novel catalysts to control and speed up chemical reactions in industrial processes such as gasoline production or natural gas power generation, which would sharply curtail or eliminate waste production and the need for costly "end of the pipe" cleanup.[57]

It would be impossible to list all of the environmental innovations and inventions one can find in just a single year, ranging from simple reuse technologies at plant sites to machines and acids that remove virtually all known pollutants from energy plant emissions.[58] Some of these technologies have been developed, as Vice President Gore suggests, in response to regulatory mandates. Others have come about as companies seek to reduce their waste disposal costs, improve the efficiency of their production processes, or find new areas of opportunity in a constantly changing economy. The key point for the purposes of evaluating corporate responsibility in environmental issues is to recognize the significance of innovation itself. It is through innovation and productivity gains, not through corporate munificence or a commitment to a theoretical environmental ethos, that American business will make its most important contribution to a cleaner world and the health and safety of the public.

One potential source of energy for consumers and businesses alike, fuel cells that use "reverse electrolysis" to generate electricity, has the potential of virtually eliminating the discharge of pollutants such as carbon monoxide and hydrocarbons. Corporations ranging from the very large—Westinghouse Electric and General Motors—to the very small are working frantically to adapt fuel cells for everyday use. (The technology is not new; fuel cells were invented in 1839 and were used to power such American spacecraft as Gemini, Apollo, and the space shuttle.) The Hyatt Regency Hotel in Irvine, California, is powered entirely from an experimental fuel cell operated by Southern California Gas Inc.[59] Will fuel cells be the answer to our energy needs? Are they cheaper, more efficient, and less environmentally troublesome than alternatives? The truthful answer is that no one knows. This is the kind of issue with which corporate innovators can reasonably be expected to wrestle—not whether America should abandon industrial society altogether because it is powered primarily by "nonrenewable resources."

CONCLUSION

For corporate decision-makers, therefore, true responsibility entails a recognition of the uncertainty that often accompanies environmental controversies and an unwillingness to put the interests of shareholders at risk by accepting environmental truisms at face value. It is by no means clear that simply recycling more, or substituting paper for plastic, or abandoning profitable enterprises because they require nonrenewable resources will necessarily serve environmental ends. Ultimately such ends are determined and valued by human beings who also value healthful and reasonably priced foods, high-quality consumer goods, and job opportunities. The chances of making a poor decision are significantly higher when corporate managers try to act like public policymakers or conservation experts.

Instead, as much as is practicable, corporations should let prices guide their decisions. In most cases, wasteful industrial practices impose measurable costs on firms, be they for waste disposal, purchasing raw materials, or lost customer revenue. Thus firms have every incentive to find alternatives. "For all environmental issues, shareholder value, rather than compliance, emissions, or costs, is the critical unifying metric," said McKinsey & Company management consultants Noah Walley and Bradley Whitehead in their noted 1994 *Harvard Business Review* essay on corporate environmentalism. "That approach is environmentally sound, but it's also hardheaded, informed by business experience, and, as a result, much more likely to be truly sustainable over the long term."[60]

An example of how truly responsible companies might make decisions about environmental issues is the case of Eco-Foam pellets, a substitute for Styrofoam peanuts in packing boxes or other containers. Texas-based American Excelsior Co. makes Eco-Foam out of corn starch and markets it as environmentally friendly. "The biggest benefit is that it's manufactured from renewable resources instead of petroleum products," said one local distributor. Should responsible companies concerned about the global environment use Eco-Foam instead of Styrofoam, then? Probably not. Managers need not evaluate all the pros and cons of the two products; they need only watch the price. In early 1995 Eco-Foam cost 25 percent more than Styrofoam. If we ever really start running out of oil, the price of petroleum products (including Styrofoam) will rise, making alternatives competitive. Until then, the environmental benefits of switching to corn starch will not be worth the cost.[61]

Another example can be found in the controversy over automobile tires with "high rolling resistance." Rolling resistance is the force required to overcome the tire's friction as it comes in contact with the road and moves a vehicle; all other things being equal, a tire with high rolling resistance uses more fuel to move the vehicle than does a tire with lower rolling resistance. While most new cars are equipped with lower-resistance tires to improve initial energy efficiency, replacement tires that consumers subsequently buy often have higher resistance. Michelin is one tire company that sells low-resistance replacements, promising consumers that the additional cost (five dollars per tire) will be repaid within a year through fuel savings. So should other tire companies, to be socially responsible, start making lower-resistance tires, too? Again, not necessarily. For one thing, independent studies of the fuel economy of tires have found contradictory results. *Consumer Reports* concluded that the different fuel economies of high and low resistance tires translate into only fifteen or twenty gallons of gas a year, far lower than Michelin claims. Also, competing manufacturers point out that in order to reduce rolling resistance, they have to sacrifice other characteristics (such as traction and handling) that have implications for safety.[62] There is no clear answer and no clear burden for responsible tire manufacturers. They and their customers will have to track fuel and tire prices to determine what type of tire seems best.

As public policymakers develop more efficient ways to regulate waste and pollution and scientists continue to gather information about the real health and environmental risks from various substances or practices, pricing structures will evolve that communicate even more accurate information to manufacturers and entrepreneurs about the true cost of commercial activities and the potential rewards from innovative solutions to environmental problems. There are many promising trends in environmental thinking and regulatory policy, from emissions markets to the increased use of cost-benefit analysis to establish realistic public priorities.[63] Once ecological and economic ends are brought closer together, the perceived clash of interests between American business and Mother Nature will largely disappear. For corporations, the complex issues of environmental responsibility will always be challenging. But dealing with them requires no redefinition of the core profit-seeking purpose of economic enterprises.

CHAPTER 9

BUSINESS AND
SOCIAL EQUALITY

A re women and minority groups consistently denied economic opportunity by corporate America? To hear some prominent social commentators tell it, American business has a shameful record on social equality: Corporate boards lack significant minority representation; minority consumers are underserved, and minority and female workers underpaid; and minorities and women cannot get financing to start their own businesses. "In most fields, there is a level beyond which people of color cannot rise," writes Stephen Carter, the well-known author and law professor.[1] "Enlightened self-interest by itself is unlikely to affect corporate actions substantially," Robert Gnaizda, a longtime activist on redlining and discrimination issues, has sorrowfully concluded.[2] Similar complaints about the economic prospects of women have been popularized in recent years by such authors as Susan Faludi and Gloria Steinem.

This picture of the business sector as an arena of continued discrimination, inequality, and despair for everyone in society except white men is often repeated, presumed accurate by reporters and politicians—and completely wrong. Not only is there great news to report for the economic accomplishments and prospects of previously downtrodden groups in America, but this good news is due almost totally to the triumph of commercial values over alternative values that have in the past put fear, racism, and insularity ahead of business success and profit.

151

William G. Mays, founder and president of Mays Chemical Co. Inc. in Indianapolis, has found success and created a multimillion-dollar business by serving the needs of his corporate customers. Mays, an African-American, supplies chemicals to such large white-owned businesses as General Motors, Eastman Kodak, and Pillsbury. He built his business not through set-asides or government programs but instead by hard work, determination, and delivering the best quality products to business customers with high standards. Mays Chemical is one of only three or four companies in the United States to be honored more than once as one of Pillsbury's annual awards for supplier quality; a Pillsbury official noted that Mays constantly reduces cost, passing those savings on to the client, and works to reduce shortages and simplify his company's inventory and ordering process. Mays has little patience with business owners who blame failure on the color of their skin. "Being black can be an obstacle, but not a complete one," he said. "Sooner or later, you have to look in the mirror and say, 'Maybe things aren't working out because I'm doing something wrong.'"[3]

THE REAL ENEMY OF DISCRIMINATION

The story of Mays Chemical is hardly exceptional in our economy today. The cornucopia of good news about social equality and American business overflows with little-noticed facts about our recent economic past. For example:

- American women were forming small businesses at twice the rate of men in the early 1990s. Businesses owned by U.S. women now employ more people than do all the firms in the Fortune 500 combined.[4] If the trends of the 1980s and early 1990s continue, women will own half of all U.S. businesses by the year 2000.[5] Similarly, the number of businesses owned by racial and ethnic minorities more than doubled from 1982 to 1994.[6]
- Before World War II only 5 percent of American blacks had middle-class incomes. In the mid-1990s the figure is about 60 percent.[7] From 1981 to 1991 the total income of blacks grew 38 percent, faster than the growth rate for the incomes of the white population. Almost half of all black households own their own homes.[8]
- Measured correctly, there is no evidence of significant discrimination in bank lending against prospective minority homebuyers.[9]

- Among full-time, college-educated workers, about the same percentage of blacks and whites have executive, administrative, or managerial jobs.[10]

Of course, racial stereotypes, discrimination, and animus still exist in America. But it is important to understand the role profit-seeking businesses play in combating these lingering problems. For corporate managers, excluding potential workers or customers because of race, gender, or other group characteristics means sacrificing future productivity and sales. It simply stands to reason that the wider you cast your net for employees or consumers, the better off you will be. To do anything less is to fail in your responsibility to the owners or shareholders of the firm. Gary Becker, Nobel laureate in economics and a professor at the University of Chicago, pointed out the antidiscrimination effect of free enterprise in 1957 and has been restating his conclusion every since. The key, he points out, is competition. Screening out job applicants because of their group means reducing the chances of hiring the best worker, who may well go to work for a competing firm. Similarly, screening out whole groups of consumers means giving up sales to competitors. "Competition forces people to face costs, and therefore reduce the amount of discrimination when compared with monopolistic situations," Becker has said.[11] So racism and discrimination are, over time, much more likely to persist in monopolistic institutions (like governments themselves) rather than in businesses. In the South, for example, desegregation occurred much more rapidly at lunch counters and in hotels then it did in public schools—where, indeed, the process is still ongoing.

Indeed, one might argue that without the largely unconscious pressure of the business sector on social attitudes, there would be a great deal more racism and social inequity. For governments, charged with protecting societies from their external or internal enemies, loyalty to one's group and the distrust of others is a virtue. It maximizes the physical safety of the society and protects its land from encroachment. But for traders, the greatest rewards lie in trusting strangers, who are the source of new products and new ideas. That means seeking out and embracing people who are different from you: the more different they are, the more likely they are to have something of value to you. The social benefits of trade—of breaking down barriers between groups in the interest of mutual economic gain—have been enjoyed by every group in American society. Past immigrants, recent immigrants, racial minorities, religious minorities, and many others have sought and obtained in the marketplace what they did not have and could not achieve through other types of activity such as politics or social activism.

American blacks have experienced the liberating power of free enterprise, too. The economic achievements of black Americans, rising in only a few generations from a state of bondage to a standard of living exceeding that of most societies in the world, are almost unparalleled in history. But the road to a better life for black Americans was not a straight one; they were forced to take some tragic detours.

The economic history of American blacks is poorly understood. Even during the days of slavery, black Americans (both free and enslaved) were able to establish enterprises, make discoveries, introduce innovations, and generally speaking improve their lot. Naturally, free blacks enjoyed the greatest economic success during the late 1700s and throughout most of the 1800s. John Sibley Butler, a sociologist who has studied black entrepreneurship in American history, notes that free blacks created businesses in every area of American economic life prior to the Civil War, including merchandising, real estate, manufacturing, construction trades, transportation, and extractive industries. Many slaves—as a result of thrift, industry, and enlightened paternalism on the part of their masters—also ran the equivalent of large business enterprises in agriculture, manufacturing, and transportation. In the Philadelphia of the early nineteenth century, for example, black-owned businesses dominated or played a major role in such industries as sail making, tanning, tailoring, and catering.[12] After the Civil War, emancipation led to a flurry of black business activity. One measure of the importance of blacks to the nineteenth-century economy is the large number of patents registered by black inventors and entrepreneurs from 1860 to 1900, for inventions ranging from the all-important transportation field (including trolley cars, railroad signals and switches, locomotive smokestacks, railroad water closets, and rotary engines) to water sprinklers, lawn mowers, breadcrumbing machines, and fountain pens. Black restaurateurs even invented modern-day ice cream.[13]

But as the Reconstruction period ended and threatened white politicians began to enact Jim Crow laws in the late 1800s, the role of black businesses and entrepreneurs in America actually declined. This was exactly the reason why many whites supported segregation; it reduced competition for jobs and economic opportunities, in addition to satisfying other emotional and psychological desires. Industries and workers that feared competition from minorities thus lobbied for segregation, though it is important to remember that such protection from competition was impossible to accomplish except through political intervention. This intervention came in the form of local laws segregating the races in public transportation, accommodations, and retail establishments, as well as state and federal laws restricting access by minorities to occupations and businesses. (A key example would be the passage of the Davis-Bacon Act by Congress in 1931, which required union-scale wages in construction jobs paid for by the federal government. Davis-Bacon, still in effect today, was promoted explicitly by its supporters as a way to keep blacks and immigrants from taking jobs from native-born white Americans.[14])

Since segregation cut off black businesses from all but a black customer base, their ability to function and innovate in the context of the larger economy disappeared. Cities with thriving black business communities endured economic dislocation and regression. Black customers correspondingly lost access to white-owned enterprises. In Tampa, Florida, for example, where blacks and other minorities had long found good jobs and economic opportunities during the nineteenth century, the advent of segregation was jarring. Blacks who had been accustomed to entering businesses through the front door suddenly found themselves directed around back. "Tampa had de facto discrimination, but [before the *Plessy v. Ferguson* case codifying segregationist law] what you didn't have was a lot of laws to make people separate," said Susan Greenbaum, an anthropologist at the University of South Florida. "It wasn't easy to mandate this."[15]

This new segregation was not to the liking of those white business owners who valued profit more than racial exclusivity. When Georgia passed a state law in 1891 to segregate the races in streetcars, the streetcar companies ignored the law for years because they did not want to offend their black riders. In Mobile, Alabama, the streetcar company refused to comply with segregation laws until its conductors were arrested for noncompliance with the law. Similarly, white owners of a Tennessee streetcar company tried to get state courts to declare that state's Jim Crow laws unconstitutional.[16]

Of course, far too many white business owners went along with Jim Crow for far too long. But the point is that their economic interests—not to mention the personal moral interests of company managers and owners—

clearly lay with integration rather than segregation, which was an artificial construct dependent (at least initially) on government regulatory power for its existence. Responsible companies, then and now, would fight racial and other segregation because it conflicts with their need and obligation to maximize return to shareholders, as well as with the proper workings of the capitalist economic system to which they owe their very existence.

RACE, GENDER, AND ENTREPRENEURSHIP

As mentioned earlier, the number of businesses owned by racial minorities and women has been increasing rapidly in recent decades. Not only has the number of firms grown, but their stake in the national economy has as well. Just from 1991 to 1995, for example, the combined revenue of the Black Enterprise 100 for industrial/service companies and auto dealers grew by 63 percent to $11.7 billion.[17] A third of the roughly 6.5 million enterprises with fewer than 500 employees were owned or controlled by women in 1994.[18] And according to research by David L. Birch of Massachusetts-based Cognetics Inc., the size distribution and industry distribution of women-owned companies are very much like those owned by men.[19]

Entrepreneurship has been a traditional route out of poverty for American minority groups of all sorts. Butler describes how Jewish, Greek, Cuban, and Japanese immigrants, for example, overcame prejudice and social barriers by entering occupations and markets ignored by native-born Americans, making themselves indispensable to the growth and development of the economy. As generations of immigrants gained economic success, their children and grandchildren pursued higher education, befriended and married individuals outside their own groups, and gradually obtained social tolerance and acceptance.[20]

Even within the artificially restricted markets left to them by Jim Crow segregation, some American blacks of the late nineteenth and early twentieth centuries were able to find opportunities for economic success. Arthur G. Gaston was born in 1892 in a log cabin his grandparents, former slaves, built in rural Marengo County, Alabama. After the early death of her husband, Gaston's mother moved to Birmingham in 1900 to be a cook for A. B. and Minnie Loveman, founders of what would later become the state's largest department store chain. Young Gaston, an admirer of Booker T. Washington, worked a number of odd jobs, including selling subscriptions for the local black newspaper. Later he moved to

Mobile and became a bellhop. After serving in the army during World War I, Gaston came home and took a job at the Tennessee Coal and Iron Company. Always looking for entrepreneurial opportunities, he began selling box lunches (prepared by his mother) and peanuts, and loaning money, to workers at the TCI plant. He started a burial society for the workers, too, which eventually acquired a mortuary and became Smith and Gaston Funeral Directors. In 1932 the burial society was incorporated as Booker T. Washington Insurance Co.[21]

New ventures followed. Gaston started a business college for black clerical workers in 1939, bought a cemetery in 1947, opened the Gaston Motel in 1954, and started the Citizens Federal Savings Bank in 1957 to lend money to blacks excluded from lending markets by segregation. Active in the civil rights movement and numerous civic and community organizations, Gaston kept adding to his business holdings during the 1960s, 1970s, and 1980s, buying radio stations and opening his own construction company. In 1994, *Black Enterprise* named A. G. Gaston, then 102 years of age, as the magazine's Entrepreneur of the Century. In Gaston's view, his business success has enabled him to advance the cause of racial equality just as his hero Booker T. Washington had predicted decades before. "Money has no color," he said. "If you can build a better mousetrap, it won't matter whether you're black or white, people will buy it."[22]

Timothy Bates, a professor at the New School for Social Research, has studied black entrepreneurship for two decades. "We're now in an era when the educated members of the African-American community are going into the business world," he said. "This transformation is immense."[23] Notable black chief executives of American corporations today include John Johnson of Johnson Publishing, Robert Johnson of Black Entertainment Television, J. Bruce Llewellyn of Philadelphia Coca-Cola Bottling, and Loida Lewis, whose TLC Beatrice International Holdings, the New York–based food processor and distributor, placed her at the top of the chief executive list in the *Black Enterprise* industrial/service rankings.[24]

On a somewhat smaller scale, Robert Gaye is one black entrepreneur with a strong drive to succeed. Gaye started Transtar Transportation Inc., a shuttle and limousine service, in Orlando, Florida, in 1986. Gaye, an immigrant from the Cayman Islands, had owned his own shuttle company back home but came to the United States in 1980 to seek his fortune. After working for other companies, Gaye finally decided to strike out on his own. His enterprise took off and did $5.6 million of business in 1994. Another transportation entrepreneur, Robin Petgrave, operates Benbow Helicopters Inc., a flight school and tour/charter company in Torrance, California. "All my life, people have been telling me what I can and can't do," Petgrave said. [I say] 'No, that's what you think I can and can't do. If I want to do something, I'm going to do it.'" Benbow Helicopters, begun in 1991, took in more than $1 million in 1994.[25] In 1990 Lynn Robinson opened the first McDonald's franchise in the state of New York owned by an African-American woman. She had worked for the company during her college days, and she continued working part-time at a McDonald's restaurant while also serving as a supervisor of computer operations at a hospital. "I was always a take-charge, I'm-going-to-make-it type of person," she said. "But I kept running into roadblocks, so I felt that it never provided me with the best opportunity in terms of my personal growth. I was going to go for it. Owning a franchise provided that chance."[26]

American women have also found entrepreneurship to be an avenue for pursuing their dreams and achieving social equality. Today's female entrepreneurs are branching out into all sorts of businesses, many traditionally dominated by males. Fran Greene started her first business, Sun State Electronics, at age fifty after twenty-five years working for a big electronics component supplier. Sun State, based in Winter Springs, Florida, sells high-tech gear to the aerospace and defense industries and did $2.5 million in business in 1994. Pleased with the success of Sun State, Greene started another venture, Cakes Across America, which contracts with bakeries nationwide to deliver cakes for all occasions. Hillary Sterba and Nancy Novinc, former employees of a cutting-tool manufacturer, founded their own tool-engineering company, S & N Engineering Services, in 1992. "We decided if we were going to put in these long hours and work this hard, we would do it for ourselves," Sterba said.[27]

RACE, GENDER, AND WORKERS

The entrepreneurial explosion among women and minorities in the past few years has demonstrated that consumers, both households and businesses, will generally buy from anyone who can supply a high-quality product or service at a low price. The same might be said about American employers, who have discovered that businesses who want to compete effectively cannot afford to discriminate against workers because of race, gender, or other characteristics. Indeed, having a workforce of people who meet high standards of quality and performance but also bring differing backgrounds and perspectives to their jobs is often a recipe for business success.

Vigorous political debates about such subjects as affirmative action and comparative worth obscure what is actually occurring in the American economy today: the gradual elimination of discriminatory hiring and firing practices, as well as rising levels of compensation and respect for minority and female workers. Joseph F. Coates, a consultant for business and government for more than thirty years, notes that "bad press presents the situation of black Americans in a manner that is totally out of balance. It fails to report that black Americans have made enormous progress in the middle and late 20th century."[28] Part of the problem, Coates continues, is that aggregate statistics showing continued economic deprivation among blacks are skewed by the depressing but relatively small percentage of poor, badly educated blacks trapped in desolate inner cities. According to economist Howard R. Bloch of George Mason University, 70 to 85 percent of observed differences in income and employment among American racial and ethnic groups disappear when you adjust the numbers for factors such as age, education, and experience. "That's been shown by studies dating back to the mid-1960s," Bloch says. "And you can't even be sure that the residual gap is due to discrimination. It could be due to factors we haven't controlled for."[29]

Job responsibilities as well as compensation have been increasing. As of 1995, more than 10 percent of managers in such fields as retail trade, transportation, communications, finance, insurance, and real estate were minorities.[30] Black managers, for example, are becoming increasingly common across the spectrum of American business. While generating some workplace conflicts and tensions, reports *Time* magazine, "the rise of the black manager has been accomplished with remarkably little upheaval."[31] At McDonald's, for example, an astounding 70 percent of restaurant managers, 25 percent of corporate executives, and about half of corporate department heads are minorities or women.[32]

In measurements of accumulated household wealth, as contrasted with annual income, minorities have also made tremendous gains. A Federal Reserve Bank of St. Louis study in 1989 found that observed differences between whites and minorities were no longer statistically significant once age and education were taken in account. "Members of minority groups are typically younger than whites, and therefore have had less time to accumulate assets," noted the author, John C. Weicher of the Hudson Institute.[33]

Similarly, apparent pay gaps between men and women do not prove the lack of "equal pay for equal work," as many critics allege. June O'Neal, head of the Congressional Budget Office, noted that when earnings comparisons are restricted to men and women with similar experience and life situations, the differences are small, particularly among today's young people. Among people aged twenty-seven to thirty-three who have never had a child, the earnings of women are close to 98 percent of men's.[34] Even for broader groups of men and women, today's pay gaps mostly reflect the impact of such factors as women's shorter average working week and women's choice of careers that allow for greater flexibility should they wish to bear and rear children later on. Full-time working women also have, on average, less work experience than comparable males, again affecting their value to firms and thus their compensation.[35] Women's perceptions of how they are being treated by employers are generally consistent with these observed trends. A 1995 survey by Lou Harris and Associates found that 59 percent of women said they were "very valued" at their workplace, and few listed "lack of opportunities to advance in their jobs" as a major worry. Furthermore, fully 80 percent of women say they expect the next generation of women to have even more opportunities.[36] In a 1994 survey by the Labor Department, 79 percent of working women said they loved or liked their jobs.[37]

As in the case of minorities, women have become increasingly likely to hold management positions in American businesses, with more than 25 percent of such jobs in transportation, communications, manufacturing, retail trade, services, and in financial services (where women hold 41 percent of management jobs).[38] Some critics have complained that women are unable to retain management jobs in business because of the need for time off and leaves to care for their families. But a 1994 Bureau of Labor Statistics study found that the difference in job tenure between men and women managers was not that significant (seven years versus five years), and a separate study by the consulting firm Wick and Co. found that only 7 percent of surveyed women executives who left their jobs did so to stay at home. Most left one management job for another, in an attempt to advance their careers or start their own enterprises.[39]

Surely government actions and political movements have played some role in the trend toward equitable treatment of workers, but progress

began long before the passage of state and federal laws banning discrimination. Thomas Sowell, a senior fellow at the Hoover Institution and the
author of numerous books on affirmative action, notes that the number of
blacks in higher-paying, professional occupations was increasing rapidly
before the passage of the 1964 Civil Rights Act.[40] Several studies have
found that the convergence of economic opportunities for blacks and
whites and men and women began before World War II.[41] Indeed, the
1940s were a decade of unusually rapid narrowing of wage differentials
between black and white workers. The black-to-white ratio of average
weekly wages for adult men increased by 24 percent during the decade,
and this shift accounted for fully 37 percent of the total rise in black
wages relative to white wages from 1940 to 1980. Much of the convergence of the 1940s appears related to diminishing racial differences in
schooling.[42] Harvard economist Richard Freeman has found that blacks
and whites with similar backgrounds and education had essentially
achieved pay equity by 1969.[43] (Of course, the fact that similarly educated workers tend to receive similar compensation does not excuse government from responsibility on pay equity; it is the differing educational
levels of students coming out of public schools today that explains much
of the differing prospects of these students in the working world.)

When evaluating issues such as pay equity, it helps to apply a little
common sense. Apparent correlations or examples of discrimination often
turn out to reflect very different conditions that have no basis in unfair-
ness. For example, researchers in several studies have found that among
married men, those whose wives stay at home earn higher average wages
than those whose wives work. Is this evidence of corporate male chauvin-
ism about working women and a preference for traditional family roles?
Many analysts believe it is. "I don't know if you call it prejudice, but I do
think the people in the top positions, who are mostly traditional men, are
more comfortable with people who seem like themselves," said Frieda
Reitman, a Pace University researcher and coauthor of one of these studies.[44] Of course, all she found in the study was a correlation. A more
straightforward explanation might be that the causality runs the other way:
families in which men earn higher average incomes have less of a need for
two incomes, leaving the spouse free to pursue other uses of time such as
child bearing, part-time work, volunteering, or education. In short, these
men do not earn more because their wives stay home; the wives stay home
because the men earn more. Interestingly, Reitman's own study found that

married women—whether they have children or not—earn about 12 percent more on average than do single women. This fact is difficult to square with the notion that patriarchal males with disdainful attitudes about working wives populate the upper reaches of corporate management.[45]

Many explanations for the pay convergence among American workers lie in the social changes wrought by an innovative business sector. Technological innovation in our economy, for example, has not only made us all collectively better off but also had the side effect of promoting greater pay equity. The substitution of machinery for human labor has reduced the value of physical strength and increased the value of mental acuity and social skills, which are distributed more evenly between genders. At the same time, labor-saving devices in the home have given married women more freedom to pursue education and employment. Household chores that previously consumed hours of tedious work (such as washing clothes and dishes, sweeping floors, cleaning ovens, defrosting refrigerators, and cooking meals) are now performed in whole or in part by electrical appliances or by outside contractors.[46] The result has been a revolution in time and family responsibility that is difficult to overstate. Advances in transportation, information technology, and computerization have affected markets, competition, and worker mobility to such an extent that employers, no matter how remotely located, must inevitably deal with suppliers, contractors, or consumers who live far away and who might well be very different from them in race, ethnicity, language, and religion. Prejudice and discrimination cannot long survive in this vastly expanded and competitive marketplace.

AFFIRMATIVE ACTION AND DIVERSITY

Of course, the notion that men and women, or blacks and whites, should be paid the same for equally valuable work and treated equitably in the workplace does not necessarily mean that businesses do or should ignore their differences. There are situations in which gender or race might significantly affect the ability of workers to perform their tasks well, at least in the sense that their unique experiences are valuable to a firm. For example, a company seeking to design and market women's clothing is likely to do a better job if its design and marketing teams include women. A company trying to increase its market share among ethnic or language groups or into minority neighborhoods would be wise to have people working on the project whose knowledge of and experience with the target audience might be valuable.[47]

Consider the experience of MacTemps, a staffing firm created in 1987 and generating $50 million in national sales by 1995. John Chuang, founder of MacTemps, has discovered that the cultural and linguistic background of his employees has had a direct impact on the ability of the firm to secure contracts. "MacTemps has two publishing clients in Miami that we would never have landed if we hadn't hired a native-Spanish-speaking assignment manager," he said. In the company's Los Angeles office, where entertainment firms are constantly looking for good animation artists, MacTemps found that its Chinese employee was invaluable in locating potential artists—since many of the best ones happen to be from China and Japan. Chuang has concluded from these and other experiences that cultural diversity among his staff is a business asset worth maintaining, though he "will never promote a less qualified person over a more qualified person."[48]

By importing the concept of political equality (including the one-person–one-vote rule and equal treatment under the law) into business and trying to apply it to economic decisions, some analysts of business forget that in commerce, individuals receive higher pay and obtain greater economic opportunity when they can offer higher value to specific firms. Sometimes where you are from, what language you speak, and whom you know determine whether you have something of value to add to a particular company's operations at a particular point in time.

In practical terms, this means that many firms with varied customers and interests cannot afford to have a monochrome or homogeneous workforce, even in the unlikely event that such a workforce was hired according to strictly nondiscriminatory principles. So when these firms make extra efforts to recruit at minority colleges and organizations, or extend generous maternity leave to valuable female employees, they are not being irresponsible or unfair. They are taking actions intended to increase the performance and profitability of their operations—the definition of business responsibility advanced in this book.[49] Of course, this approach to maximizing performance does not justify stereotyping and arbitrary racial classification: A black employee with ten years of good experience marketing products to Hispanics should not be replaced with a Puerto Rican college graduate who lacks that experience, nor should a Chinese-American manager of a bank branch in predominantly white Iowa be replaced by a white on the vague assumption that the latter will do a better job of tailoring the bank's services to its market. Job descriptions and expectations should be based on performance, and applicants judged according to that standard. That in some cases ethnic or religious background might be a "tie-breaker" among similarly qualified employees, because of the specific demands of the job at issue, is a possibility that truly responsible firms must entertain.

Unfortunately, private employment practices have becoming hopelessly politicized by well-intentioned laws and well-intentioned people. Thus we have affirmative action of a reasonable, "casting one's net widely" sort degenerating in all too many cases into quotas and statistical games in which corporate managers who ought to know better judge their organizations not by performance but by the existence of racial or gender disparities per se—as if every firm, regardless of size, type, or market, should exhibit a percentage breakdown of workers that mirrors larger society or some mythical standard of perfection.[50] George Harvey, chief executive of Connecticut-based office-equipment firm Pitney Bowes, set a quota in 1985 stipulating that at least 35 percent of all new employees hired be women and 15 percent minorities. Managers' pay and bonuses were tied to meeting the quota. Harvey defended the quota with "casting the net" rhetoric: "It doesn't make sense to cut yourself off from half of the talented people in this world."[51] Of course, there is also no need to translate this commonsense observation into a fixed numerical quota, as long as the hiring process is free from bias and focused on the value and abilities of individual applicants.

As Sowell has so eloquently pointed out, "Human beings are not random. They have very pronounced and complex cultural patterns." Distribution of ethnic groups among occupations, for example, almost never mirrors the distribution of consumers or the larger society. The fact that Koreans and Indians own many small retail establishments in black or Hispanic neighborhoods in the United States is hardly surprising when you recognize that similar patterns—of merchants and customers differing in ethnicity—have been common for centuries in Southeast Asia, Eastern Europe, West Africa, the Caribbean, Fiji, the Ottoman Empire, and numerous other places. Also, people who hail from different locations and cultures will not exhibit the same educational or job skills. Interestingly, people who come from areas where trade is made easier by geography—such as flat lands, rivers, and coasts—have generally been richer, healthier, and more technologically advanced than people who live in rugged mountains or away from navigable water. This has been true with highland and lowland Scots, Adriatic and inland Slavs, river-basin dwellers and hill dwellers in India, and coastal and inland West Africans.[52] These cultural differences do not disappear immediately when people immigrate to other societies, such as the United States. They persist, affecting the rearing, education, and life choices of subsequent generations, albeit to a progressively lesser extent.

So those who play statistical-disparity games are trying to engineer a result that will never occur in the real world in the free choices of economic actors, whose background and culture will always influence, at least in part, their choice of education, career, and lifestyle.[53] "Most of us who have benefitted from or participated in minority recruiting would be against numerical goals and quotas because all they lead to is taking the first 10 dark faces that walk through the door instead of taking people who are qualified," says Larry Thompson, deputy general counsel of the Wall Street firm Depository Trust Co.[54] And by using racial hiring quotas, some corporate executives risk reinforcing rather than reducing racist beliefs in society. Quotas "unwittingly perpetuate the inferiority myth, undermining in the process the very equality they are meant to create," says Errol Smith, president of Captains International in California and the child of Caribbean immigrants.[55]

Similarly, the sensible idea that diversity among workers can be valuable has in recent years been hijacked by self-styled "diversity consultants" and passive employers as a call for "diversity training" in many American workplaces. Diversity training has no formal definition, and can range from innocuous or even worthwhile attempts to foster teamwork or cultural understanding to bizarre and destructive ideological crusades that promote divisiveness and racial strife. The most notorious story of diversity training gone horribly awry is probably that of a public-sector employer, the Federal Aviation Administration. In June 1992 the FAA brought in a diversity consultant to conduct some training sessions. In one session, men were asked to walk through a "gauntlet" of women, who looked at and touched the men and then rated their masculinity on a scale of one to ten. Other sessions required workers to discuss personal traumas and to react to sexually explicit material. The FAA later had to settle an unfair labor practices complaint by offended workers.[56]

Private-sector employers have made their share of diversity-training

blunders. AT & T, for example, has been in the forefront of the movement. But after sending 100,000 employees through diversity programs
in the late 1980s and early 1990s, AT & T found that many of its white
male employees felt threatened and left out. When the company tried to
undo the damage with new diversity programs aimed at addressing these
concerns, other employees objected to shifting the focus of diversity
training away from the interests of women and minorities, even urging a
boycott of training sessions.[57]

Despite rhetoric about the potential economic payoff of "embracing
diversity," the diversity training movement is largely an ideological creation that dates only to the mid-1980s. Diversity trainers run the gamut
from psychologists to management consultants to educators to those with
no special expertise or degrees at all. In many cases, training sessions
become exercises in psychobabble or in victimology—dwelling on the
historical grievances of groups rather than talking about specific differences between workers today and how to bridge them.[58] There is no hard
evidence that these programs (as distinguished from more established
methods of encouraging teamwork and building company morale, such
as volunteer or sports activities outside of work) have any positive impact
on company performance. Interestingly, the results of one of the few academic studies done on diverse workforces themselves were trumpeted by
the diversity-training industry and friendly media outlets as evidence of
the value of cultural diversity, even though the study found that, if anything, the culturally *homogeneous* group actually solved problems given
to them in the experiment faster and more successfully than did the culturally heterogeneous group.[59] The proper conclusion from this is not that
cultural diversity is harmful, but instead that a diverse workforce is not
inherently more productive across the entire population of economic
enterprises. To put it more bluntly: general rules about these matters are
simply impossible to formulate.

Nevertheless, either because of good intentions, the ideological fervor
of middle managers, or neglectful or defensive upper management, diversity programs have proliferated. About two-thirds of the companies polled
by the Conference Board in 1992 said they were initiating diversity programs. Daily fees for these programs run from $1,500 to $4,000, so companies with many programs and employees spend millions of dollars a
year on diversity training. Some firms have wisely moved away from hiring outside consultants with few qualifications or little understanding of

company operations, opting instead for in-house programs. Amoco Corporation, for example, began to run cultural awareness and training programs with in-house staff after having to dismiss previous consultants whose work generated employee complaints. "It typically does not work to have an off-the-shelf program that does not know what Amoco and all its different divisions need in terms of training," said the company's Phyllis Hayes. "The topic of diversity is very inflammatory, so it's very important to be clear on objectives and have a consultant who is receptive."[60]

Just like successful skills training, or safety and health programs, or waste reduction programs, company efforts to improve social relations among workers and build a sense of teamwork and commitment to a common goal must be part of the everyday operation of the firm, rather than single-shot classes or feel-good programs designed for internal or external appearances.[61] "Diversity training has the greatest impact when people who work together are trained together," wrote H. B. Karp and Nancy Sutton, both consulting psychologists, in *Training* magazine. "It's often more effective to deal with diversity as a component in a training program focused on another organizational need such as team-building or leadership."[62] Richard Orange, a New York City–based consultant, noted that "diversity training is like hearing a good sermon on Sunday. You must practice what you heard during the week, and refer to the Bible."[63]

Training and information that focuses on understanding real cultural differences—in areas like language, dress, holidays, consumer preferences, and social graces—can be valuable in a way that "white-male bashing" and victimology are clearly not. Focusing on changing unproductive *behavior* at the workplace, rather than changing the deep-seated attitudes or beliefs of workers, is also important. "The danger of leaving the focus too long on past injustices is that the whole things turns into a game—a competition involving whose group has suffered the most," Karp and Sutton continued. "It quickly devolves into a whining contest, then moves into a final stage called 'Get the Straight White Males.'"[64]

RACE, GENDER, AND CONSUMERS

If the logic of business success works against unfair and capricious treatment of workers on the basis of race or gender, then it virtually mandates that companies with the desire to maximize revenue not discriminate against potential customers. The fact that some businesses have done so, and continue to do so, reflects only that they are run by people who put their own personal biases above profit. Flagstar Companies, which operates Denny's and Hardee's restaurants throughout the South and West, is clearly not one of these businesses, despite some well-publicized cases of discrimination in the early 1990s.

In 1991 reports began to trickle in to Flagstar CEO Jerry Richardson of racial discrimination at some of his Denny's restaurants in California. Some black customers charged that they were denied service, while others said they were forced to prepay for food when white customers were not. Richardson (who was in the process of seeking a National Football League franchise in Charlotte, North Carolina, and thus could ill afford such bad publicity) immediately took action to fire managers who had discriminated, to apologize to offended customers, and to institute programs to train restaurant managers and workers about racism. In a restaurant chain with thousands of employees across many states, it would have been impossible not to inadvertently hire some racists. The key issue was how company management saw its responsibility to correct problems as they arose. "It makes no sense that we would condone racism," said Richardson. "Denny's needs all the customers it can get.[65]

In reality, today's business world is full of white males trying to sell things to females and minorities (as well as the latter trying to sell to the former, of course). One of the most important business trends of the 1990s is *niche marketing*—attempts by businesses, ranging from retailers to restaurateurs, to tailor specific products or marketing campaigns to ethnic or religious minorities. Target Stores, for example, has invested a great deal of time and money developing an inventory and distribution process to keep stores stocked with items likely to be popular in the particular neighborhoods where the stores are located.[66]

The pool of potential non-white consumers is vast and growing. They spent $600 billion in 1994, up 18 percent since 1990, and by the year 2000 are expected to account for 30 percent of the domestic demand for goods and services.[67] Black Americans alone buy about $213 billion of consumer products a year, and they spend proportionally more than whites on things like boys' clothing, pork products, sugar, and appliance rentals—giving companies a strong incentive to gather information about what these consumers want and how to deliver it to them. Sometimes, seemingly minor nuances matter a lot. StoveTop Stuffing, for example, found in its research that black Americans usually referred to its kind of product as "dressing" rather than "stuffing." After the company prepared a marketing campaign using the term dressing, sales among blacks improved. Other marketing research shows that blacks and whites differ on how they consume rare meat, coffee, milk products, and alcohol.[68]

Groups such as Hispanics and Asians who are more recent immigrants to America and who may be relatively new English speakers exhibit even more significant differences from white consumers. Chinese Americans, for example, drink nearly twice as much cognac per person as the average American. Koreans eat more Spam than any other ethnic group. Companies that discover these kinds of differences and tailor their products and campaigns accordingly stand to gain tremendously by tapping previously unpenetrated markets. Miami-based health maintenance organization CareFlorida Inc. has seen its share of the managed care market grow rapidly because of a marketing pitch aimed at Hispanics. Universal Casket, based in Michigan, grew to $3 million in sales by 1995 by marketing to black-owned funeral homes.[69] Procter & Gamble spends about 5 percent of its $2 billion advertising budget on ethnic-oriented ads, while AT & T sponsors Chinese Dragon Boat Festival races and Cuban folk festivals. Its domestic broadcast and print ads run in twenty different languages, including Korean and Tagalog (Asians make three times as many overseas calls as the average U.S. consumer). "Marketing today is part anthropology," said the company's director of multicultural marketing, Jacqueline Morey.[70]

The efforts of corporations to cultivate regular customers among minority groups has been largely obscured in the public mind by the lingering controversy over "redlining" by banks, insurers, realtors, and similar types of businesses. Discussion of redlining is complicated by the fact that historically, some lenders and insurers were clearly willing to forgo the business of blacks and others in order to reinforce a social consensus of segregation in their communities. But this despicable—and economically unwise—practice would seem to be extremely rare today, despite incessant claims by activists and the media that redlining remains the rule.

The problem is that studies purporting to show discrimination in bank lending or insurance focus almost exclusively on rejection rates for loans and policies. These rejection rates often do, indeed, differ significantly among racial groups in studies. But these studies ignore many important factors that provide a more plausible explanation for the apparent disparity than does racism.[71] Sometimes the studies promoted so widely by the mass media, like the celebrated 1992 Federal Reserve Board of Boston study purporting to show higher black rejection rates than those of whites with similar incomes, are simply invalid; the Boston Fed study contained transcription and mathematical errors, inappropriate generalizations, and the skewing of average results by a few exceptional cases.[72] Ironically, higher rejection rates are often found for those very institutions (including minority-owned banks) that are trying to extend credit in inner-city and minority neighborhoods, since banks in predominantly white areas are more likely to receive applicants from a smaller, more select group of minorities with better-than-average financial resources, work histories, or business prospects. To open a branch in a minority community and try to attract more minority loan applicants means necessarily that you will reject more minority applications than you did before.[73] Furthermore, when observers point to high rejection rates for lenders with branches in minority communities, they ignore the possibility that such decisions are being made for sound business reasons to protect the interests of depositors—including minority depositors who live in those communities. "We should ask: Where is the social good in asking or requiring people in a poor community to earn less on their money?" wondered T. Carter Hagaman, editor of *Management Accounting*.[74]

It is, indeed, the personal characteristics of loan applicants—the items in their financial history likely to communicate to potential lenders the likelihood that their loans will be repaid—that explain virtually all racial or ethnic disparities. The most important measure of discrimination is not rejection rates, which are affected by a host of racially neutral factors, but instead the rates at which customers of different races or communities *default* on their loans. If those households or businesses in black areas tend to default at lower rates than those in white areas do, that would be evidence of discrimination, since it would imply that blacks have to meet higher credit standards than whites do in order to get loans. Conversely, if the default rates of blacks are higher, that would suggest discrimination in favor of them. In reality, the available evidence on default rates suggests that there is no significant difference between households and businesses of predominantly white and predominantly minority communities, suggesting that the latter are not being redlined.[75] Other studies that have tried to identify actual racial discrimination by interviewing loan applicants have often failed to find any significant evidence of it.[76]

Similar problems exist with common arguments that such industries as insurance and telecommunications "redline" minority communities. Premiums for auto and homeowners insurance, for example, are typically higher in inner-city communities than in suburban communities, but as economist Catherine England observes, this occurs "because expected claims costs are higher for city residents than for residents of suburban or rural neighborhoods." There are more traffic accidents, fires, and home break-ins per capita. Also, these inner-city communities not only tend to generate higher insurance premiums but also attract fewer competing insurance competitors. If the higher premiums were solely discriminatory, resulting in higher revenues, then other insurers would enter the market in droves. Since that does not happen very often, it is likely that the higher rates simply reflect higher expected costs.[77]

The fact of the matter is that banks and insurers have a significant incentive to seek out productive investments in minority communities, no less than in other communities. As with other kinds of businesses, this effort requires innovative thinking and an attempt to understand the demands of minority consumers. By acquiring several faltering savings and loans, First National Bank of Chicago grew from 5 to 77 branches from 1986 to 1994 in inner-city Chicago. To serve its new customer base, First National had to adjust its business practices. One branch manager essentially converted her bank into a "currency exchange" that cashed paychecks and issued money orders, because that was what many people in the surrounding Hispanic neighborhood expected the bank to do. Similarly, bank branches in immigrant communities arranged to pay for depositors' utility bills with large, official-looking seals stamped on the receipts—a device that recent immigrants could use to display their creditworthiness. First Chicago also sought out employees who could speak second languages; at one branch, employees collectively could speak 46 languages.[78]

THE ELDERLY AND DISABLED

Discussions of discrimination in the workplace get more complicated when the subject is changed from racial minorities or women to groups such as the elderly and the disabled. The latter groups have traditionally had unique characteristics that might very well make them less employable or more difficult to serve as customers than other groups. A decision not to hire a Hispanic woman because of her race and gender is difficult to defend, but a decision not to hire someone with physical handicaps because he or she might not be able to perform the job adequately is more understandable. Nor do regulatory interventions by governments magically wipe the problem away. A law that outlaws discrimination against the disabled, for example, does not change the fact that a particular individual's disability might limit his or her ability to perform as well as alternative workers. If employers are simply forced to ignore that fact by law, the result will be lower-quality services or lower productivity in affected firms.[79]

Fortunately, business innovations are making these sorts of zero-sum games increasingly unnecessary. One of the least-recognized impacts of the automation or computerization of the American workplace has been the empowerment of millions of Americans with physical handicaps who are now able to produce goods and services. At E. I. duPont de Nemours & Co. in Wilmington, Delaware, a 1990 sampling of the company's more than three thousand employees with disabilities included a staff research chemist and a computer programmer who were blind, a systems analyst with muscular dystrophy, a deaf machine operator, and a wheelchair-bound assistant store manager. Company studies have found that their disabled workers are more likely than the workforce as a whole to receive average or above average ratings in safety, attendance, and job performance.[80]

Similarly, the elderly have benefited from medical innovations that have extended their lives, reduced their physical limitations, and increased their ability to remain involved in business well beyond the standard retirement age (see Chapter 6). "Age is a different thing than it used to be," said Joan Kelly of the American Association of Retired Persons. "The 50-year-old of today is like the 35-year-old of 20 years ago. People are living longer; therefore, they're going to be working longer."[81] Businesses that have hired and retained older workers have often found them to be extremely productive. Days Inn of America finds that older reservations agents sell more than their younger colleagues, and they actually cost less per year even when higher health insurance costs are taken into account. And Ford Motor Company, with a workforce almost twice the average age of its Japanese rivals, credits its financial turnabout largely to the ability of older employees to work in teams. "We have found that the more people have been around, the more they contribute," said Ernest Savoie, former director of employee development at Ford. "We attribute a lot to the older workers."[82]

Hardware and software manufacturers continue to introduce new products onto the market to give those with physical limitations more power to work or to consume. A joint venture by AT & T and NCR offers engineering consulting services and adaptive hardware and software to firms and individuals. Both IBM and Apple Computer have produced assistive technologies for their systems that range from graphics-based speech-synthesis systems to sticky-key software (which electronically locks and holds several keyboard buttons at once—for example, "shift" and "control" keys—thus making it easier for people with typing handicaps to operate computers). Computerized electrical stimulation devices allow paralyzed persons to "move" their limbs for exercise. Sip-and-puff air tubes connected to computers control the movements of motorized wheelchairs. Vision-impaired users can buy magnification, braille, and speech-operated technology. One $700 software package called Window Bridge can verbalize both MS-DOS and Windows-based applications, allowing users to operate them by listening and responding. Similarly, modems and other devices have allowed the hearing-impaired to perform tasks or consume services that previously required talking on the telephone. Even severely handicapped people can operate computers and do work by using Morse-code devices and head-mounted pointing devices that in 1993 cost less than $1,500.[83]

Companies have developed these products because there is a huge potential demand for them. Some 14 million working-age Americans are disabled to some degree, and about a third of these individuals currently work. Of course, many of these workers and consumers do not need elaborate computer technologies; simple and inexpensive products such as ergonomically reengineered chairs have helped many workers perform their jobs better.[84] Indeed, most workplace accommodations for disabled workers now average less than $1,000 in cost, often because of innovative new ideas or products.[85] Joseph Jarke, who at age nineteen became paraplegic in an automobile accident, noticed that wheelchair-bound people had a hard time traveling long distances because of narrow airplane aisles and inaccessible hotel rooms. Rather than agitate for regulations to address this problem, Jarke saw "a chance to do something I'd always wanted to do: create a product." He invented a wheelchair that could fold up to the size of a briefcase, thus making it easier for the handicapped to take their own wheelchairs on trips, and started SeatCase Inc. in 1990.

Airlines loved the idea and helped market the product. SeatCase had $1 million in sales by 1993. "We really have changed the world in a small way," Jarke said.[86]

CONCLUSION

On the contentious issue of social equality, it would be absurd to argue with two propositions: (1) there remain significant differences in incomes, job prospects, and economic opportunities among various social groups in our society, and (2) racism, sexism, and other forms of discrimination or stereotyping persist in America. What is important for our purposes here is to understand the role of profit-seeking business in changing these two conditions. The fact is that actions taken on the basis of personal prejudice by corporate managers violate not only the standards of personal morality that most of us hold dear, but also the properly understood social responsibility of business, which is to maximize the productivity and profitability of economic enterprises. Those who ignore this responsibility pay a price in the marketplace in the form of lower worker performance, lower market share, and ultimately lower profits.[87] Of course, the damage competition does to racist and sexist firms is not always obvious and often takes some time to appear. But, as Auburn University author Steven Yates points out, "while the free market may permit private racist attitudes to survive—for not even market forces can regulate thought—bottom-line business considerations will render them impotent."[88]

For this reason, it is most likely that institutions other than businesses, such as public schools and government regulators, are primarily responsible for continuing gaps in living standards and opportunities. As monopolies, these types of institutions need not face competitors and thus have no bottom-line incentive to police discriminatory actions or results. Furthermore, business innovation has even begun to resolve the hard cases of discrimination—the elderly and disabled—by generating new technologies and management strategies that minimize barriers to employment and success, thus unleashing talents and energies previously unavailable to employers and consumers. For groups kept from realizing the American dream by the prejudices and failures of the past, the best hope for progress in the future is an economy populated with companies whose managers put performance and profitability first.

CHAPTER 10

FAMILY VALUES AND
THE WORKPLACE

Fran Rodgers wants businesses to pay more attention to the needs of
employees and their families. In her view, firms should help workers
obtain good-quality care for their children or elderly parents, provide
more leave and flexible working hours, and steer troubled workers into
counseling. Is Rodgers simply a political activist or cloistered academic?
No. Her interest in work and family issues is pecuniary as well as social.
She is founder and CEO of Work/Family Directions, a Boston-based
provider of referral services for work-and-family issues that employs 250
people and took in $44 million in revenues in 1993. For Rodgers, reconcil-
ing the demands of the workplace with those of family is not simply a
question of social conscience or fairness. "The work my company does is
socially responsible in that it contributes not only to business results but
also to society," she said. "But that's not why our clients choose us. They
buy our services primarily to enhance their profitability and performance."[1]

Rodgers came to the business of helping families through personal
experience. In 1978, while working at an educational consulting firm,
Rodgers discovered that her infant daughter had a severe case of asthma.
To be able to spend more time with her, Rodgers set out to consult from
her home. In 1983 IBM was looking for child-care referral services at
some of its facilities and came to Rodgers because of her published

175

research on the demands of the changing workforce. At its plant in Boca Raton, Florida, for example, IBM employed 12,000 employees in an area with few good-quality day care providers. Rodgers decided the company needed to actively recruit such providers, going so far as advertising on billboards and handing out flyers at lunchtime in supermarkets. The message, she said, to prospective day care providers was that "if you're thinking of staying home with this child, here's a way to do it—by caring for others as well." Her efforts to improve day care offerings for IBM led to other contracts with Xerox, American Express, and NationsBank. Gradually she added services such as elder care, educational assistance, and counseling. "Smart companies acknowledge that with dual-income families, women in the workforce, and other changes, people have more family issues," she said. "You don't have to look too far to know that people can take only so much change before they crack. Employees get sick, they give a marginal performance, they snap at the next customer."[2]

On social responsibility, Rodgers makes the point that businesses cannot successfully address family issues at the workplace by thinking of them as charitable activities. "To the extent that socially responsible concepts are seen as the nice thing to do, it's not so good for me to be seen in that light," she said. "In fact, if clients see my work as irrelevant to getting business results, their employees will not be well served in the long run because the companies won't be examining the basic business rationale for those socially responsible decisions."[3]

Over the past several decades, the composition of the American workforce—and the condition, it must be said, of the American family—has been changing dramatically. The most obvious change is that more mothers with young children have entered the job market. According to the U.S. Bureau of Labor Statistics, of all mothers with children under the age of six in 1993, almost 60 percent worked outside home, compared with less than 40 percent in 1975 and only 20 percent in 1960 (many of these mothers, however, worked outside of the home only part-time).[4] A less obvious, but also important, development is that longer life spans mean more workers with responsibilities to their aging parents. A survey of large companies by Rodgers' Work/Family Directions found that about 15 percent of employees had an aging or infirm dependent.[5] The abuse of alcohol and illegal drugs is common, and a host of other social pathologies has made parents afraid for their children's safety and for the future they will inherit.

But the news is by no means all bad. Economic changes also have led to the creation and wide distribution of labor-saving devices such as washers and dryers, dishwashers, and microwave ovens that have saved families time and money.[6] Productivity gains have improved the lives of families in countless ways. "As hard as it may be for many Americans to believe," noted a Federal Reserve Bank study of living standards, "surveys show the country has never had as much leisure. . . . Americans are starting work later in life and, perhaps even more significant, they are enjoying longer periods of retirement." The study goes on to show that the typical employee spends less than one-third of all waking hours working, either at home or on the job. "When totaled, the results are mind-boggling," the Fed stated. "Workers, on average, have added nearly five years of waking leisure to their lifetimes since 1973." Increases in expenditures for recreation and community activities show how much of that leisure time is being used.[7]

Nevertheless, though families may have benefited overall from economic changes in recent decades, they are still faced with problems of reconciling work and family responsibilities. Part of the problem, no doubt, is that while economic conditions have improved, social conditions have deteriorated. There are fewer intact families and more single parents who must work outside the home to feed their children. There is little reason to believe in a correlation between rising prosperity and falling family stability, since previous periods of American history have seen simultaneous improvements in both economic and family conditions. Social scientists have debated the causes and effects of family breakup and rising rates of unwed births, but the key implication for the workplace is that even in the midst of increased prosperity and leisure time, there are many workers today whose family responsibilities are complex and time-consuming.

As Rodgers points out, these problems do not just affect workers. They affect employers and the performance of companies. That is why responsible businesses have been exploring ways to accommodate family values in the workplace, through such policies as family leave, "flextime," employee assistance programs, and telecommuting. These innovations have not spread to every corner of the American workforce—nor should anyone expect them to—but they do suggest a private-sector, incentive-led response to the needs of families that calls into question the large public-sector role some analysts have recommended. The search for profit, particularly as we approach the end of the 1990s, will not hamper the development of family-friendly workplaces. It will hasten it.

THE CHILD-CARE CHALLENGE

The American child-care industry is huge and diverse—encompassing large proprietary chains, small for-profit centers, churches and nonprofit providers, and informal day care homes where a mother might care for her own children as well as the children of neighbors or other working parents. American families' child-care arrangements also include a lot of uncompensated assistance from extended family and friends; indeed, most child care is provided in homes, not in centers.[8] These arrangements are of varied quality, no doubt, and the cost of especially for-profit care is a major concern of many families. But to say (as many self-styled advocates for children do) that working parents lack alternatives, and particularly the help and understanding of their employers, in making child-care arrangements is to ignore the extent of corporate involvement and to misdiagnose the real problems that many parents face.

Business managers have several salient reasons to help their employees find reliable, good-quality child care. The most important one is probably the market for labor. In the competition to attract good workers, companies often find they can offer valuable benefits due to their size and experience. For example, experience in hiring and managing employees from the same community over many years exposes employers to useful information about local child-care offerings, which they can offer to prospective workers. Tax considerations also affect the labor market; contributions to flexible spending accounts and child-care benefits are not taxed like regular compensation and thus may be more valuable to workers than extra salary. A 1992 survey found that 87 percent of corporate benefit managers said they had observed increased demand from employees for work-family benefits.[9] "In the 1990s and beyond, a hefty salary without concerns about the family and individual needs of the employee may cost a company a good job candidate," American Management Associates observed. "Job candidates know that if Company Z doesn't offer them child care or flextime, Company Q probably will."[10]

Still another issue for employers is that workers from families where child-care arrangements are satisfactory and reliable are likely to be more committed and productive than workers who must take absences to pick up children or who are distracted by family concerns. For example, Fel-Pro, an automotive-parts maker with two thousand employees in Skokie, Illinois, subsidizes its workers' day care. The company often has a waiting list for prospective employees and has been consistently profitable for three decades. "We are not a charity," said David Weinburg, co-chairman of Fel-Pro. "We are enhancing profits by keeping employees satisfied."[11] A University of Chicago study of Fel-Pro's program found that participating employees had the highest job-performance evaluations and the highest commitment to the company of all Fel-Pro employees. "We characterized it as a culture of mutual commitment between employee and employer," said the university research team leader, Susan J. Lambert. "That's how it's translated into work performance."[12] Sandra Hamilton, employee benefits director for Illinois-based Allstate Insurance Co., makes a similar point: "We truly believe dedicated and motivated employees who balance work and personal lives will give us a competitive advantage." Allstate offers its workers child-care referral, flexible spending accounts, and long-term care insurance.[13]

Most of the time, a company's involvement in child care is limited to helping employees locate good programs or day care alternatives in their communities. Some companies also provide funds to employees for child-care expenses, while only a few actually operate their own day care centers (those that do, however, have received an incredible amount of attention from corporate social responsibility advocates).[14] A Hewitt Associates survey of 1,034 U.S. companies found that almost 80 percent of the firms offer child-care support and referral programs, but only 9 percent had on-site centers.[15] Other studies have shown similar results; the most popular benefit is referral, followed by spending accounts and subsidies and, for a very few firms, on-site child-care centers.[16]

This is not at all surprising and certainly should not be troubling. After all, the fact that a company is good at milling steel or processing insurance claims does not mean it has the expertise or resources to run a child-care center.[17] Also, running a center increases the company's liability and steers money away from some of their employees who simply do not like formal day care settings or who do not have children. Gayle M. Evans, manager of human resources at Standard Insurance, noted that "a lot of people don't want their children around 30 other snotty-nosed little children."[18] Since company funds devoted to in-house centers are almost invariably funds that otherwise would be paid directly to workers in the form of wages or fringe benefits, most firms are better off passing the compensation along to employees and serving as advisor and facilitator.[19] U.S. West Inc., the telecommunications giant, provides a national resource and referral service to its employees. Company CEO Richard D. McCormick said that "child care referral services are among the least costly and most-appreciated services a company can provide." He related that many employees have written him to express their appreciation for the company's aid.[20] Indiana-based insurer Lincoln National set up a series of seminars, support groups, newsletters, and an annual child-care fair to help its employees make good child-care decisions.[21]

Charity Benedict and Joy Blackhurst exemplify the stake both employers and employees have in meeting child-care needs. Both have young children and both picked their employer, Pro Tem Temporary Services, for its child-care benefits. The Portland, Oregon, personnel company contributes 75 cents an hour toward child-care expenses for each hour worked by employees, whose pay typically ranges from $7.50 to $8 an hour. The company policy increases take-home pay without increasing payroll and income taxes for the workers. "If people don't get benefits, I don't see how they do it," Blackhurst commented. "I'm trying to raise a good family, and they're giving me help with it. It's a big reason why I took this job." Not only did Pro Tem attract Blackhurst with the policy, but she is also an enthusiastic worker who is likely to remain with the company for a long time. "I would do anything for them," she said. "They're a great company." Pro Tem employees receiving the subsidy have a turnover rate about half that of other company employees.[22] Apparently, the potential bottom-line benefits of this policy have not escaped corporate managers. A survey of U.S. manufacturers, service firms, and financial institutions by the Financial Executives Institute found that 61 percent offered child-care spending accounts of some type.[23]

Despite these corporate investments in helping employees with child-care needs, there are problems with the availability and cost of child care. Many of these problems can be traced to local or state government regulations that unnecessarily increase cost without really improving quality very much. For example, government regulations covering providers, facilities, supplies, and location boost the price of both formal and informal day care centers by a substantial amount. Local governments particularly complicate work and family problems by imposing rigid zoning rules that separate residential from commercial or industrial areas, even as companies and workers are trying to find more cost-effective and convenient ways to reconcile work and family responsibilities.[24] Studies have shown that by and large, these regulations serve to benefit large child-care providers at the expense of their competitors and of families.[25]

LEAVE AND FLEXTIME

As the composition of the workforce has been changing, advances in technology and new thinking on the part of corporate managers has led to new ways to reconcile work and family responsibilities. Even before the 1993 passage of the Family and Medical Leave Act, many firms had instituted leave policies so that employees could take care of family needs. Businesses have also become more flexible about work hours, introducing such concepts as flextime, compressed work schedules, and job-sharing to the workplace.

It is difficult to estimate the extent of family friendliness among businesses. Some firms do not have formal policies in place but nevertheless work flexibly with employees, while others might offer benefits that are not significantly taken advantage of (or, in some cases, known about) by their workers. One survey in 1992 found that 93 percent of companies offered some sort of unpaid leaves for reasons such as disability, adoption or new parenthood, child or elder care, and military service (the 1993 federal law required that all businesses with fifty or more workers provide twelve weeks of unpaid leave following childbirth or adoption, to care for a seriously ill child, spouse, or parent, or for an employee's own serious illness). The survey found that 63 percent of companies offered flexible hours, 30 percent offered compressed workweeks (such as working forty hours in four days rather than five), and 27 percent offered an employee the opportunity to share a job with another worker, thus reducing hours for both.[26]

As one might expect, large businesses tend to offer more in the way of formal work/family programs than small businesses do—there are economies of scale in most employee benefits. A 1991 study of 188 large firms by the Families and Work Institute found that all offered maternity leave, 88 percent offered part-time work, 77 percent offered flextime, and 48 percent offered job-sharing.[27] But the existence of formal programs is not necessarily the only evidence of family friendliness, and smaller businesses also tend toward flexibility in accommodating worker needs. A

Gallup Organization survey of small employers in 1991 found that 73 percent would accommodate an employee's request for indefinite time off, while 94 percent said they had granted the most recent employee request for family or parental leave.[28]

Again, the motivation behind these endeavors need not be charitable or social. The experience of many companies shows that family-friendly firms often improve productivity and morale among employees while saving hiring and training costs for new employees. Johnson & Johnson, for example, found that workers who used flextime and family-leave policies had 50 percent lower absentee rates when compared to the total workforce. The company also found that almost 71 percent of participating employees said such policies were "very important" in their decision to stay at the company. AT & T studied its leave policies and found that a year of unpaid parental leave cost 32 percent of an employee's annual salary, but replacing the leave-taker would have cost 150 percent of his or her salary.[29] At NationsBank, based in Charlotte, North Carolina, a program to let professionals work part-time seems to have helped the company retain valuable employees. A survey found that two-thirds of the participants would have left the bank rather than continue full-time, and most workers and their managers said their part-time work was more productively spent than their full-time work because they were more focused and spent less time on non-work activities.[30] Other studies have found part-timers to be as productive, and in some cases more productive, than full-time counterparts.[31]

Turnover is a key consideration. By introducing flexible work rules, New York insurance company Continental Corporation halved its voluntary employee turnover rate to less than 5 percent a year.[32] Aetna Life & Casualty Co. made a similar discovery when it created a Work/Family Strategies unit in 1988 after years of losing talented female workers after childbirth. Instituting flexible scheduling, the insurance company found by 1993 that roughly 2,000 of its 44,000 employees worked part-time, shared a job, worked at home, or worked a compressed week. It also concluded that it was saving $1 million a year in training expenses.[33] New York–based Corning Inc. estimates that it saves $2 million a year through increased employee retention attributable to career and family initiatives.[34] At these companies, in other words, it made financial sense to retain a valuable employee who needed time off—using temps and other measures to bridge the gap—rather than hire and train a new one.

Historically, leave policies and other family benefits have been instituted in large part by companies that wanted to retain valuable employees.[35]

While some companies have experimented with these policies and found success, it would be a mistake to assume that all companies can and should implement flexible scheduling and other work/family programs. Analysts agree that two conditions must exist before leave and flextime strategies can be successfully implemented. First, upper management must understand the need for flexibility in accommodating employee needs; simply introducing programs without establishing an organizational consensus about their goals can lead to little measurable benefit. "One of the most cost-effective ways of dealing with family-and-work conflicts," wrote Bonnie Michaels and Elizabeth McCarty, authors of *Solving the Work/Family Puzzle,* "is educating upper managers and training employees and managers in how to deal with work and family conflicts."[36]

Effective training programs can clear away inertia and misunderstanding on the part of corporate managers, but that is not the only reason why firms do not offer work and family benefits. Particularly when one is looking at flexible scheduling and leave policies, the characteristics of the individual businesses involved can also make a big difference. Some firms are simply unsuited for many work/family programs. They may track employee performance on the basis of hours worked rather than measurable output—and while there are many methods and reasons for changing that practice, some firms may never be able to. Service businesses, for example, that require on-site personal interactions between clients and employees may not have the same capacity for flexible hours and generous leaves as manufacturers or information-processing businesses do. For those businesses, both managers and workers may want compensation packages to lean less toward leave and flextime benefits and more toward salary, health care, and child-care benefits. Other firms are simply too small to accommodate worker demands for generous leave time. Workers having such needs probably should look for a different employer, and indeed most already have: A study by the Kessler Exchange in 1995 found that among small employers exempt from federal leave laws, those who offer leave anyway have much lower rates of worker participation than larger firms do.[37] There is no right answer for every situation—which is why social responsibility should not be evaluated simply on the basis of whether a company offers a particular benefit.

TECHNOLOGY AND TELECOMMUTING

One answer that seems to be "right" for a growing number of American workers is telecommuting: working at home, typically using computers and communications technology, rather than spending all of their time in an office. This variation on the flextime theme deserves special attention because it represents the best in corporate responsibility—the search for better performance, coupled with the development of new technologies and management innovations, leading to a result with profound and positive social implications.

Telecommuting is not a completely new idea. McCormick's U.S. West, in its previous incarnation as part of the Bell system, had telephone switchboards in employees' homes in the 1920s.[38] And, of course, most economic production occurred in or around workers' homes for most of human history. But the advent of cheap and portable computers, modems, on-line services, phone mail, and cellular phones have given workers virtually all the technological "horsepower" available to them at an office, thus liberating many companies and workers to think through home-based work arrangements. "Telecommuting has gone from a curious oddity or novelty to a very well-accepted and proven business practice," said Gil Gordon, head of a New Jersey–based workplace reengineering firm. "It is no longer experimental, no longer new. The evolution of an innovation has occurred."[39]

The extent of telecommuting is surprising, particularly given the fact that its modern incarnation has appeared only in the past few years. By 1995, there were approximately 11 million telecommuters in the American workforce, estimates Link Resources Corporation, up from only 2.2 million in 1988.[40] That includes only salaried workers. Paul and Sarah Edwards, authors of *Working from Home,* report that in 1993 some 32 million Americans worked at home either for themselves or for someone else.[41] Nor do telecommuters all work from home full-time. A *USA Today* poll in 1995 identified 27 million people who worked on a computer at work and at home in some combination, representing 41 percent of all computer users.[42] But even using new technologies to work at home part of the week, these telecommuters and home-based entrepreneurs are revolutionizing not only work and family relationships but also business productivity.

Telecommuting does not necessarily resolve a worker's child-care needs; bouncing a child on one knee and balancing a laptop computer on the other is not likely to lead to either good parenting or good work. But by freeing workers from a 9-to-5, drive-to-work-and-back straightjacket, telecommuting lets families make better use of their time and thus accommodate more attention to children and family needs without sacrificing careers. Alison Holt Brummelkamp gave up her title as vice president at Golin-Harris Communications Inc., a public relations agency in Los Angeles, to work a compressed four-day week, three of those days from home. "I was working 70 hours a week," Brummelkamp said. "I never saw my kids."[43] Susan Sears, a public relations manager for AT & T in the company's New Jersey district, lives in Phoenix, Arizona. She telecommutes from 6 A.M. (8 A.M. Eastern time) to 3 P.M. "My husband helps get the kids off to school, so I don't see them a lot in the morning," she said. "But I'm there for the afternoon activities, which takes the pressure off him."[44] Joyce Wilcox, a medical transcriptionist for Florida Hospital in Altamonte Springs, Florida, typically works from 6 A.M. to 2 P.M. "It's wonderful because you can be available for your kids," she said. "You are physically there. And if they were sick, I didn't miss a day of work."[45] Graphics designer Mary Stoddard found that having her studio at home gave her more time with her children. "By being [at home] where everything's in one central location, I save on baby-sitting costs and get work done in the time I used to spend driving my kids here and there," she said. By scheduling their work during times in which children are at school or asleep, some home-based workers can even afford to be essentially full-time parents.[46] Computers and other home-office technology, said Tom Miller of New York–based Emerging Technologies Research Group, "allow you to juggle work and home life a lot more flexibly than you could 10 years ago."[47]

Companies and workers, however, do not just use telecommuting as a way to improve work and family situations. Experience demonstrates that many workers are more productive when they work from home and have more direct control over their workday. "We're finally coming to the conclusion that the office is a terrible place to work," Gordon said. "It's not just the wear and tear of getting there. It's the noise, the interruptions, the endless meetings." In a recent Conference Board study of 155 employers, almost 50 percent of respondents said that the greatest benefit of telecommuting programs was increased employee productivity.[48] Hewlett-Packard Co. found that its work-at-home employees in technical support handled 20 percent more calls than its on-site workers did. Ameritech Corporation in Chicago had similar results with its telecommuting program.[49] AT & T, with more than eight thousand telecommuting employees, reports that productivity in some areas has improved by 45 percent. Nancy Montrone, a higher-education client representative for IBM in Buffalo, New York, found that working from home allowed her to manage her time more efficiently. "You set your own agenda for the day," she said. "This is the first time in my job that I have been able to write a to-do list for the day and finish it. I feel more like an entrepreneur." Overall, IBM says its productivity has improved between 15 and 20 percent due to telecommuting.[50]

Another reason an increasing number of companies and workers are embracing telecommuting is that it has the potential to save such costs as office rent, insurance, and transportation. IBM saved more than $1 million in real estate costs by increasing the number of telecommuters like Montone at its Buffalo office. "We used to occupy three floors of this building and now we take up only one-third of one floor," said Mike Guerinot, the office's senior manager. "Now we can do contracts right from our living rooms."[51] Similarly, by moving twelve thousand account representatives into their homes, AT & T saved $80 million in 1994 in real estate costs.[52]

The latest impetus for companies and employees to rethink workplace flexibility has been the development of affordable, powerful laptop computers that give workers opportunities to translate previously wasted time, at home or on the road, into work time. Laptop sales grew by 45 percent in 1994 alone, and industry analysts expect some 21 million will be sold by the turn of the century. In New Jersey, IBM closed its regional sales headquarters, gave its sales personnel laptops, and sent them on the road.[53] The development of the laptop is a good example of how businesses seeking profit can have a tremendous impact on society by introducing new goods and services, in this case by revolutionizing the use of information and by allowing more flexible work and family arrangements.

As with other work and family programs, telecommuting requires the acceptance of managers and, in some cases, the development of new, performance-based ways to measure employee work effort. Also, to repeat an earlier point, telecommuting will have only limited usefulness for some businesses that must manufacture products or provide services to customers on-site. But for many other firms and entrepreneurs, working from home—which is made possible by the private development of new communications and information technologies—represents an effective way to reconcile work and family responsibilities. For them, it is a win-win proposition.

EMPLOYEE ASSISTANCE PROGRAMS

Another benefit that many companies offer their workers is an employee assistance program (EAP). Such a program often includes free or subsidized counseling by private therapists on issues such as substance abuse, marriage, and parenting. Some companies hold employee workshops on personal finance, finding a good school, or dealing with stress. They do this not just because they care about their employees, but because they believe the company's interests are served by addressing family and social problems.

Advocates of EAPs point to examples like that of Engelhard Corporation, a New Jersey–based chemical manufacturer. In 1981 Joseph Steinreich came to Huntsville, Alabama, to manage two Engelhard plants. He found the plants had a 150 percent turnover rate, 18 percent product waste, and a high number of serious worker injuries. Steinreich came to the conclusion that most of these problems stemmed from excessive absenteeism, particularly among workers with substance abuse or other problems. "There were some Friday nights we couldn't even run," said plant superintendent Sharon Hobbs. "It was horrible." Steinreich established an EAP, hired an on-site psychologist available to workers one day a week and by beeper, and introduced flexible work hours and other family initiatives. The company saw absentee rates fall from twenty days a year to three, and annual turnover and product waste rates dropped below 1 percent.[54]

The Hay Group, a management consulting firm, estimated in 1994 that almost 70 percent of U.S. companies offer EAPs of some sort. Firms view reduced absenteeism, greater productivity, and lower costs for health and workers' compensation claims as the key reasons for offering such programs.[55] Drug and/or alcohol abuse counseling is the most frequently provided service, but this may soon be eclipsed by family and parenting counseling.[56] Great Western Bank in Northridge, California, has offered parenting classes to its employees (whose average age is thirty-four and who are 70 percent female) since 1990. Attendance has been consistently strong. San Francisco–based Pacific Gas and Electric Co. saw similar interest after it began offering seminars on child development and education; of 2,500 employees, 50 percent attended at least one seminar. Apple Computer Inc. in Cupertino, California, also offers parenting assistance. "Our average age is thirty-four, and our employees are feeling more stress due to greater workloads and reorganization in the Silicon Valley," said Courtney Murrell, manager of fitness programs. "The programs give the employees peace of mind and the tools to handle their personal lives better, making them more productive on the job because they can better balance life as a whole." Renee Noll, senior human resources representative at New York–based Bausch & Lomb Inc., said the same about her company's employee assistance program, noting that "by helping our workforce deal more effectively with family issues, our employees will be more productive and more focused."[57] Effective programs can also reduce company costs for benefits such as leaves or health claims. A 1992 study at Waste Management Inc., which offers parenting support groups, found that among those employees who attended the training, benefits usage decreased by 50 percent, leading to a savings of $1,600 for each employee who attended.[58]

Other companies have had less success with employee assistance programs, however, demonstrating that it is important to evaluate family-friendly policies on the basis of quantifiable benefits rather than intention. The decision to offer counseling or seminars to workers is similar to those made by corporate managers in other areas of their operations: Should I do it in-house or outsource it instead? Money spent on EAPs is presumably money not spent on other employee benefits or on salary (with which employees can purchase their own counseling or education). To be worthwhile, company programs must be based on expertise or experience not obviously available to workers, or tied closely to reducing company costs and increasing company productivity.[59] For some firms offering EAPs, these standards do not seem to have been met. A survey by A. Foster Higgins & Co. Inc. of New York found that 41 percent of employers offering EAPs had no idea what effect their programs had on their costs, while only 25 percent said their program had reduced costs, 20 percent reported no change, and 15 percent reported increased costs.[60]

Employee assistance programs may not be worth their investment, but that should not be a company's only concern. Another pitfall for companies with counseling programs is that questions of confidentiality can lead to worker disaffection or even legal liability. In one case, employee Robert Bratt sued IBM after being asked to go on leave by the firm, which had found out that its own company-paid psychologist had diagnosed Bratt as paranoid and mentally unstable. Bratt contended that his privacy had been invaded and that his diagnosis should have been considered confidential.[61]

CONCLUSION

Helping employees cope with family responsibilities, personal problems, and stress makes good financial sense for businesses, which is why most do so. But that does not mean that all firms will offer generous child-care benefits, leave policies, or other particular programs. Of greatest value, especially to workers at small companies, may simply be flexibility—the ability of managers to accommodate family needs and to support employees as they address their own personal problems. "The need for flexibility to solve work and family problems," noted *Business Week* in an editorial, "is beginning to look like nothing more than an extension of the growing corporate need for flexibility in all its staffing requirements."[62] Donna Wagner of the National Council on the Aging made the same point in the context of elder care. "Employers don't need to turn themselves into aging-service providers to address this issue, nor do they have to spend a lot of money," she said. "They need to alter the culture within the company so it supports family caregiving." Flexible scheduling and referral services are two ways to do this, she added.[63]

A 1995 survey for the Families and Work Institute by Louis Harris & Associates demonstrates the extent to which companies and working parents already seem to have come to satisfactory arrangements regarding work and family responsibilities. Of working women surveyed, 59 percent said they were "very valued" by others for fulfilling their responsibilities at work and at home, with another 35 percent saying they were "somewhat valued." These are hardly the responses of women in the throes of despair. A majority of respondents also disagreed with the statement "I wish I could give up some of my responsibilities," although working women also picked "balancing work and family life" as their second greatest worry among workplace issues (employee benefits was number one). At the same time, only 15 percent of working mothers said they would work full-time if they didn't have to for financial reasons, with a third (and 28 percent of men surveyed) opting for part-time work and another 31 percent (21 percent of men) saying they would rather work at home caring for their families.[64] There is a strong sense of progress in work and family issues, in other words, but also a continuing interest in more flexible arrangements, involving part-time or home-based work, that allow parents to spend more time at home.

Companies cannot afford to be surrogate parents or constant thera-pists, but they also cannot afford to ignore personal problems of workers that inevitably intrude on their job performance. Responsible companies recognize that valuable employees with years of training and experience are assets that are not easily replaceable. Often it will be worth the time, effort, and expense to retain them. "You cannot make business decisions about competing in today's world without considering the people who have to 'buy' the change," said Rodgers of Work/Family Directions. "If you can figure out how to compete and figure out how your people will help you do it, you'll be way ahead of the game."[65]

CONCLUSION

Corporate social responsibility, despite its prominence in legal and academic debates for almost half a century, remains more a set of complaints and criticisms than it is a real managerial alternative to traditional views of corporate organization and purpose. By detaching management decisions from their moorings to shareholder value, corporate social responsibility would in practice leave managers with the impossible task of trying to balance competing claims from workers, consumers, lenders, social activists, and other so-called stakeholders.[1] In juggling these claims, managers would lack the decision rule—returning the highest value to shareholders—that currently allows them to set priorities and that makes markets work. "At the end of the day," said Nell Minow of the Lens consultancy in Washington, "the calculus has to come down to what is good for shareholders. Otherwise, what have you got?"[2] Should unexpected corporate revenues be given to workers in higher wages? To consumers in lower prices? To shareholders in higher dividends? To local charities in higher donations? Without a clear function in mind for the organization they head, managers would be left to make essentially political rather than economic decisions. As Friedman pointed out in his famous 1970 essay on corporate responsibility: "Here the businessman—self-selected or appointed directly or indirectly by stockholders—is to be simultaneously legislator, executive, and jurist. . . . He becomes in effect a public employee, a civil servant, even though he remains in name an employee of a private enterprise."[3]

191

Of course, some corporate critics are comfortable with the notion that corporate managers should be, in effect, public servants. In the Fall 1994 issue of *Business and Society Review,* a journal popular with corporate social responsibility advocates, business scholar S. Prakesh Sethi called on corporations to elevate their CEOs to the status of public figures. Under his "investiture" system, executives would make the equivalent of campaign promises, which would later be evaluated by journalists and regulators. Business leadership, he argued, should be made more like leadership in other social institutions. "Philosopher kings are not unknown in history," Sethi wrote. "Philosopher scientists are common-place today. Isn't it time that we asked for philosopher managers to run our major economic institutions?"[4]

Economists who understand the nature of information in a market and the inefficiency of central planning would cringe at this application of political thinking to corporate management, as well they should. But even Plato, from whom the concept of the philosopher king comes, set limits to the power of rulers in his ideal Republic that modern-day business analysts would be wise to study. In his society, philosopher kings of the "guardian class" would, indeed, make political decisions; the fighting class of warriors would protect the city from internal or external enemies; and the remaining citizens would conduct the commercial life of the Republic. For Plato, the source of the greatest injustice in this ideal society would be for members of one class to attempt to do the work or emulate the behavior of another class. The result would be corruption, inefficiency, and vice. A "craftsman who is a moneymaker by nature" would be disastrous as a guardian or soldier, he noted, just as a guardian or soldier would be a horrible craftsman. "The meddling and interchange between the three classes would be the greatest damage to the city, and would rightly be entitled ... injustice."[5] More specifically, *The Republic*'s Socrates suggests, the political decisions of guardians should not extend to "contracts which different classes of people make in the market."[6]

REALITY AND RESULT

In the real world of pension-fund stockholding, *Money* magazine cover stories on "hot" mutual funds, competition for consumers and workers on a worldwide scale, and "quicksilver capital" flowing in and out of investments and countries at the touch of a button, there is neither a principled nor a practical alternative to the corporate goal of maximizing share-holder return. In today's economy, corporate managers who ignore their contract with providers of equity and liability often find themselves with a declining company or even without a job.

The corporate social responsibility movement is trapped in an unrealistic, ahistorical view of commercial activity. Critics of corporations zero in on the stories like the *Exxon Valdez* oil spill or the Bhopal chemical-plant disaster because they are well-known to the public, who have been told ceaselessly by news and entertainment media that businesses are corrupt, destructive institutions. The positive, indeed revolutionary, ways in which corporations have made the everyday lives of Americans better over the past half-century are rarely recognized. All too often we take for granted what goes right and dwell on disasters and villains—which are notable precisely because of their exceptional status. In the search for heroes, we enshrine political leaders or military commanders or TV cops or movie action heroes or the glorious protagonists of our mythical and legendary past. But those who create the amenities we enjoy and the innovations that make our lives safer, healthier, and happier exist, with very few exceptions, in relative obscurity. Business innovation may determine our standard of living and solve the basic problems of humanity, but it is not often seen as heroic.[7]

This is unfortunate. "The creation and distribution of goods and services elevate the quality of life," said business author Charles E. Watson. "To view the creation of wealth as an evil suggests that lives spent in the miseries of hunger and privation are better than those living with plenty."[8] When Yvon Chouinard wrote in the mail-order catalog of Patagonia, the company he heads, that he wanted his firm to offer fewer products in order to "save the planet," he was, indeed, equating material comfort with evil. "Last fall, you had a choice of five ski pants," he told his customers, "now you may choose between two. This is, of course, un-American, but two styles of ski pants are all that anyone needs."[9] (Fortunately, other firms also sell ski pants, so those customers who can no longer find what they want from "socially responsible" Patagonia can find it elsewhere.) Paul Solman, business correspondent for public television's "MacNeil/Lehrer NewsHour," echoed Chouinard with a call for lower economic expectations. "Many of us, I imagine, can in fact make do with less—less stuff for Christmas, fewer electronic gadgets, even, let's face it, less food," he said.[10]

One need not be a materialist to understand how profoundly silly such thinking is. Commerce is not an evil to be combated or a superfluous luxury to be minimized. It is not subject to "limits to growth," as the neo-Malthusians of the 1960s and 1970s warned. It is merely the process by which human beings better their lives and their families' lives. Some corporate executives have confidently defended the benefits of business. Robert Mercer, CEO of Goodyear Tire & Rubber Co., said he saw his firm as "a corporation that's providing freedom and mobility to people in this country and around the world." Former K-Mart CEO Bernard M. Fauber reflected that he saw the company's mission as being "the best place to shop . . . not just price, but to get something for your price, to be treated well, and to shop in pleasant surroundings." Ted Saenger, president of Pacific Bell, explained that his company was "part of the infrastructure. If we don't do our job right, a lot of people can't do their thing right. And so quality telecommunications and allowing business and social interaction and movement of information to take place over our network . . . are pretty important."[11]

The commercial search for profit not only expands the choices available to consumers but also generates the wealth required to accomplish non-commercial objectives. John Nelvin, former chairman and CEO of Firestone, never felt defensive about the social responsibilities of his corporation:

> I don't apologize for being a businessman. . . . The fact is that most of the good things that happen in this world can only happen because somebody else is also generating wealth. So generating wealth is a *sine qua non*. There is no way you have educational communities in this country, there is no way you have hospitals, there is no way you have homes for the aged, there's no way you have the social programs that deal with poverty and all, unless you're also generating wealth.[12]

As we have seen, American business creates jobs, treats workers fairly, supports educational innovation, trains employees, contributes to the health of cities, discovers new drugs and medical treatments, makes workplaces and products safer, conserves resources, invents ways to save energy and reduce or eliminate waste, gives women and minorities unparalleled economic opportunities, and contributes to the stability and quality of life of families. It does all these things not in spite of its search for the highest possible return to shareholders, but because of it.

American businesses contribute to the progress and well-being of society because they must. If firms mistreat workers, they cannot be productive. If firms ignore issues of education and skills among young people, they will not be productive in the future. If they discriminate against women and minorities, they pay the price in the market for employees and for consumers. If they ignore the wastes they generate, they pay higher energy bills and disposal fees. Most importantly, if firms fail to take advantage of the opportunities they see to create new products or services to solve society's problems, then they will surely lose profits to their competitors.

It is through invention and innovation—a process that extends from the laboratory to the factory floor to the delivery truck to the retail store— that business makes its most significant social contribution. Governments are not good at promoting innovation. The history of government research and development efforts is largely one of false starts, misallocation of resources, and manipulation of markets by politically connected monopolists. Billions of dollars have been spent over the years by the U.S. government in an attempt to foster technological innovation. In contrast, government policymakers have consistently missed the boat on technologies that proved to be invaluable. Samuel Morse, for example, conducted the first successful test of his telegraph design in 1844. Shortly afterward, he and his antsy business partners tried to sell the design to the federal government for $100,000. Congress said no; private industry said yes. Some thirty years later Alexander Graham Bell tried to sell his telephone to the government for the same amount, and he also was refused.[13] The country is, of course, fortunate that neither sale occurred, but the point is that governments have an extremely poor track record of recognizing true innovation and rewarding it.

Some corporate critics contend that businesses, seeking profit in a marketplace, will always underinvest in new ideas and new technologies because they cannot capture all the benefits of the innovation for themselves. The patent and copyright system helps protect corporate investments to some extent, but it by no means eliminates the possibility of imitation (just ask Apple, which lost its infringement suit against Microsoft over the Windows operating system). American inventiveness, however, is not a new phenomenon related to government expenditures for education and research. It predates government research budgets and large state universities. Throughout the late eighteenth and nineteenth centuries, American entrepreneurs—often with little to no schooling—were responsible for many of the world's most important industrial and technological discoveries.[14] Obviously, innovation on the whole is related more to markets and competition than it is related to the growth of governmental or philanthropic endeavors.

Moreover, these critics have an extremely narrow view of how businesses make decisions. In many cases, firms patent and produce new products that they know could be imitated by competitors. It is frequently still in their interest to do so, as a 1995 study in the *Southern Economic Journal* demonstrated. In many industries where the future path of innovation is uncertain, the most profit-maximizing policy for individual firms is to invest strongly in research and development. "It pays to be an innovator rather than an imitator," stated the study's author, Illinois State University researcher Rajeev K. Goel, because the initial boon to the bottom line is often larger than the subsequent costs of imitation.[15] Of course, investing in innovation does not simply mean spending money. Even as formal corporate R & D budgets have grown slowly if at all in recent years, the productivity and effectiveness of corporate R & D has increased significantly. Companies are using labor-saving devices, closer cooperation among business units, and productive relationships with outside sources of technology to get more bang out of the research buck.[16]

SOCIETAL DIVISION OF LABOR

"The basic idea of corporate social responsibility," stated University of Pittsburgh scholar Donna J. Wood, "is that business and society are interwoven rather than distinct entities; therefore, society has certain expectations for appropriate business behavior and outcomes."[17] Despite the pronouncements of corporate social responsibility advocates like Wood, different institutions do have different purposes to serve and roles to play in society, as Plato recognized many centuries ago. Modernity and technological sophistication have not invalidated these long-recognized differences. Commercial activity conducted by corporations and other forms of business is fundamentally different from the type of activity conducted by coercive governments or by voluntary, philanthropic organizations. For the society to function, each institution must operate according to its own unique purpose. A simple demarcation of responsibilities might go something like this:

- *Businesses exist to make and sell things.* They thrive on competition, on prices, on freely negotiated contracts, on optimism, and on a search for innovation and productivity.
- *Governments exist to take and protect things.* They thrive on a monopoly of sovereignty and authority, on providing necessary services to all without separate prices or negotiations, on realism, and on a search for justice and safety.
- *Charities exist to give things away.* They thrive on cooperation, on gifts, on volunteerism and services, on altruism or religious values, and on a search for compassion and enlightenment.

Each type of institution helps to solve society's problems and advance the common good. Consider the issue near and dear to the hearts of most critics of American corporations: the environment. Government clearly has a role to play defining and protecting individual rights to clean air and water. That means setting reasonable standards for emissions of potentially hazardous substances. Charities, too, have a role to play by collecting donations and marshaling volunteer efforts to protect endangered species and to ensure that ecological values are appreciated by citizens and policymakers. The role of business is no less crucial: to find ways to produce the goods and services that individuals want and need at the lowest possible cost in resources and energy output. To expect these institutions to mix and match responsibilities—for businesses to act as standard-setting governments or as environmental charities—is to compromise the unique benefits that each form of social organization can provide.

Social responsibility, then, must be defined according to the type of social institution to which it is applied. Corporations and governments clearly have different social responsibilities; what is proper in one context is improper in another. Author Jane Jacobs examined this issue at length in a remarkable 1992 book called *Strategies of Survival,* which took the form of a modern-day version of a Socratic dialogue. Following Plato's lead, Jacobs' characters identified two distinct "syndromes" of ethical behavior: commercial and guardian. Ethical problems occur when people "syndrome-hop"—that is, when they apply the expectations and methods of one form of activity to another. She noted that when businesses pay employees by commission to motivate greater sales, the resulting incentives help maximize return to shareholders. When governments pay police officers by the number of traffic citations they write, however, the result is injustice and corruption. Similarly, to attempt to run commercial institutions such as corporations as if they were governments or charities is to invite inefficiency and to harm the common good.[18]

Advocates of corporate social responsibility have tried to invalidate the distinction between commercial activity and guardian activity by arguing that, in effect, whatever is socially responsible (according to their definition) is also best for business. As we have seen, sometimes this is true. Businesses that concern themselves with the skills, health, safety, and productivity of their workers tend to do better than businesses that shortsightedly neglect these issues. Nevertheless, successful businesses undertake these activities with a close eye on the bottom line: the payoff in productivity must be worth the cost. Moreover, some policies that advocates say are socially responsible—such as the environmental extremism of Patagonia, or the implementation of racial or gender quotas to match some supposedly "correct" mix of workers—clearly do not advance profitability. The notion that there exists a set of common principles and standards (other than profitability) with which corporate managers can judge their efforts is false. Studies seeking a correlation between profits or stock-market performance on the one hand, and particular "socially responsible" views on the part of corporate managers or workers on the other, have generally failed to find any.[19]

TRUE CORPORATE IRRESPONSIBILITY

The major way in which corporations can and do become irresponsible is precisely when they employ tactics and behaviors of other institutions. When businessmen kill their competitors or extort money from them at the point of a gun, we properly call them gangsters. Similarly, when corporate leaders use political contributions and lobbyists to protect themselves from competition and to obtain taxpayer subsidies, they are no longer engaged in commercial activity—characterized by Friedman as the search for *justly obtained* profit.[20] When corporations bargain in bad faith or distribute misinformation to workers and consumers, they fail Friedman's test as well. The use of force (directly or indirectly through the manipulation of government power) and fraud make freely negotiated and mutually beneficial contracts impossible. They strike at the very heart of why a corporation exists and how it should function.[21]

To identify justly obtained profit as the proper function of corporations is to define their social responsibilities in a way very different from that proposed by most corporate social responsibility advocates. Rather than measuring social responsibility by such yardsticks as layoffs, charitable donations, health insurance coverage, or racial quotas, analysts should instead seek answers to these important ethical questions:

- Are corporations obtaining their profits through force or fraud?
- Are corporations putting the investments at their disposal to the most economically productive use?
- Are corporate managers fulfilling their contractual obligations to shareholders by allocating resources and investments to achieve the highest return to those who supply equity and liability to the enterprise?
- Are corporate managers competing successfully for workers and customers by employing innovative technologies and management strategies, training workers to be productive and safe, and avoiding racial or other prejudices?
- Are corporations (through example and through participation in philosophical, social, and political debate) upholding and defending the principles of voluntary exchange, free markets, and societal division of labor on which their existence is predicated?

These are some of the questions that a truly responsible corporate leader would want to be able to answer in the affirmative. In order for American business to fulfill its unique role in our society, those who lead and manage corporations must be willing to defend the benefits of markets and the morality of profit-seeking behavior.[22] Business schools must teach their students that the search for owner or shareholder return is the process by which economic enterprises add value to society.[23] As General Motors executive Henry Grady Weaver observed half a century ago, business has the ultimate responsibility for explaining and promoting its own contribution to the common good:

> In the role of salesmen for America, perhaps we might become more appreciative of our own product, more steadfast in holding to the faith of our fathers, more alert in resisting the alluring promises of false Utopias, which . . . have kept the vast majority of people underfed, poorly clothed, embroiled in wars, and surrounded by famine, pestilence, and human degradation.[24]

NOTES

Introduction

1. Henry Grady Weaver, *The Mainspring of Human Progress* (Irvington-on-Hudson, New York: Foundation for Economic Education, 1984 [13th edition]), p. 11.
2. Ibid., pp. 11–12.
3. See Nicholas Eberstadt, "Population, Food, and Income: Global Trends in the Twentieth Century," in Ronald Bailey, editor, *The True State of the Planet* (New York: Free Press, 1995), pp. 7–48.
4. Ibid., p. 12.
5. Karl Zinsmeister, "Payday Mayday," *American Enterprise,* September/October 1995, p. 48.
6. Ibid., p. 15.
7. S. Robert Lichter, Linda S. Lichter, and Stanley Rothman, *Video Villains: The TV Businessman 1955–1986* (Washington, D.C.: Center for Media and Public Affairs, 1987), pp. 17–21.
8. S. Robert Lichter, Linda S. Lichter, and Daniel Amundson, "Does Hollywood Hate Business or Money?" (Washington, D.C.: Center for Media and Public Affairs, 1994), p. 27.
9. Ibid., p. 26.
10. Ibid., p. 28.
11. Karlyn H. Bowman and Everett Carll Ladd, editors, "Public Opinion and Demographic Report," *American Enterprise,* November/December 1993, pp. 86–88.
12. Bowman and Ladd, "Opinion Pulse," *American Enterprise,* January/February 1995, p. 106.

13. Bowman and Ladd, 1993, p. 86.
14. Edwin M. Epstein, "The Corporate Social Policy Process: Beyond Business Ethics, Corporate Social Responsibility, and Corporate Social Responsiveness," *California Management Review,* Vol. 29, No. 3, Spring 1987, p. 101.
15. Donna J. Wood and Philip L. Cochran, "Business and Society in Transition," *Business and Society,* Spring 1992, p. 1.
16. Burton W. Folsom, Jr., *Entrepreneurs vs. the State: A New Look at the Rise of Big Business in America, 1840–1920* (Reston, Virginia: Young America's Foundation, 1987).
17. Jerry Mander, "The Myth of the Corporate Conscience," *Business and Society Review,* Spring 1993, p. 62.
18. LynNell Hancock, "Breaking Point," *Newsweek,* March 6, 1995, p. 58.
19. *These Are the Good Old Days,* 1993 Annual Report, Federal Reserve Bank of Dallas, 1994, pp. 7–8. The "overworked American" thesis is based almost totally on public opinion surveys, not on employment data. It relies "heavily on people's ability to estimate, in response to a snap survey question, where their time goes during the week." See John P. Robinson and Geoffrey Godbey, "Are Average Americans Really Overworked?" *American Enterprise,* September/October 1995, p. 43.
20. Bowman and Ladd, 1995, pp. 105–106.
21. Paul Hawken, "The Ecology of Commerce," *Inc.,* April 1992, pp. 93–94.
22. Bowman and Ladd, 1993, pp. 84, 88.
23. Michael Novak, *Free Persons and the Common Good* (Lanham, Maryland: Madison Books, 1989), pp. 100–102.
24. Students, in particular, need to gain a better understanding of how the search for economic return can drive social progress. Surveys of business executives and business students often show that the two groups differ in how they view corporate social responsibility and the importance of economic performance. See Nabil A. Ibrahim and John A. Angelidis, "Corporate Social Responsibility: A Comparative Analysis of Perceptions of Top Executives and Business Students," *Mid-Atlantic Journal of Business,* Vol. 28, No. 3, December 1993, pp. 303–314.
25. Franklin invented a stove, the rocking chair, bifocal spectacles, and experimented with electricity. Jefferson's innovations ran the gamut from botany and agricultural techninque to engineering, architecture, and law. Paine drew up the plans and supervised the construction of the first single-span iron bridge with crisscross struts. See Weaver, p. 234.
26. Ibid.

Chapter 1. Responsible to Whom?

1. Lawrence J. Haas, "Corporate Do-Gooders," *National Journal,* August 1, 1992, p. 1779.
2. Ibid.
3. Peter Hong, "Invasion of the MBA Liberals," *Business Week,* October 19, 1992, p. 33.

4. Richard Evans, "Business Ethics and Changes in Society," *Journal of Business Ethics,* No. 10, 1991, p. 872.
5. "Can Slower Growth Save the World?" *Business and Society Review,* Spring 1993, No. 85, p. 10.
6. U.S. Department of Commerce, *Survey of Current Business,* March 1995, Vol. 75, No. 3.
7. Thomas M. Jones, "Corporate Social Responsibility Revisited, Redefined," *California Management Review,* Vol. 22, No. 2, Spring 1980, p. 61.
8. Shelby D. Green, "Corporate Philanthropy and the Business Benefit: The Need for Clarity," *Golden Gate University Law Review,* Vol. 20, 1990, p. 246.
9. Daniel J. Morrissey, "Toward a New/Old Theory of Corporate Social Responsibility," *Syracuse Law Review,* Vol. 40, 1989, p. 1008.
10. Ibid., p. 1011.
11. Green, pp. 248–249.
12. *New York Stock Exchange Fact Book* (New York: New York Stock Exchange, Inc., 1995), p. 83.
13. Bill Shaw and Frederick R. Post, "A Moral Basis for Corporate Philanthropy," *Journal of Business Ethics,* No. 12, 1993, pp. 748–749.
14. Robert Kuttner, "The Corporation in America: Is It Socially Redeemable?" *Dissent,* Winter 1993, p. 35.
15. R. Eric Reidenbach and Donald P. Robin, *Ethics and Profits: A Convergence of Corporate America's Economic and Social Responsibilities* (Englewood Cliffs, New Jersey: Prentice Hall, 1989), p. 65.
16. Green, p. 251.
17. Ibid.
18. Milton Friedman, "The Social Responsibility of Business Is to Increase Its Profits," *New York Times Magazine,* September 13, 1970, p. 33.
19. Ibid., p. 125.
20. Ibid., p. 33.
21. Ibid., p. 124.
22. Jeffrey Nesteruk, "Corporations, Shareholders, and Moral Choice: A New Perspective on Corporate Social Responsibility," *Cincinnati Law Review,* Vol. 58, 1989, p. 460.
23. Colin Grant, "Friedman Fallacies," *Journal of Business Ethics,* Vol. 10, 1991, p. 908.
24. Jones. p. 61.
25. Grant A. Brown, "Are Profits Deserved?" *Journal of Business Ethics,* No. 11, 1992, p. 110.
26. "Milton Friedman Responds," *Business and Society Review,* Spring 1972, p. 6.
27. Stephen M. Bainbridge, "In Defense of the Shareholder Wealth Maximization Norm: A Reply to Professor Green," *Washington and Lee Law Review,* Vol. 50, No. 4, Fall 1993, p. 1426.
28. Friedman, p. 9.
29. Ibid.
30. *New York Stock Exchange Fact Book,* pp. 79–81.
31. Bainbridge, p. 1429.

32. "Milton Friedman Responds," p. 7
33. Ibid.

Chapter 2. A Social Investment Balance Sheet

1. The first recipient of the prize was William Bolander, an automotive engineer recognized for his inventions in General Motors' Saturn and Powertrain divisions. His work has made cars better, cheaper, and safer. The lifetime achievement award was given to William Hewlett and David Packard, whose familiar company's first innovation was an audio oscillator that Walt Disney used to make the music for *Fantasia*. See Joanne Kenen, "New $500,000 Prize Aims to Make Inventing Admirable," Reuters News Service, March 29, 1995 (downloaded from CD NewsBank).
2. Anne Lowrey Bailey, "This Inventor's Latest: a New Foundation," *Chronicle of Philanthropy*, August 10, 1995, p. 8.
3. "General Patent," *Entrepreneur*, March 1994, p. 93.
4. Otis Port, "Inspiration, Perspiration—or Manipulation?" *Business Week*, April 3, 1995, p. 56.
5. Srikumar S. Rao, "Tomorrow's Rosetta Stones," *Financial World*, November 22, 1994, p. 71.
6. "General Patent," p. 93.
7. Hanna Rosin, "The Evil Empire," *New Republic*, September 11, 1995, p. 22.
8. Shelby D. Green, "Corporate Philanthropy and the Business Benefit: The Need for Clarity," *Golden Gate University Law Review*, Vol. 20, No. 239, 1990, pp. 248–249.
9. Craig Smith, "The New Corporate Philanthropy," *Harvard Business Review*, May–June 1994, pp. 107–108.
10. Ann Kaplan, editor, *Giving USA 1994: The Annual Report on Philanthropy for the Year 1993* (New York: AAFC Trust for Philanthropy, 1994), pp. 20–21.
11. Patricia Donovan Wright, "Amoco Refines Its Giving," *Philanthropy*, Vol. 8, No. 2, Spring 1994, p. 8.
12. Nelson Schwartz, "Giving—and Getting Something Back," *Business Week*, August 28, 1995, p. 81.
13. Menlo F. Smith, "Can Corporations be Charitable?" *CEI Update*, Washington, D.C.: Competitive Enterprise Institute, Vol. 6, No. 9, September 1993, p. 3.
14. Schwartz, p. 81.
15. Irving Warner, "Corporations Have Lost Sight of Philanthropy," *Chronicle of Philanthropy*, August 10, 1995, p. 46.
16. Smith, p. 105.
17. Marc J. Epstein, "The Fall of Corporate Charitable Contributions," *Public Relations Quarterly*, Vol. 38, No. 2, Summer 1993, pp. 37–40.
18. Mescon and Tilson, p. 56.
19. Ibid., pp. 56–57.
20. Edward J. Stendardi, Jr., "Corporate Philanthropy: The Redefinition of Enlightened Self-Interest," *Social Science Journal*, Vol. 29, No. 1, p. 26.

21. Smith, p. 109.
22. Mescon and Tilson, p. 54.
23. Mescon and Tilson, p. 57.
24. Smith, p. 112.
25. Ken Barun, "McGiving," *Philanthropy,* Vol 8, No. 2, Spring 1994, p. 13.
26. Don Oldenburg, "Big Companies Plug Big Causes for Big Gains," *Business and Society Review,* Spring 1992, p. 23.
27. Barbara Ettorre, "Charity Begins at Home," *Management Review,* February 1995, p. 35.
28. "1993–94 Bowl Games," *Information Please Sports Almanac,* CompuServe, 1995.
29. Mescon and Tilson, p. 52.
30. Udayan Gupta, "Cause-Driven Companies' New Cause: Profits," *Wall Street Journal,* November 8, 1994, p. B1.
31. Justin Martin, "Good Citizenship Is Good Business," *Fortune,* March 21, 1994, p. 15.
32. In 1984 Harry Darling, a vice president of the American Marketing Association, said that "there's a strong feeling among companies who have researched the subject that deeds speak louder than words." Actually, deeds don't speak at all. Philip Maher, "What Corporations Get by Giving," *Business Marketing,* December 1984, p. 84.
33. Ettorre, p. 34.
34. Avery Hunt, "Strategic Philanthropy," *Across the Board,* July/August 1986, p. 23.
35. Shari Caudron, "Volunteerism and the Bottom Line," *Industry Week,* February 21, 1994, pp. 14–15.
36. Diane Filipowski, "Structure Supports Volunteer Efforts," *Personnel Journal,* March 1993, pp. 79–81.
37. Jo Thornton, "Employee Involvement in Community Activities: Can It Be a Matter of Choice?" *Bank Marketing,* October 1991, p. 37.
38. Caudron, p. 14.
39. Louis W. Fry, Gerald D. Keim, and Roger E. Meiners, "Corporate Contributions: Altruistic or For-Profit?" *Academy of Management Journal,* Vol. 25, No. 1, 1982, pp. 94–106.
40. Schwartz, p. 81.
41. Kaplan, pp. 164–167.
42. Stuart Nolan, *Patterns of Corporate Philanthropy* (Washington, D.C.: Capital Research Center, 1994), p. 9.
43. Hunt, p. 24.
44. Lois Therrien, "Corporate Generosity Is Greatly Depreciated," *Business Week,* November 2, 1992, p. 118.
45. Milton Moskowitz, "When Your Conscience Needs a Guide," *Business and Society Review,* No. 83, Fall 1992, p. 71.
46. Robert H. Stovall, "When Do-Gooders Do Good," *Financial World,* September 1, 1992, p. 68.
47. Neil Peirce, "Sabotaging Social Investment," *Charlotte Observer,* June 17,

1995, p. A11; also see Marc J. Epstein, "Pension Funds Should Practice What They Preach," *Business and Society Review,* Fall 1992, pp. 60–61.

48. These issues are discussed at greater length in M. Bruce Johnson, "Socially Responsible Investing," *Altenatives in Philanthropy,* Washington, D.C.: Capital Research Center, July 1992.

49. Linda Marsa, "Cashing In on Environmentally Sound Investments," *Information Please Almanac,* CompuServe, 1995, p. 1.

50. Jerome S. Dodson, "Social Investing Comes of Age," *Business and Society Review,* Spring 1992, p. 25

51. See, for example, Peter Arlow and Martin J. Gannon, "Social Responsiveness, Corporate Structure, and Economic Performance," *Academy of Management Review,* Vol. 7, No. 2, 1982, pp. 235–241; Kenneth E. Aupperle, Archie B. Carroll, and John D. Hatfield, "An Empirical Examination of the Relationship Between Corporate Social Responsibility and Profitability," *Academy of Management Journal,* Vol. 28, No. 2, 1985, pp. 446–463; and Gordon J. Alexander and Rogene A. Buchholz, "Corporate Social Responsibility and Stock Market Performance," *Academy of Management Journal,* Vol. 21, No. 3, 1978, pp. 479–486.

52. Assets numbers for the funds were obtained from CompuServe's FundWatch service, produced by *Money* magazine. Equity holdings data were obtained from the New York Stock Exchange.

53. For more discussion of how socially responsible investing should be defined, see Richard E. Wagner, "Free Markets and Responsible Investing," *Alternatives in Philanthropy* (Washington, D.C.: Capital Research Center, July 1993), pp. 1–2.

54. Martin Morse Wooster, "Using Their Own Judgment," *Alternatives in Philanthropy* (Washington, D.C.: Capital Research Center, May 1990),

55. Richard B. McKenzie, "The Market Foundations of Philanthropy," *Philanthropic Prospect* (Indianapolis: Philanthropy Roundtable, 1994), p. 50.

Chapter 3. Employment, Layoffs, and Social Responsibility

1. Bruce Nussbaum, "Downward Mobility: Corporate Castoffs Are Struggling Just to Stay in the Middle-Class," *Business Week,* March 23, 1992, pp. 56–57.

2. Louis S. Richman, "America's Tough New Job Market," *Fortune,* February 24, 1992, p. 61.

3. Marianne M. Jennings, Larry R. Smeltzer, and Marie F. Zener, "The Ethics of Worker Safety Nets for Corporate Change," *Journal of Business Ethics,* No. 12, 1993, p. 459.

4. Leslie Wayne, "U.S. Official in Plea to Pension Funds," *New York Times,* October 12, 1993, p. D2.

5. Richman, "When Will the Layoffs End?" *Fortune,* September 20, 1993, p. 54.

6. Daniel J. McConville, "The Upside of Downsizing," *Industry Week,* May 17, 1993, p.14.

7. Joann S. Lublin, "Don't Stop Cutting Staff, Study Suggests," *Wall Street Journal,* September 27, 1994, p. B1.

8. Richman, "When Will The Layoffs End?" p. 56.

9. Mark D. Fefer, "How Layoffs Pay Off," *Fortune,* January 24, 1994, p. 12.

10. Susan Pulliam and Lee Berton, "A Restructuring of Write-Offs is in the Making," *Wall Street Journal,* November 2, 1994, p. C1. The use of immediate write-offs for restructuring costs has become controversial in the accounting industry, with the Financial Accounting Standards Board, apparently under pressure from the federal Securities and Exchange Commission, promulgating new rules to distribute expense write-offs more equally over the course of a firm's restructuring process. Nevertheless, even under the new rules investors are likely to view many restructuring announcements as good news for the long-term profitability of firms.

11. Dan L. Worrell, Wallace N. Davidson III, and Varinder M. Sharma, "Layoff Announcements and Stockholder Wealth," *Academy of Management Journal,* Vol. 34, No. 3, 1991, p. 670.

12. "1994 AMA Survey on Downsizing: Summary of Key Findings," *AMA News,* American Management Association, New York, September 1994, pp. 1–4.

13. Beth Belton, "Profits Pedal Economic Growth Cycle," *USA Today,* October 31, 1994, p. 1B.

14. George J. Church, "We're #1 and It Hurts," *Time,* October 24, 1994, p. 54.

15. Ronald Brownstein, "America's Anxiety Attack," *Los Angeles Times Magazine,* May 8, 1994, p. 14.

16. *Employee Benefits: Survey Data from Benefit Year 1992,* U.S. Chamber of Commerce Research Center, Washington, D.C., 1993, p. 33.

17. *Handbook of Labor Statistics,* Bureau of Labor Statistics, U.S. Department of Labor, Bulletin 2340, August 1989, p. 349; with 1990–1993 data provided in Sylvia Nasar, "Most New Jobs in Areas That Pay More Than Average," *New York Times* (reprinted in *News & Observer* [Raleigh, N.C.], September 11, 1994, p. 12C.)

18. The flaws of the CPI became a political issue for the new Republican Congress in 1995 as it grappled with budget and tax issues. Even Federal Reserve chairman Allen Greenspan has called for new measurement. See David Wessel, "GOP Seeks Change in Inflation Estimate," *Wall Street Journal,* January 17, 1995, p. A2; Michael J. Mandel, "The Real Truth About the Economy," *Business Week,* November 7, 1994, pp. 110–118.

19. *These Are the Good Old Days,* p. 15.

20. When hourly earnings numbers are adjusted according to Greenspan's revised inflation measure, they show a 19 percent (or 1 percent annual) increase on average since 1970. See Rich Thomas and Michael Meyer, "Do the Numbers Lie?" *Newsweek,* February 13, 1995, p. 43. Total family income, including benefits, is up about 30 percent. See Karl Zinsmeister, "Payday Mayday," *American Enterprise,* September/October 1995, p. 46.

21. These wage and income trends are summarized in Michael Walden, *Economic Issues: Rhetoric and Reality* (Englewood Cliffs, New Jersey: Prentice Hall, 1995), pp. 3–15. One key point to remember is that categories such as "rich" and "poor" are only snapshots in time. From year to year, the people who make up these categories are constantly changing. Eighty-five percent

of tax filers in the bottom 20 percent of households had risen to a higher quintile by 1988. See John Cunniff, "Politics Muddies the Issue of Caste," *Portsmouth Herald,* August 18, 1995, p. A16.

22. Lawrence B. Lindsey, "Why the 1980s Were Not the 1920s," *Forbes,* October 19, 1992, pp. 78–89; see also John C. Weicher, "Getting Richer (at Different Rates)," *Wall Street Journal,* June 14, 1995, p. A10. One way to contrast measured income and actual well-being is to compare reported income to reported consumption. Many households spend a great deal more than they appear to take in. See Ed Rubenstein, "The Inequality Industry," *National Review,* May 15, 1995, p. 21.

23. Gene Koretz, "Be Your Own Boss, Earn Less?" *Business Week,* November 28, 1994, p. 32.

24. Albert B. Crenshaw, "So Much for the Myth of a Mobile Work Force," *Washington Post National Weekly Edition,* January 2–8, 1995, p. 22.

25. James Overstreet, "Survey: Baby Boomers Outwhine X-ers," *USA Today,* December 13, 1994, p. 1B.

26. See, for example, "How It's Going," *American Enterprise,* November/December 1994, p. 99.

27. Marc Levinson, "Hey, You're Doing Great," *Newsweek,* January 30, 1995, pp. 42–42A.

28. Overstreet, p. 1B.

29. Jerry Flint, "Keep a Resume on the Floppy, But Don't Panic," *Forbes,* April 26, 1993, p. 70.

30. The "falling wages" myth is but one example of how skewed government data gathering and data reporting can tell a misleading story about the performance of the economy or individual workers. When evaluating the impact of layoffs on individual communities or states, many observers have pointed to U.S. Labor Department surveys of business establishments in each state. From August 1992 to August 1993, for example, the department's establishment survey found a significant 1.3 percent drop in employment in cutback-buffeted California, a 0.6 percent drop in New York, and a 1.4 percent drop in New Jersey. But establishment surveys miss an important fact: many laid-off workers rejoin the labor market as home-based entrepreneurs, consultants, or contractors, which are not included in the establishment survey. A different Labor Department analysis based on household surveys and covering the same time period (August 1992 to August 1993) found that employment dropped only slightly in California, stayed the same in New York, and shot up by 2.2 percent in New Jersey. By looking at wage and employment numbers in different ways, one can come to radically different conclusions about the impact of layoffs and economic change on particular communities. See Lucinda Harper, "Employer Survey May Not Provide Best Jobs Measure," *Wall Street Journal,* October 8, 1993, p. A2.

31. Church, p. 52.

32. *These Are the Good Old Days: A Report on U.S. Living Standards,* Federal Reserve Bank of Dallas, 1993 Annual Report, p. 7.

33. Flint, p. 69.

34. Fleming Meeks and Dana Wechsler Linden, "Trickle-Down Bosses," *Forbes,* November 7, 1994, p. 207.

35. Paul and Sarah Edwards, *Working From Home* (New York: G. P. Putnam's Sons, 1994), p. 11.

36. Harper, "Despite Big Layoffs, Employment Grows," *Wall Street Journal,* October 8, 1993, p. A2.

37. Nasar, p. 12C; also John M. Berry, "The Economy's Surprise: More High-Wage Jobs," *Washington Post,* September 2, 1994, p. A1.

38. Meeks and Linden, p. 207.

39. Richman, "America's Tough New Job Market," p. 58.

40. Jonathan Eig, "Temporary Workers Alter Face of Business," *Dallas Morning News,* June 5, 1994, p. 1A.

41. Janice Castro, "Disposable Workers," *Time,* March 29, 1993, p. 42.

42. Jaclyn Fierman, "The Contingency Work Force," *Fortune,* January 24, 1994, p. 31.

43. Janet Novack, "Is Lean, Mean?" *Forbes,* August 15, 1994, p. 88.

44. Marvin Kosters and Deirdre McCullough, "Does Part-Time Work Pay?" *American Enterprise,* November–December 1994, pp. 90–95.

45. Novack, p. 88.

46. Ida L. Walters, "Temping Fate," *Reason,* April 1994, p. 51.

47. Tatiana Pouschine and Manjeet Kripalani, "'I Got Tired of Forcing Myself to Go to the Office,'" *Forbes,* May 25, 1992, p. 104.

48. Donald J. McNerney, "A New Look at Entrepreneurism," *HR Focus,* August 1994, p 1.

49. Kirk Johnson, "Franchise Stores Lure Corporate Refugees," *New York Times,* May 13, 1994, p. A1.

50. Edwards, pp. 11–12.

51. Pouschine and Kripalani, p. 108.

52. Jane Applegate, "From Executive to Entrepreneur," *Working Woman,* July 1992, pp. 33–34.

53. Steven Kaufman, "Dispelling the Myths: Most Small Businesses Succeed, Study Shows," *News & Observer* (Raleigh, N.C.), February 26, 1995, p. 1F.

54. Richman, "America's Tough New Job Market," p. 58.

55. Edwards, p. 7.

56. Beth Brophy, "After the Layoff, an Invitation Back," *U.S. News & World Report,* October 31, 1994, p. 100.

57. Personal interview, November 7, 1994.

58. Edwards, p. 10.

59. Ibid., p. 12.

60. Flint, pp. 65–66.

61. *These Are the Good Old Days,* p. 4.

62. U.S. firms spent 6.1 percent of payroll on pension plans in 1992, compared to 5.4 percent in 1979, 4.0 percent in 1967, and 3.6 percent in 1951. See *Employee Benefits,* p. 23; and also *Employee Benefits: Historical Data 1951–1979,* U.S. Chamber of Commerce Research Center, Washington, D.C., 1981, p. 24.

63. Personal interview, November 7, 1994.
64. Under the Consolidated Omnibus Budget Reconciliation Act (COBRA) of 1985, most organizations with twenty or more employees that offer group health benefit plans are required to continue coverage for former employees and their families for between eighteen months and three years, depending on the situation. See "Severance Benefits and Outplacement Services," Personnel Policies Forum Survey No. 143, Bureau of National Affairs, Washington, D.C., December 1986, p. 11.
65. *Severance: The Corporate Response,* Right Management Consultants Inc., Philadelphia, 1990, p. 19.
66. "1994 Survey on Downsizing," p. 4.
67. William J. Barkley, Jr., and Thad B. Green, "Safe Landings for Outplaced Employees at AT & T," *Personnel Journal,* June 1992, p. 144.
68. Joe A. Bowden, "The Anatomy of a Plant Closing," *Personnel Journal,* May 1992, p. 60.
69. Peggy Stuart, "Workers Upgrade Skills at Training Center," *Personnel Journal,* March 1993, p. 66 (sidebar).
70. Linda Stockman Vines, "Workplace Rainmakers: The Outplacement Industry Comes Into Its Own," *Solutions,* March 1994, p. 25.
71. Karen Matthes, "The Pink Slip Turns Into Something Rosier," *Management Review,* April 1992, p. 5.
72. See Dyan Machan, "Meet the Undertakers," *Forbes,* November 11, 1991, pp. 384–388, for a skeptical look at outplacement.
73. Robert J. Werner, "IRS Draws Map for Exclusion of Outplacement Services as Working Condition Fringe," *Journal of Taxation,* December 1992, Vol. 77, No. 6, p. 350.
74. Betsy Carter, "My Life and (Surprisingly Good) Times at an Outplacement Center," *Working Woman,* September 1992, p. 109.
75. McNerney, p. 9.

Chapter 4. Business and the Education Challenge

1. Personal interview, January 24, 1995.
2. Timothy Ehrgott, "A CHOICE Success Story," fact sheet from the Educational CHOICE Charitable Trust, May 1994.
3. Personal interview, January 24, 1995.
4. Peter M. Flanigan, "Private Capital Flows to School Choice," *Philanthropy,* Vol. 7, No. 3, Summer 1993, pp. 18–19.
5. Statistics obtained from "Privately Funded Tuition Grant Program Summary," a fact sheet distributed by CEO America in Bentonville, Arkansas.
6. Ann E. Kaplan, editor, *Giving USA: The Annual Report on Philanthropy for the Year 1993* (New York: AAFRC Trust for Philanthropy, 1994), pp. 75–77.
7. Bud Spillane, superintendent of schools in Fairfax County, Virginia, quoted in "Getting Off the Sidelines," *America's Agenda,* Spring 1992, p. 22.
8. Charles Brown, "Empirical Evidence on Private Training," *Research in Labor Economics,* Vol. 11, 1990, p. 98.

9. Debbie Goldberg, "Education at Work: Employers Spend Billions on Job and Management Training," *Washington Post Education Review,* August 6, 1989, p. 12.

10. A study by the U.S. Census Bureau in 1995 found a strong correlation between educational quality and productivity gains. A 10 percent increase in the educational attainment of a business's workforce results in an 8.6 percent increase in productivity, the study found. "How To Increase Productivity? Find More Educated Workers," *Daily Report Card,* May 16, 1995, p. 3.

11. John Hood, "When Business 'Adopts' Schools: Spare the Rod, Spoil the Child," Policy Analysis No. 153, Cato Institute, Washington, D.C., June 5, 1991, p. 5.

12. See, for example, Eric A. Hanushek, "Impact of Differential Expenditures on School Performance," *Educational Researcher,* May 1989, p. 45.

13. Troy Segal, "Saving Our Schools," *Business Week,* September 14, 1992, p.78.

14. Tom Soter, "A Business Plan for Education," *Management Review,* September 1993, p. 15.

15. Anna David, "Public-Private Partnerships: The Private Sector and Innovation in Education," Policy Insight No. 142, Reason Foundation, Los Angeles, CA, July 1992, p. 1.

16. Soter, p. 16.

17. Susan E. Kuhn, "How Business Helps Schools," *Fortune,* Spring 1990, p. 92.

18. "Delta Sponsors Landmark Geography Programs," Delta Air Lines press release, September 8, 1992, pp. 1–3.

19. Betsy Wagner, "Our class Is Brought to You Today By . . . ," *U.S. News & World Report,* April 24, 1995, p. 63.

20. "Comunity Help & Involvement Program at McDonnell Douglas: Education Programs," company brochure.

21. Nancy Ramsey, "What Companies Are Doing," *Fortune* (Special Report on Education), November 29, 1993, pp. 142–162.

22. Walter L. Kaus, "Inner-City Innovations," *Across the Board,* December 1992, pp. 56–57.

23. Ann Bradley, "Corporate School's Plan to Merge with Chicago District Is a Done Deal," *Education Week,* August 3, 1994.

24. Steffer Johnson, "Corporate Efforts in Education," *Law & Politics,* April 1992, p. 11.

25. Shari Caudron, "New Curriculum Benefits Students and Helps Industry," *Personnel Journal,* March 1993, p. 85.

26. Ramsey, p. 162.

27. "Minneapolis Corporate School: Open for Business," *Education '92,* LRP Publications, Alexandria, Virginia, Vol. 1, No. 12, p. 4.

28. Christine Woolsey, "Education and Training Benefits," *Business Insurance,* September 14, 1992, p. 12.

29. Ramsey, pp. 142–144.

30. Personal interview, January 23, 1995.

31. For further analysis of government job-training programs, see Patrick F. Fagan, "Liberal Welfare Programs: What the Data Show on Programs for

Teenage Mothers," Heritage Foundation, Washington, D.C., Backgrounder No. 1031, March 31, 1995; Marc Levinson, "Everyone's Magic Bullet; Why 'Job Training' Is No Cure for the Economy's Ills," *Newsweek,* September 21, 1992, p. 44; and Jonathan Walters, "The Truth About Training," *Governing,* March 1995, pp. 32–35.

32. "1994 Industry Report," *Training,* October 1994, pp. 29–60.
33. As discussed in Gary Becker, *Human Capital* (New York: Columbia University Press, for the National Bureau of Economic Research, 1964).
34. Alan Eck, "Job-Related Education and Training: Their Impact on Earnings," *Monthly Labor Review,* October 1993, pp. 21–36.
35. Kevin Kelly, "Motorola: Training for the Millennium," *Business Week,* March 28, 1994, pp. 158–159.
36. Ibid., p. 163.
37. "Manpower's Success Clearly Not Temporary," *Triangle East Business Journal,* May 1995, p. 7.
38. Peggy Stuart, "Employees Launch ESL Tutoring at the Workplace," *Personnel Journal,* November 1994, p. 53.
39. Stephanie Barlow, "Reality Check," *Entrepreneur,* July 1993, p. 73.
40. Michael Ryan, "Go to School, and I'll Pay for It," *Parade,* September 18, 1994, pp. 20–21.
41. Personal interview, August 26, 1994.
42. Edwin Reingold, "America's Hamburger Helper," *Time,* June 29, 1992, p. 66.
43. "1994 Industry Report," p. 54.
44. Nan Stone, "Does Business Have Any Business in Education?" *Harvard Business Review,* March–April 1991, p. 48.
45. See, for example, Stephen F. Hamilton, *Apprenticeship for Adulthood: Preparing Youth for the Future* (New York: Free Press, 1990).
46. James J. Heckman, "Is Job Training Oversold?" *Public Interest,* Spring 1994, pp. 91–115.
47. Brian S. Moskal, "Apprenticeships: A Few Good Crusaders," *Industry Week,* January 4, 1993, pp. 23–24.
48. Dawn Gunsch, "Job Training Shows Youth How to Apply Knowledge," *Personnel Journal,* March 1993, pp. 69–70.
49. Jennifer J. Laabs, "Mentors Offer Students the Tools for Job Success," *Personnel Journal,* March 1993, p. 59.
50. See, for example, "Business' Role in Education," *Congressional Quarterly Researcher,* November 22, 1991, pp. 879–880.
51. Bernard Avishai, "What Is Business's Social Compact?" *Harvard Business Review,* January–February 1994, p. 47.
52. See Mike Bowler, "Sylvan Project Reaps Results in Pupil Scores," *Baltimore Evening Sun,* July 28, 1994; and *Devry Institute of Technology: 1994 Academic Catalog,* DeVry National Office of Admissions, Oakbrook Terrace, Illinois, 1994.
53. Linda Brown Douglas, "Home-Improvement Stores Tackle Classes," *News & Observer* (Raleigh, N.C.), June 27, 1995, p. 1D.
54. See Belinda Thurston, "Selling in the Schools: Does It Pay to Let Businesses Advertise?" *USA Today,* March 1, 1995, p. 7D.

55. Martin Anderson, "The Answer Is in the Boardroom," *Philanthropy,* Vol. 7, No. 3, Summer 1993, pp. 8–9.

56. Laurie J. Bassi, "Workplace Education for Hourly Workers," *Journal of Policy Analysis and Management,* Vol. 13, No. 1, 1994, pp. 55–73. Bassi also found that employer-sponsored consortia to provide education and training would be more common if antitrust regulations were liberalized.

57. Quoted in "Educating the Workforce of the Future," *Harvard Business Review,* March–April 1994, p. 46.

Chapter 5. Revitalizing America's Cities

1. Samuel Greengard and Charlene Marmer Solomon, "The Fire This Time?" *Personnel Journal,* February 1994, p. 60.

2. Stephen Bennett, "Combining Good Businesses and Good Works," *Progressive Grocer,* December 1992, pp. 65–67.

3. Bradley Johnson, "Supermarkets Move Back to Inner Cities," *Advertising Age,* January 25, 1993, p. 41.

4. Bennett, p. 67.

5. Sam Staley, "Bigger Is Not Better: The Virtues of Decentralized Local Government," Policy Analysis No. 166, Cato Institute, Washington, D.C., January 21, 1992, p. 5; see also Wendell Cox, Jean Love, and Samuel A. Brunelli, "The Livable American City: Toward an Environmentally Friendly American Dream," *State Factor,* Vol. 19, No. 3, American Legislative Exchange Council, Washington, D.C., August 1993, p. 1.

6. Cox, Love, and Brunelli, p. 1.

7. Warren Cohen, "Cities Try to Bring Home the Bacon," *U.S. News & World Report,* January 31, 1994, p. 59.

8. These issues are discussed in Staley, p. 5; also Peter D. Salins, "Cities, Suburbs, and the Urban Crisis," *Public Interest,* Fall 1993, pp. 91–104.

9. Cox, Love, and Brunelli, p. 2.

10. Mark Alpert, "The Ghetto's Hidden Wealth," *Fortune,* July 29, 1991, p. 170.

11. "A Sip of Something Good," *Economist,* October 10, 1992, p. 24.

12. "Supermarkets Shun Inner Cities," Associated Press On-Line (CompuServe), May 16, 1995, p. 1.

13. Neil R. Peirce, "A New Way to Bring Home the Bacon," *National Journal,* October 8, 1994, p. 2359.

14. Janean Huber, "Urban Renewal: Franchising Breathes New Life into Inner Cities," *Entrepreneur,* January 1994, pp. 105–106.

15. Amy Barrett, "Talk About Doing Well by Doing Good," *Business Week,* December 6, 1993, p. 162.

16. Cohen, p. 60.

17. Alpert, p. 170.

18. Don L. Boroughs, "The Bottom Line on Ethics," *U.S. News & World Report,* March 20, 1995, p. 66.

19. Morgan O. Reynolds, "Using the Private Sector to Deter Crime," NCPA Policy Report No. 181, National Center for Policy Analysis, Dallas, Texas, March 1994, p. 8.

20. "A Sip of Something Good," p. 25.
21. Johnson, p. 41.
22. Evelyn Gilbert, "Insurers Wrestle with Inner-City Risks," *National Underwriter,* January 17, 1994, p. 41.
23. Ibid., p. 22.
24. Martin Anderson, *The Federal Bulldozer* (New York: McGraw-Hill, 1967).
25. These projects are discussed in Bernard J. Frieden and Lynne B. Sagalyn, *Downtown, Inc.: How America Rebuilds Cities* (Cambridge, Massachusetts: MIT Press, 1989).
26. Jonathan Walters, "After the Festival Is Over," *Governing,* August 1990, p. 28–29.
27. Alpert, p. 168.
28. Ibid., p. 174.
29. Dolores Palma, "Downtown Trends, Downtown Success," *Public Management,* December 1992, p. 3.
30. Sam Staley, "Changing Course in America's Cities: Revitalization Through Entrepreneurship," Urban Policy Perspective No. 1, Urban Policy Research Institute, Dayton, Ohio, August 28, 1992, p. 4.
31. Janet Rothenberg Pack, "BIDs, DIDs, SIDs, SADs: Private Governments in Urban America," *Brookings Review,* Fall 1992, pp. 18–21.
32. "Let the Landlords Do It," *Economist,* April 25, 1992, p. 23.
33. Giannini's story is told in a new biography: Felice A. Bonadio, *A.P. Giannini: Banker of America* (Berkeley: University of California Press, 1994).
34. Typically, banks and other for-profit institutions will handle loans of $20,000 and up, with nonprofits—sometimes in association with banks—handling smaller loan amounts. "Behind the Boom in Microloans," *Inc.,* April 1994, p. 114.
35. Michael Schuman, "The Microlenders," *Forbes,* October 25, 1993, p. 166.
36. Alpert, p. 173.
37. Barrett, p. 162.
38. Edward O. Welles, "It's Not the Same America," *Inc.,* May 1994, p. 92.
39. Jonathan D. Glater, "Lenders Discover Small Is Beautiful," *Washington Post,* March 8, 1995, p. C1.
40. John S. Benton, "Ending the Redlining Lie," *Best's Review,* May 1993, pp. 46–48.
41. Gilbert, p. 41.
42. Greengard and Solomon, p. 63.
43. Ibid., p. 67.
44. Dawn Gunsch, "Urban Renewal Is an Investment," *Personnel Journal,* March 1993, p. 53.
45. Charles L. Young, Jr., "Insurers Can Help Spur Inner-City Recovery," *National Underwriter,* June 8, 1992, p. 15.
46. Huber, p. 106.
47. Diane Filipowski, "More Working Ideas," *Personnel Journal,* March 1993, p. 64.
48. Sylvester Monroe, "The Gospel of Equity," *Time,* May 10, 1993, p. 55.

49. "Start-Ups from Scratch: Eight Companies Launched with No (Almost No) Money Down," *Inc.,* September 1994, pp. 76–77.
50. Marc Hequet, "Blight Busters," *Training,* September 1992, pp. 32–33.
51. Marc Hequet, "Can Two Wrongs Make a Right?" *Training,* August 1994, pp. 37–38.
52. Cox, Love, and Brunelli, p. 4.
53. Ibid., p. 11.
54. Ibid.
55. Jennifer J. Laabs, "Shuttle Service Moves Inner-City Residents to Jobs," *Personnel Journal,* March 1993, p. 78.
56. Dawn Gunsch, "Creativity Can Extend Resources," *Personnel Journal,* March 1993, p. 93.
57. Bennett, p. 70.
58. Gunsch, p. 93.
59. Ellyn E. Spragins, "Making Good," *Inc.,* May 1993, p. 116.
60. Diana Filipowski, "Homeless Workers Contradict Myths," *Personnel Journal,* March 1993, p. 51.
61. Charlene Marmer Solomon, "McDonald's Links Franchisees to the Community," *Personnel Journal,* March 1993, p. 61.
62. Ibid., p. 64.
63. Diane Gingold, "American Corporate Community Service," *Fortune* (special advertising section), November 30, 1992, pp. 134–135.
64. Murray and Neil Raphel, "Myths of the Inner City," *Progressive Grocer,* March 1993, p. 14.
65. Michael E. Porter, "The Rise of the Urban Entrepreneur," *Inc.,* June 1995, p. 108.
66. Johnson, p. 41.
67. Ideas for fixing urban American's problems can be found in such publications as Welles, pp. 82–98; Sam Staley, "Changing Course in America's Cities: Revitalization Through Entrepreneurship," Urban Policy Perspective No. 1, Urban Policy Research Institute, Dayton, Ohio, August 28, 1992; and William D. Eggers, "Rightsizing Government: Lessons from America's Public-Sector Innovators," How to Guide No. 11, Privatization Center, Reason Foundation, Los Angeles, January 1994.
68. Porter, p. 104.
69. Alpert, p. 174.

Chapter 6. Promoting Health and Wealth

1. Newt Gingrich, "What Good Is Government and Can We Make It Better?" *Newsweek,* April 10, 1995, p. 20.
2. Jerry Flint, "The Goose That Laid the Golden Pill," *Forbes,* May 9, 1994, p. 52.
3. "Merck & Co. Profile," *Hoovers Company Database* (Austin, Texas: Reference Press, 1994 [retrieved on CompuServe]).
4. "Baxter International Profile," *Hoovers Company Database.*

5. Ray Jordan, "Freeing Pharmaceutical Funding," *Philanthropy*, Vol. 8, No. 3, Summer 1994, p. 6.
6. Tim Beardsley, "Big-Time Biology," *Scientific American*, November 1994, p. 90.
7. Shannon Brownlee, "Biotech Finally Finds the Bottom Line," *U.S. News & World Report*, July 17, 1995, p. 45.
8. James Vincent, "Profits, Research, and Progress," *The Charlotte Observer*, September 16, 1994, p. 12A.
9. Murray Weidenbaum, "Are Drug Prices Too High?" *Public Interest*, Summer 1993, p. 85.
10. Jeffrey H. Birnbaum and Michael Waldholz," *Wall Street Journal*, February 16, 1993, p. A1.
11. Ruth Shalit, "Bitter Pills," *New Republic*, December 13, 1993, p. 19.
12. Ibid.
13. Doug Levy and Anita Manning, "Market Forces Work Against 'Me-Too' Efforts," *USA Today*, July 11, 1995, p. 1A.
14. Patrick Flanagan, "Drug Prices: What's the Rationale?" *Management Review*, July 1993, p. 11.
15. Birnbaum & Waldholz, p. A9.
16. Flint, p. 52.
17. Raymond V. Damadian, "The Story of MRI," *Saturday Evening Post*, May/June 1994, p. 92.
18. Ibid., p. 58.
19. Weidenbaum, p. 87.
20. Regina Herzlinger, "The Quiet Health Care Revolution," *Public Interest*, Spring 1994, p. 79.
21. Flanagan, p. 13. Also see Herni Termeer, "The Cost of Miracles," *Wall Street Journal*, November 16, 1993, p. A14.
22. Birnbaum and Waldholz, p. A9.
23. Weidenbaum, p. 87.
24. John Merline, "Do We Spend Too Much on Health Care?" *Consumers' Research*, March 1994, p. 20.
25. "The Upjohn Company Profile," *Hoover Company Database*.
26. Beardsley, p. 93.
27. Herzlinger, p. 79.
28. "U.S. Surgical Corporation Profile," *Hoover Company Database*.
29. Herzlinger, p. 80.
30. Gene Bylinsky, "Got a Winner? Back It Big," *Fortune*, March 21, 1994, p. 69.
31. "Abbott Laboratories Inc. Profile," *Hoover Company Database*.
32. John Carey, "Science-Fiction Medicine Is Fast Becoming Fact," *Business Week*, p. 169.
33. Jason Forsythe, "Breakthroughs: Products and Ideas That Shatter the Walls of Possibility," *Success*, October 1994, p. 40.
34. "Bristol-Myers-Squibb Profile," *Hoover Company Database*.
35. Beardsley, p. 90.

36. Marcia Clemmitt, "U.S. Drug Industry's Research Support," *Nature,* February 25, 1993, p. 757–759.
37. Jerry E. Bishop, "Plan May Blow Lid Off Secret Gene Research," *Wall Street Journal,* September 28, 1994, p. B1.
38. Naturally, there is much discussion among the medical research community about the pros and cons of the commercialization of research. See E. S. Browning, "Change in Health Care Shakes Up the Business of Drug Development," *Wall Street Journal,* March 28, 1995, p. A1.
39. Eliot Marshall, "Fewer Young Researchers Are Seeking NIH Grants," *Science,* July 1994, p. 314.
40. Patrick Fleenor, Three Decades of Government-Financed Health Care in the United States," Special Report, Tax Foundation, Washington, D.C., August 1994, p. 4.
41. John Merline, "Do We Spend Too Much on Health Care?" *Consumers' Research,* March 1994, p. 20.
42. "Changes in the Ownership, Control, and Configuration of Health Care Services," *For-Profit Enterprise in Health Care* (Washington, D.C.: National Academy Press, 1986).
43. Herzlinger, pp. 73–74.
44. George Anders, "More Patients Get Quick Surgery and Go Home," *Wall Street Journal,* August 11, 1994, p. B1.
45. "Merck & Co. Profile."
46. Shawn Tully, "Remedy: Educate the Patient," *Fortune,* February 7, 1994, p. 134.
47. Tim Friend, "Patients Find 'Direct Line' to Doctors," *USA Today,* February 8, 1995, p. 1D.
48. Jerome P. Kassirer, "Transforming the Delivery of Health Care," *Consumers' Research,* March 1995, pp. 27–28.
49. Jolie Solomon, "With or Without You," *Newsweek,* August 15, 1994, pp. 58–59.
50. George Anders, "Mergers of Hospitals Surge Amid Pressures to Cut Costs," *Wall Street Journal,* December 1, 1993, p. B1.
51. Herzlinger, pp. 76–77.
52. Suzanne Tregarthen, "Statistics Overstate Health Care Costs," *Wall Street Journal,* August 18, 1993, p. A12.
53. Sandra Lotz Fisher, "Wellness in the Workplace," *Sales & Marketing Management,* January 1992, p. 88.
54. Julie Cohen Mason, "The Cost of Wellness," *Management Review,* July 1994, p. 29.
55. Christine Woolsey, "Encouraging Workers to Care for Themselves," *Business Insurance,* May 3, 1993, p. 4.
56. Gillian Flynn, "Companies Make Wellness Work," *Personnel Journal,* February 1995, pp. 64–65.
57. Mason, p. 30.
58. Judy Greenwald, "Programs Educate Employees on Health, Cut Costs," *Business Insurance,* February 21, 1994, p. 4.

59. Chris Roush, "Wellness Can Mean a Trim Bottom Line," *Business Week*, p. 112.
60. Louis S. Richman, "Health Care Fears Don't Stop Job Hoppers," *Fortune*, February 21, 1994, p. 24.
61. Christine Gorman, "Can Drug Firms Be Trusted?" *Time*, February 10, 1992, p. 42.
62. Merline, p. 18.

Chapter 7. Selling Safety

1. Associated Press report, "Jackson Revisits Hamlet: Town Linked to Cities of Rights Movement," *News & Observer* (Raleigh, N.C.), November 26, 1991, p. 5B.
2. David Warner, "Protecting OSHA from 'Reform,'" *Nation's Business*, February 1992, p. 17.
3. Van Denton, "Wreath, Blame Placed at State's Doors: Luring Businesses to State Fosters Lack of Safety Concern, Some Say," *News & Observer* (Raleigh, N.C.), September 8, 1991, p. 1B.
4. John Drescher, "USDA Inspector OK'd Locking of Door at Hamlet Plant," *Charlotte Observer*, November 13, 1991, p. 1A; also Steve Riley, "U.S. Agency Knew About Locked Door: Flies Caused Hamlet Plant to Block Exit," *News & Observer* (Raleigh, N.C.), November 13, 1991, p. 8A.
5. J. N. Kocsis, "Employees Pump Real Power into Utility Safety," *Safety & Health*, February 1994, pp. 74–75.
6. *Statistical Abstract of the United States*, U.S. Government Printing Office, 1993, Table 196, p. 131.
7. *Accident Facts*, National Safety Council, Washington, D.C., 1994 edition, pp. 26–27.
8. See a discussion of employer incentives to report in *Report on the American Workforce*, U.S. Department of Labor, Washington, D.C., 1994, pp. 99–100. Increases in worker's compensation and disability coverage have significantly increased workers' incentives to report real or exaggerated claims of occupational injury or illness. Consumers have also been encouraged to pursue accident claims, given changes in liability law and perceived likelihood of a generous jury verdict.
9. Adam Pertman, "Life in U.S. Is Becoming Less Risky, Studies Say," *Boston Globe*, July 18, 1994, p. 1.
10. *Accident Facts*, pp. 26–27.
11. W. Kip Viscusi, "Consumer Behavior and the Safety Effects of Product Safety Regulation," *Journal of Law & Economics*, Vol. 28, October 1985, p. 553.
12. Daniel Seligman, "Unsafe in Washington," *Fortune*, March 22, 1993, p. 179.
13. David Ball, "Regulating Risk: A Primer on How Markets, Government Address Worker Safety," *Carolina Journal*, Vol. 1, No. 3, p. 17.
14. Kathy Pitman, "Workplace Safety Comes with a Price, Duke Economist Says," Duke University press release, June 24, 1992, p. 2.
15. Worker's compensation rates aren't directly rated to accident rates. Premiums

reflect not only a firm's experience rating but also industry classifications that reflect the average level of risk each industry presents over time. This has the effect of averaging out risks to some extent, subsidizing relatively unsafe firms and penalizing relatively safe ones within the same industry. Also, state legislators have tended to try to please both labor and management by hiking benefits levels and keeping rates artificially low. This eventually results in rates that make many employers unprofitable customers for insurers, who cannot charge a high enough rate to offset expected claims paid. These companies do not just lose coverage, however, which might serve as a strong warning to workers about the risk of working for them. Instead, states require companies to retain coverage, and they offer it to high-risk firms through assigned-risk pools that, through government subsidies, again artificially keep premiums low and discourage companies from making appropriate investments in safety. In some states, a surprising number of companies are in assigned-risk pools; in Maine, the percentage was 90 percent in 1991. See James R. Chelius, "Role of Worker's Compensation in Developing Safer Workplaces," *Monthly Labor Review,* September 1991, pp. 23–24.

16. Mark Calvey, "Safety Programs Benefit with Worker Incentives," *Business Journal* (Charlotte, N.C.), August 22, 1994, p. 20.
17. Mark D. Fefer, "Taking Control of Your Workers' Comp Costs," *Fortune,* October 3, 1994, p. 131. The cost of mandated worker's compensation coverage on American business skyrocketed during the latter half of the 1980s, not so much because of an actual increase in danger at the workplace but because of federal court decisions liberalizing eligibility requirements. Workers found it easier to file claims, while state governments made mandatory benefit levels more generous. The result was a surge in worker claims. While this development had many negative consequences for economic growth, particularly for states with higher benefit levels, it also meant that the insurance market had to be more competitive than ever, as American companies sought ways to cut down of one of their most explosive labor costs.
18. Ball, p. 17.
19. Linda Johnson, "Preventing Injuries: The Big Payoff," *Personnel Journal,* April 1994, p. 61.
20. Ibid., p. 64.
21. Dawn Gunsch, "Employees Exercise to Prevent Injuries," *Personnel Journal,* July 1993, p. 59.
22. Jack Anderson and Michael Binstein, "Putting Low Value on Worker Safety," *Washington Post,* September 6, 1992, p. C7.
23. Fefer, p. 134.
24. Calvey, p. 24.
25. Dennis Pillsbury, "Worker Safety: New Approaches to Reducing Worker's Compensation Costs" (special advertising supplement), *Forbes,* October 19, 1992, p. 245.
26. Carolyn T. Geer, "Exorcising Demons from the Boiler," *Forbes,* April 15, 1991, p. 118.
27. *Report on the American Workforce,* p. 123. For an extended discussion of the

media's role in hyping CTDs, see Edward Felsenthal, "An Epidemic or a Fad? The Debate Heats Up Over Repetitive Stress," *Wall Street Journal,* July 14, 1994, p. A1; also Michael Meyer, "A Pain for Business," *Newsweek,* June 26, 1995, p. 42.

28. Janet Novack, "Ergonomical Correctness," *Forbes,* October 24, 1994, p. 224.
29. Fefer, p. 132.
30. *Report on the American Workforce,* p. 101.
31. Eileen Norris, "Mine Safety Starts with Mind Safety," *Safety & Health,* February 1994, p. 63.
32. Ibid., p. 64.
33. *Report on the American Workforce,* pp. 97–107.
34. Bernard L. Cohen, "How to Assess the Risks You Face," *Consumers' Research,* June 1992, p. 13.
35. Cited by Nancy Harvey Steorts, "Consumer Product Safety: A Public Policy Issue," *Thurmond Institute Lectures,* Strom Thurmond Institute, Clemson University, Clemson, South Carolina, 1984, p. 7.
36. Paul Rubin, Dennis Murphy, and Gregg Jarrell, "Risky Products, Risky Stocks," *Regulation,* 1988, No. 1, pp. 35–39.
37. Quoted in W. Bruce Chew and Timothy B. Blodgett, "The Case of the High-Risk Safety Product," *Harvard Business Review,* May–June 1992, p. 19.
38. Ibid., p. 26.
39. William Barrett, "Testing for Money," *Forbes,* July 6, 1992, p. 96.
40. Faye Rice, "Secrets of Product Testing," *Fortune,* August 21, 1994, p. 104.
41. W. Kip Viscusi and Michael J. Moore, "Product Liability, Research and Development, and Innovation," *Journal of Political Economy,* Vol. 101, No. 1, 1993, p. 162.
42. Many observers have noted that a surprising number of injuries and illnesses involving consumer products occur because consumers misuse them, often in ways impossible for product designers to predict. See John Merline, "Ten Ways Congress Can Help the U.S. Consumer," Backgrounder No. 702, Heritage Foundation, April 24, 1989, p. 7.
43. Robert P. Charrow, "Good Science and Bad Law: Liability and Basic Research," Legal Backgrounder, Vol. 5, No. 26, Washington Legal Foundation, June 22, 1990, p. 2.
44. Viscusi and Moore, pp. 161–183.
45. Janet Novack, "Entrepreneur on Board," *Forbes,* October 25, 1993, pp. 122–124.
46. Cynthia E. Griffin, "Brush with Greatness," *Entrepreneur,* June 1994, p. 168.
47. Alison Sprout, "Air-Filled Car Seat," *Fortune,* October 18, 1993, p. 122.
48. Cohen, p. 11.
49. Terrence Scanlon (interview), "We Want to Work with Companies, Not Against Them," *U.S. News & World Report,* January 15, 1985, p. 40.
50. *Accident Facts,* pp. 26–27.
51. Stephen R. Godwin and Mark R. Dayton, "Real Numbers on Airline Deregulation," *Consumers' Research,* July 1992, p. 32.
52. Richard B. McKenzie, "Airline Regulation Can Be a Killer—on the Ground," *Wall Street Journal,* March 7, 1989, p. A14.

53. Krystal Miller, "Insurance-Claims Data Don't Show Advantage of Some Auto Devices," *Wall Street Journal*, March 17, 1994, p. A1.

54. Peter L. Spencer, "The Trouble with Air Bags," *Consumers' Research*, January 1991, p. 10.

55. Miller, p. A7.

56. Personal interview, Colin Pease, Guilford Rail System, May 22, 1995.

57. Pitman, p. 2.

58. For a discussion of what employer practices can help reduce worker injuries, see David Lewin and Steven Schecter, "Four Factors Lower Disability Rates," *Personnel Journal*, May 1991, pp. 99–103.

59. See, for example, Robert A. Reber, Jerry A. Wallin, and David L. Duhon, "Safety Programs That Work," *Personnel Administrator*, September 1989, pp. 66–69.

Chapter 8. Nurturing Nature

1. Terry Anderson and Donald R. Leal, "Enviro-Capitalists," *Philanthropy*, Vol. 8, No. 4, Fall 1994, p. 27.

2. Anderson and Leal, p. 13.

3. Jo Kwong Echard, *Protecting the Environment: Old Rhetoric, New Imperatives* (Washington, D.C.: Capital Research Center, 1990), p. 103.

4. Dan McGraw, "A Fistful of Dollars," *U.S. News & World Report*, July 24, 1995, pp. 36–38.

5. Paul Hawken, "A Declaration of Sustainability," *Utne Reader*, September/October 1993, p. 54.

6. Noah Walley and Bradley Whitehead, "It's Not Easy Being Green," *Harvard Business Review*, May–June 1994, p. 48.

7. This position was advanced more recently in John Carey, "Are Regs Bleeding the Economy?" *Business Week*, July 17, 1995, p. 75.

8. This is not a theoretical example. See Eric Peters, "The False Promise of Electric Cars," *Consumers' Research*, August 1995, pp. 10–15.

9. The difficulties of using moral suasion and voluntary standards to promote environmental ends are discussed in a sympathetic analysis of the "Valdez Principles" by Rajih N. Sanyal and Joao S. Neves, "The Valdez Principles: Implications for Corporate Social Responsibility," *Journal of Business Ethics*, Vol. 10, 1991, pp. 883–890.

10. "3M's Conservation Ethic Pays Off," *Philanthropy*, Vol. 7, No. 2, Spring 1993, p. 8.

11. Art Kleiner, "What Does It Mean to Be Green?" *Harvard Business Review*, July–August 1991, p. 46.

12. Sul-Jin Yim, "Investment Group Sees Profit in Forests," *News & Observer* (Raleigh, N.C.), July 16, 1995, p. 1D.

13. Joseph L. Bast, Peter J. Hill, and Richard C. Rue, *Eco-Sanity: A Common Sense Guide to Environmentalism* (Lanham, Maryland: Madison Books, 1994), pp. 185–186.

14. Fred L. Smith, "Autonomy," *Reason*, August/September 1990, p. 25.

15. Ibid.

16. Bob Williams, "Tuning Up Automobile Pollution Assumptions," *Oil and Gas Journal,* September 7, 1992, p. 13.
17. Kleiner, pp. 39–40.
18. Bast et al., pp. 135–136.
19. The market prices for most natural resources suggest that we have a long way to go before scarcity becomes much of a problem. See Stephen Moore, "The Coming Age of Abundance," in Ronald Bailey, editor, *The True State of the Planet* (New York: Free Press, 1995), pp. 109–140.
20. Anita Manning, "Cancer Drug Alternative Approved," *USA Today,* December 13, 1994, p. 1D.
21. See Anderson, "Water Options for the Blue Planet," in Bailey, *The True State of the Planet,* pp. 267–294.
22. Joel Makower, "Thought for Food," *Green Consumer,* Universal Press Syndicate, June 20, 1995, p. 1.
23. Ronald Bailey, "Thwarting the Grim Reaper," *Forbes,* November 8, 1993, p. 124.
24. Henry Grady Weaver, *The Mainspring of Human Progress* (Irvington-on-Hudson, New York: Foundation for Economic Education, 1984 [13th edition]), p. 11.
25. Avery, "How Pesticides Help Prevent Cancer," *Consumers' Research,* June 1995, pp. 10–11.
26. Scott LaFee, "Promise, Menace of Biotech Create Sharp Debate," *San Diego Union-Tribune,* September 28, 1994, p. A1.
27. Rhonda L. Rundle, "Mycogen, Ciba Unit Get U.S. Approval to Sell Genetically Modified Corn Seed," *Wall Street Journal,* August 10, 1995, p. B5.
28. Jane Brooks, "High-Tech Helps Raise Crop Yields," *Montgomery* (Md.) *Journal,* July 26, 1995, p. 7A.
29. Bast et al., pp. 133–137.
30. Lester Lave, Tse-Sung Wu, Chris Hendrickson, and Francis McMichael, "My Shopping Trip with Andre," *Consumers' Research,* March 1995, pp. 24–25.
31. "Dow Chemical," *Hoover Company Database* (Austin, Texas: Reference Press, 1995 [CompuServe version]).
32. Lave et al., p. 25.
33. Virginia I. Postrel and Lynn Scarlett, "Talking Trash," *Reason,* August–September 1991, p. 27.
34. These examples are taken from an exhaustive summary of the last fifty years of the plastic industry, found in "How Plastics Changed America," *Plastics World,* April 1993, pp. 7–59.
35. Bernie Miller, "Green FR Resin Protects Sales, Molds Better," *Plastics World,* November 1993, pp. 24–25.
36. Victor Wigotsky, "The Chlorine Issue," *Plastics Engineering,* February 1995, pp. 19–20.
37. David Stipp, "Life-Cycle Analysis Measures Greenness, But Results May Not Be Black and White," *Wall Street Journal,* February 28, 1991, p. B1.
38. David Biddle, "Recycling for Profit: The New Green Business Frontier," *Harvard Business Review,* November–December 1993, p. 148.

39. Beatrice Trum Hunter, "The Pros and Cons of Aseptic Packaging," *Consumers' Research,* August 1991, pp. 15–17.
40. Task Force Report, "Progressive Environmentalism: A Pro-Human, Pro-Science, Pro–Free Enterprise Agenda for Change," National Center for Policy Analysis, Dallas, Texas, April 1991, p. 68.
41. Andrew D. Blechman, "Recycling: What Goes Around Often Profitable to Be Around," *Sacramento Bee,* November 26, 1994, p. A1.
42. Esher D'Amico, "The Growing Pains Continue," *Plastics World,* April 1994, pp. 26–28.
43. Douglas Smock, "Law and Logic Don't Always Concur," *Plastics World,* November 1993, p. 7.
44. Robert Engelman, "Technology Paves Way for Greener Future," *Safety & Health,* April 1993, pp. 31–33.
45. "Shrinking Waste," *Progressive Grocer,* October 1993, pp. 85–86.
46. Allayne Barrilleaux Pizzolatto and Cecil A. Zeringue II, "Facing Society's Demands for Environmental Protection: Management in Practice," *Journal of Business Ethics,* Vol. 12, 1993, p. 445.
47. Jan H. Schut, "Recycled Plastic Is Quietly Making Some Big, Fancy Car Parts," *Plastics World,* October 1994, p. 21.
48. Seema Nayyar, "A Film Worth Eating," *Adweek's Marketing Week,* May 18, 1992, p. 26.
49. Elizabeth Pennisi, "The Search for an Edible Coating," *Consumers' Research,* March 1992, p. 23.
50. Dawn Stover, "Toxic Avengers," *Popular Science,* July 1992, p. 70.
51. Tom Davey, "East Bay Cleanup Company Takes Microbes to Dinner," *San Francisco Business Times,* April 15, 1994, p. 7A.
52. Bioremediation has even become a popular industry for franchising. Environmental Biotech Inc. of Sarasota, Florida, began in 1989 and already had franchises in seventy-five U.S cities and eighteen countries by 1995. See Dave Bryan, "Grease-Eating Bacteria Give Rise to Franchise," *Triangle Business Journal,* June 30, 1995, p. 4.
53. Stover, pp. 71–74.
54. "Environmental Research," *Research & Development Magazine,* October 1993, pp. 48–49.
55. Ibid., pp. 48–50.
56. "Mobile System Recovers 99% of Mercury from Waste," *Research & Development Magazine,* September 1994, p. 39.
57. Gene Bylinsky, "How to Leapfrog the Giants," *Fortune,* October 18, 1993, p. 80.
58. See "System NOx the SOx Off Competing Methods" and "Unit Cuts Emissions from Coal-Fired Boilers," *Research & Development Magazine,* September 1994, pp. 35–39; also Joseph Haggin, "Catalytic Oxidation Process Cleans Volatile Organics from Exhaust," *Chemical & Engineering News,* June 27, 1994, p. 42.
59. James Glanz, "Can Fuel Cells Go Where No Device Has Gone Before?" *Research & Development Magazine,* May 1993, pp. 36–40.
60. Walley and Whitehead, p. 52.

61. Ilana DeBare, "New Eco-Foam Packs a Lot of Promise," *Sacramento Bee,* February 1, 1995, p. C1.

62. Joel Makower, "The Path of Least Resistance," *Green Consumer* (syndicated column accessed via CompuServe), July 23, 1995, p. 1.

63. The literature on market-oriented environmental thinking and policy alternatives is growing rapidly. The basics of the issue are covered in Bast et al.; Kwong; Terry Anderson and Donald Leal, *Free-Market Environmentalism;* Roger E. Meiners and Bruce Yandle, editors, *Taking the Environment Seriously* (Lanham, Maryland: Rowman & Littlefield, 1993).

Chapter 9. Business and Social Equality

1. Stephen Carter, "The Glass Ceiling for Blacks Is All Too Real," *Fortune,* November 2, 1992, p. 124.

2. Robert Gnaizda, "Dismal Record for Minorities," *Business and Society Review,* Spring 1993, p. 27.

3. Tawn Parent, "Risky Career Moves Pay Off for Civic-Minded Mays," *Indianapolis Business Journal,* January 27, 1992, p. 13A.

4. "Women Entrepreneurs: 'A Pretty Big Game,'" *Nation's Business,* August 1992, p. 53.

5. E. Holly Butler, "Female Entrepreneurs: How Far Have They Come?" *Business Horizons,* March/April 1993, p. 59.

6. James Overstreet, "Minority Businesses Riding a Wave of Success," *USA Today,* October 25, 1994, p. 4B.

7. Peter Drucker, "The Age of Social Transformation," *Atlantic Monthly,* p. 62. Of course, this increase in income potential is not due solely to the actions of firms, since minority workers are employed by government and nonprofits as well as by businesses.

8. Paul Klebnikov, "Showing Big Daddy the Door," *Forbes,* November 9, 1992, p. 150.

9. Benjamin Zycher and Timonthy A. Wolfe, "Mortgage Lending, Discrimination, and Taxation by Regulation," *Regulation,* Vol. 17, No. 2, 1994, pp. 61–71.

10. John Leo, "Our Addiction to Bad News," *U.S. News & World Report,* June 5, 1995, p. 20.

11. Peter Brimelow and Leslie Spencer, "When Quotas Replace Merit, Everybody Suffers," *Forbes,* February 15, 1993, p. 80.

12. John Sibley Butler, *Entrepreneurship and Self-Help Among Black Americans: A Reconsideration of Race and Economics* (Albany: State University of New York Press, 1991), pp. 38–39.

13. Ibid., pp. 49–55.

14. Mark Wilson, "Four Reasons Why Congress Should Repeal Davis-Bacon," Backgrounder No. 252, Heritage Foundation, Washington, D.C., June 7, 1995, p. 1.

15. Tiffany Anderson, "Blacks: Heritage Out of Hardship," *Tampa Tribune,* September 25, 1994, p. 13.

16. Elizabeth Wright, "Preferential Policies: An International Perspective," *Associates Memo,* Manhattan Institute for Policy Research, August 2, 1990, p. 3.

17. Angela G. King, "Black-Owned Businesses: Lean but Healthy," *USA Today,* May 10, 1995, p. 4B.

18. Wendy Zellner, "Women Entrepreneurs," *Business Week,* April 18, 1994, pp. 104–105.

19. Ibid., p. 53.

20. Butler, pp. 1–33.

21. Harold Jackson, "True Grit," *Black Enterprise,* June 1994, pp. 230–234.

22. Ibid.

23. "Black Entrepreneurs: A New Generation," *Inc.,* June 1994, p. 32.

24. King, p. 4B.

25. *Entrepreneur,* November 1994, pp. 118, 131.

26. Regine Styron, "African-American Entrepreneurship: An Option Worth Considering?" *Black Collegian,* March/April 1991, p. 115.

27. Zellner, p. 104.

28. Joseph F. Coates, Black Americans: Bad Press but Good Prospects for Employment," *Employment Relations Today,* August 1993, Vol. 20, No. 3, p. 267.

29. Brimelow and Spencer, p. 86.

30. Jonathan Kaufman, "How Workplaces May Look Without Affirmative Action," *Wall Street Journal,* March 20, 1995, p. B1.

31. "When the Boss Is Black," *Time,* March 13, 1989, p. 60.

32. Edwin M. Reingold, "America's Hamburger Helper," *Time,* June 29, 1992, p. 66.

33. John C. Weicher, "Getting Richer (at Different Rates)," *Wall Street Journal,* June 14, 1995, p. 10A.

34. June Ellenoff O'Neill, "The Shrinking Pay Gap," *Wall Street Journal,* October 7, 1994, p. 12A.

35. Christina Hoff Sommers, "Figuring Out Feminism," *National Review,* June 27, 1994, p. 34.

36. Dorian Friedman, "Working Women: Findings from a Sweeping New Study," *U.S. News & World Report,* May 22, 1995, p. 55.

37. Michele Ingrassia and Pat Wingert, "The New Providers," *Newsweek,* May 22, 1995, p. 38.

38. Kaufman, p. B1.

39. Janice Castro, "Get Set: Here They Come!" *Time,* November 8, 1990, p. 50.

40. Wright, p. 2.

41. See, for example, Mary C. King, "Occupational Segregation by Race and Sex, 1940–88," *Monthly Labor Review,* April 1992, pp. 30–36.

42. Robert A. Margo, "Explaining Black-White Wage Convergence, 1940–1950," *Industrial and Labor Relations Review,* Vol. 48, No. 3, April 1995, p. 470. Margo reports the fascinating fact that "surveys of common laborers' pay taken by the [Bureau of Labor Statistics] in the late 1930s reveal that, in the vast majority of cases, blacks and whites employed in the same job at the same firm earned identical hourly wages. Exceptions were more fre-

quent in the South, but even in the South, cases of pure racial wage discrimination in low-wage occupations appear to have been in the minority" (p. 472).

43. Brimelow and Spencer, p. 86.

44. Tamar Lewin, "Study: Dads Earn More If Moms Stay Home," *Austin American-Statesman,* October 12, 1994, p. A1.

45. Martha H. Peak, "Fathers Earn the Most . . . When Their Wives Stay Home," *Management Review,* Vol. 83, No. 2, February 1994, p. 6.

46. *These Are the Good Old Days*, 1993 Annual Report, Federal Reserve Bank of Dallas, 1994, pp. 7–8.

47. The advent of niche marketing to ethnic groups is "the compelling force that's causing a lot of executives" to pay attention to workforce diversity, said Ann M. Morrison of the Center for Creative Leadership in La Jolla, California. Quoted in Sharon Nelton, "Winning With Diversity," *Nation's Business,* September 1992, p. 19.

48. John Chuang, "On Balance," *Inc.,* July 1995, pp. 25–26.

49. Casting the net wide makes a lot of sense when recruiting new workers from colleges and universities, which demonstrate at best a rough correlation between the perceived quality and reputation of schools and the actual knowledge and performance of graduates. "In recruiting, if I only go to the Big 10 schools and only interview MBAs, am I overlooking talent?" asks Bob Taylor, director of training for the Memphis Race Relations & Diversity Institute. Probably. See Laurel Campbell, "Diversity in Workplaces Is New Strategy of Businesses," *Commerical Appeal,* August 21, 1994, p. C3.

50. The history of how affirmative action become a de facto quota system is described in Paul Craig Roberts and Lawrence M. Stratton, Jr., "Color Code," *National Review,* March 20, 1995, pp. 36–51.

51. Faye Rice, "How to Make Diversity Pay," *Fortune,* August 8, 1994, p. 84.

52. Thomas Sowell, "Assumptions Behind Affirmative Action," *Conservative Chronicle,* March 8, 1995, p. 10.

53. For a forceful statement of the opposite view, see Frank McCoy, "Rethinking the Cost of Discrimination," *Black Enterprise,* January 1994, pp. 54–58.

54. William A. Henry III, "What Price Preference?" *Time,* September 30, 1991, p. 30.

55. Errol Smith, "New Visions for Black America," *Corporate Board,* July/August 1993, Vol. 14, No. 18, p. 22.

56. Kara Swisher, "Diversity's Learning Curve: Multicultural Training's Challenges Include Undoing Its Own Mistakes," *Washington Post,* February 5, 1995, p. H1.

57. Ibid.

58. For a particularly spirited critique of the state of "diversity training" in America, see Thomas Sowell, "Effrontery and Gall, Inc.," *Forbes,* September 27, 1993, p. 52. The willingness of corporate managers to pay thousands of dollars to crackpot consultants is, in Sowell's words, either evidence of "a death wish" or done "for the sake of public relations."

59. The study, by Warren Watson and other researchers at the University of North Texas, was published as "Cultural Diversity's Impact on Interaction

Process and Performance" in the *Academy of Management Journal,* 1993, Vol. 16, No. 3. It examined the behavior of 173 students enrolled in a business-management course at a large, unnamed university in the southwestern United States. The students were divided into 36 teams—17 composed only of whites and 19 composed of whites, blacks, Hispanics, and immigrants. Media reports about the study varied. *Training* magazine headlined its report "Cultural Diversity Works, Study Says" (September 1993, p. 13) and *Fortune* magazine reported that the results of the study showed "diversity can enhance performance" ("How to Make Diversity Pay," August 8, 1994, p. 79). But *the Economist,* in an article headlined "The Melting Pot Bubbles Less" (August 7, 1993, p. 63), did a more even-handed treatment, noting that the study could be viewed as "gloomy results for the cause of cultural diversity" and that, in reality, "the results of this experiment have to be taken with a pinch of salt."

60. Swisher, p. H1.
61. Even in cases where shareholders or owners wish to use hiring to ameliorate social disadvantages of aggrieved groups (an unlikely scenario), there are better ways of doing so than imposing quotas. See Dennis L. Weisman, "Why Employer Discretion May Lead to More Effective Affirmative Action Policies," *Journal of Policy Analysis and Management,* Vol. 13, No. 1, 1994, pp. 157–162.
62. H. B. Karp and Nancy Sutton, "Where Diversity Training Goes Wrong," *Training,* July 1993, p. 32.
63. Rice, p. 84.
64. Karp and Sutton, pp. 32–33.
65. Andrew E. Serwer, "What to Do When Race Charges Fly," *Fortune,* July 12, 1993, p. 95.
66. Gregory Patterson, "Different Strokes: Target Micromarkets Its Way to Success," *Wall Street Journal,* May 31, 1995, p. A1.
67. Thomas McCarroll, "It's a Mass Market No More," *Time,* December 2, 1993, p. 80.
68. Eugene Morris, "The Difference in Black and White," *American Demographics,* January 1993, pp. 44–48.
69. Michael E. Porter, "The Rise of the Urban Entrepreneur," *Inc.,* June 1995, p. 108.
70. McCarroll, p. 80.
71. Benjamin Zycher and Timonthy A. Wolfe, "Mortgage Lending, Discrimination, and Taxation by Regulation," *Regulation,* Vol. 17, No. 2, 1994, pp. 61–71.
72. Stan Liebowitz, "A Study That Deserves No Credit," *Wall Street Journal,* September 1, 1993, p. A14; see also Joseph Blalock, "Testing Fair Lending," *Savings & Community Banker,* June 1994, pp. 44–48.
73. See Jeff Taylor, "Ratings Present Misleading Picture," *Consumers' Research,* October 1992, p. 23; and Tim W. Ferguson, "The Next Lender Wave: Mortgage Bias," *Wall Street Journal,* May 25, 1993, p. A15.
74. T. Carter Hagaman, "Beware of Hidden Subsidies," *Management Accounting,* July 1993, p. 18.

75. Jonathan R. Macey, "Banking by Quota," *Wall Street Journal,* September 7, 1994, p. A14.
76. See George J. Benston and Dan Horsky, "The Relationship Between the Demand and Supply of Home Financing and Neighborhood Characteristics: An Empirical Study of Mortgage Redlining," *Journal of Financial Services Research,* Vol. 8, No. 3, February 1992; pp. 235–260.
77. Catherine England, "Redlining by the Numbers," *American Enterprise,* September/October 1994, pp. 13–15.
78. Edward O. Welles, "It's Not the Same America," *Inc.,* May 1994, p. 92.
79. For a discussion of the impact of such regulations, see Robert P. O'Quinn, "The Americans with Disabilities Act: Time for Amendments," Policy Analysis No. 158, Cato Institute, Washington, D.C., August 9, 1991.
80. Meg Fletcher and Sara J. Harty, "How Doing the Right Thing Is Paying Off," *Business Insurance,* July 13, 1992, p. 25.
81. Sharon Nelton, "The Rising Tide of Older Workers," *Nation's Business,* September 1992, p. 22.
82. Charles Strouse, "Respecting the Elders," *News & Observer* (Raleigh, N.C.), March 19, 1995, p. 1F.
83. Joseph J. Lazzaro, "Computers for the Disabled," *Byte,* June 1993, pp. 59–63.
84. Blayne Cutler, "Hot Gadgets for Disabled Workers," *American Demographics,* January 1993, pp. 23–24.
85. Fletcher and Harty, p. 26.
86. "Big Wheel," *Entrepreneur,* September 1993, p. 75.
87. Of course, as has been discussed in previous chapters, the responsibility of corporate managers to maximize profit is only a presumption. It is possible that shareholders of publicly traded firms—and, much more commonly, the owners of privately held corporations—might want to sacrifice some economic return in order to strive for the betterment of a particular racial, religious, or social group. A firm's owners may wish to make hiring decisions on the basis of quotas, knowing full well that they are sacrificing profits to do so. Despite the persistence of social inequality in the United States and continued concern about the plight of disadvantaged minorities, though, there is no evidence that corporate owners as a whole view this social mission as more important than economic return. Indeed, when researchers surveyed corporate shareholders in 1992, asking them where "more corporate funds should be allocated," the answers "improve programs to benefit women" and "improve programs to benefit racial minorities" were ranked at the very bottom of the scale. Marc J. Epstein, "The Annual Report Report Card," *Business and Society Review,* Spring 1992, p. 83.
88. Steven Yates, "Affirmative Action: The New Road to Serfdom," *Freeman,* December 1990, p. 472.

Chapter 10. Family Values and the Workplace

1. Tom Ehrenfeld, "Friend of the Family," *Inc.,* December 1994, p. 94.
2. Ibid.

3. Ibid.
4. Jaclyn Fierman, "Are Companies Less Family Friendly?" *Fortune,* March 21, 1994, p. 65; and Kenneth R. Sheets, "A Bevy of Bills Would Sock Firms for Parental Leave, Even Damages," *U.S. News & World Report,* May 21, 1990, p. 53.
5. Ibid.
6. The average daily time devoted to household chores has fallen consistently—from 4 hours, 12 minutes in 1950 to 3 hours, 48 minutes in 1973 and an estimated 3 hours, 30 minutes in 1990. This amounts to an extra four days off a year. See *These Are the Good Old Days,* 1993 Annual Report, Federal Reserve Bank of Dallas, 1994, p. 7.
7. Ibid., p. 8.
8. Virginia I. Postrel, "Who's Behind the Child-Care Crisis?" *Reason,* June 1989, p. 27.
9. Christine Woolsey, "Continued Growth Seen in Work-Family Benefits," *Business Insurance,* September 14, 1992, p. 13.
10. Richard D. McCormick, "Family Affair," *Chief Executive,* May 1992, p. 31.
11. Amy Saltzman and Leonard Wiener, "Family Friendliness: What Workplace Revolution?" *U.S. News & World Report,* February 22, 1993, p. 60.
12. Charlene Marmer Solomon, "Work/Family's Failing Grade: Why Today's Initiatives Aren't Enough," *Personnel Journal,* May 1994, p. 78.
13. Woolsey, p. 16.
14. An example of a company that has received a great deal of attention is Stride Rite Corporation. Their on-site child-care and elder-care centers, however, have not served that many employees' needs. See Saltzman and Wiener, p. 61; also Jennifer J. Laabs, "Family Issues Are a Priority at Stride Rite," *Personnel Journal,* July 1993, pp. 48–56.
15. Fierman, p. 65.
16. Dee Lane, "Becoming Family Friendly," *Oregonian* (Portland), November 6, 1994, p. F1.
17. See discussion in Saltzman and Wiener, pp. 59–64.
18. Lane, p. F1.
19. To accommodate the varied preferences of their employees, firms are best off providing the greatest possible flexibility in the use of child-care benefits under existing tax law. Employees should be able to choose among day care centers, day care homes, or spending their dollars to support care by their own spouses or extended family members.
20. McCormick, p. 32.
21. William B. Werther, Jr., "Childcare and Eldercare Benefits," *Personnel,* September 1989, p. 43.
22. Ibid.
23. Mimi Deitsch, "Work and Family—What Are Companies Doing?" *Financial Executive,* May–June 1992, p. 60.
24. Postrel, pp. 21–26.
25. See, for example, Anton D. Lowenberg and Thomas D. Tinnin, "Professional Vs. Consumer Interests in Regulation: The Case of the U.S. Child

Care industry," *Applied Economics,* 1992, Vol. 24, pp. 571–580: "We conclude that professional interests dominate consumer interests in the setting of licensure requirements for child care."

26. Ibid.

27. Solomon, p. 76.

28. Matthew Bordonato, "Parental and Family Leave: Does Government Know Best?" *State Factor,* American Legislative Exchange Council, Washington, D.C., Vol. 17, No. 10, August 1991, p. 5.

29. Michele Galen, "Work and Family," *Business Week,* June 28, 1993, p. 82.

30. Solomon, p. 80.

31. Fran Sussner Rodgers and Charles Rodgers, "Business and the Facts of Family Life," *Harvard Business Review,* November–December 1989, p. 127.

32. Lori Bongiorno, "Business Is Still Structured Like Fourth Grade," *Business Week,* June 28, 1993, p. 86.

33. Chris Roush, "Aetna's Family-Friendly Executive," *Business Week,* June 28, 1993, p. 83.

34. Solomon, p. 83.

35. A study by the U.S. Census Bureau found that maternity leave and similar benefits have proven to be effective in retaining employees. From 1981 to 1984, 71 percent of women who had received maternity-leave benefits returned to work within six months of their child's birth, compared to 43 percent of women who had not received such benefits. See Richard T. Gill, "Day Care or Parental Care?" *Public Interest,* No. 105, Fall 1991, p. 6.

36. Bonnie Michaels and Elizabeth McCarty, "Family Ties and Bottom Lines," *Training & Development,* March 1993, p. 70.

37. "Small-Business Owners Should Follow Family Leave Law," *Business Journal* (Charlotte, N.C.), June 26, 1995, p. 25.

38. McCormick, p. 32.

39. Ellen Hoffman, "Telecommuting: Working at Home Goes from Fantasy to Fact," *USAir Magazine,* April 1995, p. 54.

40. Carrie A. Liberante, "More People Are Riding Telecommuter Highway," *Buffalo News,* July 24, 1994, p. B13.

41. Paul and Sarah Edwards, *Working from Home* (New York: G. P. Putnam's Sons, 1994), p. 7.

42. Julie Schmit, "Computer Blurs Line Between Job, Home," *USA Today,* June 20, 1995, p. 2E.

43. Larry Armstrong, "The Office Is a Terrible Place to Work," *Business Week,* December 27, 1993, p. 46.

44. Hoffman, p. 54.

45. Vicki Vaughan, "Flexible Time—It Works," *Orlando Sentinel,* October 25, 1994, p. E1.

46. Edwards, pp. 23–24.

47. Mary Beth Marklein, "Technology Helps People Keep Tasks In-House," *USA Today,* June 20, 1995, p. 8E.

48. Hoffman, p. 56.

49. Armstrong, p. 46.

50. Liberante, p. B13.
51. Ibid.
52. Marklein, p. 8E.
53. Charles Haddad, "Slimmer, More Powerful, and Cheaper: Laptops Are Stars of Computer Industry," *Atlanta Journal-Constitution,* September 19, 1994, p. E4.
54. Galen, p. 86.
55. Lisa Genasci, "Employee Assistance a Mixed Blessing," *News & Observer* (Raleigh, N.C.), September 18, 1994, p. 5F.
56. Stanley D. Nollen, "The Work-Family Dilemma: How HR Managers Can Help," *Personnel,* May 1989, p. 28.
57. Nancy L. Breuer and Cindy S. Moskovic, "Parenting Education Helps Employees Focus on Work," *Personnel Journal,* October 1994, p. 60.
58. Charlene Marmer Solomon, "Work/Family Is a Delicate Balance," *Personnel Journal,* May 1994, p. 82.
59. See Karen E. Carney, "Choosing an EAP," *Inc.,* July 1994, p. 95.
60. "Does Counseling Work?" *Small Business Reports,* June 1992, p. 42.
61. Genasci, p. 5F.
62. "The Right Family Values in the Workplace," *Business Week* (editorial), June 28, 1993, p. 134.
63. Sue Shellenbarger, "In Caring for Elders, Sometimes Less Can Accomplish More," *Wall Street Journal,* August 2, 1995, p. B1.
64. Dorian Friedman, "Working Women: Findings from a Sweeping New Study," *U.S. News & World Report,* May 22, 1995, p. 55.
65. Ehrenfeld, p. 94.

Conclusion

1. For an example of how a serious attempt to develop managerial guidelines from corporate social responsibility swiftly degenerates into obtuse gobbledygook, see Simon Zadek, "Trading Ethics: Auditing the Market," *Journal of Economic Issues,* Vol. 28, No. 2, June 1994, pp. 631–645.
2. Tim W. Ferguson, "Corporations, Do-Gooders and the Law," *Wall Street Journal,* February 7, 1995, p. A23.
3. Milton Friedman, "The Social Responsibility of Business Is to Increase Its Profits," *New York Times Magazine,* September 13, 1970, p. 122.
4. S. Prakesh Sethi, "Conversion of a Corporate CEO into a Public Persona," *Business and Society Review,* Fall 1994, No. 91, p. 43.
5. Eric H. Warmington and Philip G. Rouse, editors, *Great Dialogues of Plato: The Republic,* Book IV, p. 289.
6. Ibid., p. 278.
7. What's worse, in many cases analysts attribute social progress to government rather than to the businesses that are actually responsible. *Newsweek* writer Jonathan Alter, for instance, dedicated his July 3, 1995, column to the summer film *Apollo 13* and its message of government heroism. In addition to sending men to the moon, he wrote, "the U.S. government essentially ended

hunger (through food stamps), cleaned up polluted air and water (through federal regulation), [and] transformed the role of women and blacks (with routes for upward mobility). Almost no one stopped to notice." What Alter apparently didn't stop to notice was that profit-seeking and innovative firms were equally or more responsible than was government for all three of these positive trends. See Jonathan Alter, "The Moral Equivalent of Apollo," *Newsweek,* July 3, 1995, p. 56.

8. Charles E. Watson, "The Meaning of Service in Business," *Business Horizons,* January–February 1992, p. 58.
9. "Will Slower Growth Save the World," *Business and Society Review,* No. 85, Spring 1993, p. 10.
10. Paul Solman, "A Heresy: What About Lower Expectations?" *Mother Jones,* March/April 1994, p. 42.
11. Watson, p. 59.
12. Ibid., p. 58.
13. John Steele Gordon, "Technology of the Future," *American Heritage,* October 1993, p. 16.
14. B. Zorina Khan and Kenneth L. Sokoloff, "'Schemes of Practical Utility': Entrepreneurship and Innovation among 'Great Inventors' in the United States, 1790–1865," *Journal of Economic History,* Vol. 53, No. 2, June 1993, p. 289–307.
15. Rajeev K. Goel, "Spillovers, Rivalry, and R & D Investment," *Southern Economic Journal,* Vol. 62, No. 1, July 1995, pp. 71–76.
16. Peter Coy, "Blue-Sky Research Comes Down to Earth," *Business Week,* July 3, 1995, p. 79. For a discussion of innovation in both large and small firms, see Zoltan J. Acs, "Where New Things Come From," *Inc.,* May 1994, p. 29.
17. Donna J. Wood, "Corporate Social Performance Revisited," *Academy of Management Review,* Vol. 16, No. 4, 1991, p. 695.
18. Jane Jacobs, *Strategies of Survival: A Dialogue on the Moral Foundations of Commerce and Politics* (New York: Random House, 1992), pp. 151–153.
19. See Chapter 2.
20. For examples of how corporations use the federal government to protect themselves from competition and to obtain subsidies, see Stephen Moore and Dean Stansel, "Ending Corporate Welfare As We Know It," Policy Analysis No. 225, Cato Institute, Washington, D.C., May 12, 1995.
21. Fred L. Smith, Jr., "Two Cheers!" *World & I,* March 1988, pp. 381–393.
22. William E. Simon, "Taking Philanthropy Seriously: Giving as Though Our Future Depended on It," *Alternatives in Philanthropy,* Capital Research Center, Washington, D.C., September 1988, p. 3.
23. Unfortunately, the trend in business schools today appears to be to suggest that profit-seeking business is not an arena where social benefits can be accomplished. See Mary Lord, "Making A Difference," *U.S. News & World Report,* March 20, 1995, pp. 87–91.
24. Henry Grady Weaver, *The Mainspring of Human Progress,* Irvington-on-Hudson, New York: Foundation for Economic Education, 1953, p. 263.

INDEX